To Ann!
Had a ball
Seattle
Enjoy the "ride"!

Russ Tornstrom
- Son of "Swede"

DAREDEVIL
CAMERAMAN

The Saga of
Ray "Swede" Fernstrom

Russell and Beverly Fernstrom

ENGLAND · USA · SCOTLAND

PUBLISHED BY PENTLAND PRESS, INC.
5124 Bur Oak Circle, Raleigh, North Carolina 27612
United States of America
919-782-0281

ISBN 1-57197-063-0
Library of Congress Catalog Card Number 97-65962

Fernstrom, Russell and Beverly
Daredevil Cameraman/by Russell and Beverly Fernstrom

Printed in the United States of America

This book is dedicated to Ray's talent and the awards he certainly deserved, but never received and to all of the pioneering early cameramen, especially those daredevils of the fabulous Newsreel Era . . .

Foreword

Ray "Swede" Fernstrom not only saw the world during one of its most exciting eras, but through his "third eye," his beloved camera lens, he photographed it for all to see and remember. He was THE master photographer; the daredevil cameraman for Paramount News, The Eyes of the World. If it was happening, he was there. From the Hindenburg disaster to the only flight of the Spruce Goose, while in radio contact with Howard Hughes; along winding roads of thrills behind the newsreels; the discovery of "Monetta" in Dallas, who was to become a '40s famous movie star; dangerous aerial films made during World War II and in motion pictures; the legendary people he knew as friends; Walt Disney, Clark Gable, Dorothy Provine, the Warner Brothers, Ronald Reagan, from stardom to Death Valley Days on television, always a personal friend during Reagan's political career, and many more!

This same man filmed and interviewed that great American genius, Thomas Alva Edison. Swede was a Texas Ranger, friends with presidents from Hoover to Reagan; they all knew him and his ability with the camera.

He was in the cockpit of the first Navy plane to land on America's first aircraft carrier, the original Saratoga, his camera faithfully recording the event. He filmed the unusually exciting Circarama for Disneyland that the world enjoyed for so many years. He was responsible for influencing an entire fleet of ships to change their color because the old color was unphotogenic. To this day, white is now associated with luxury vacation liners.

The authors have striven for several years to document as accurately as possible each bit of Swede's history, as they carefully sorted through notes, war memorabilia and small items, and recalled hours of conversation, before his death ten years ago, in which he recalled story after story from his colorful, almost total recall memory of his childhood, and later the newsreels and photos he presented through Paramount News. Much of the book is taken from Swede's own memoirs, thus he voices his opinions and feeling through quotes many times, as one follows his life through the years. The authors add to this their own experiences as son and daughter-in-law to bring together the giant crossword puzzle that was Ray "Swede" Fernstrom's life. We have no intent to blemish any reputation, only to bring to life the sparkling era in which Swede lived.

Anything written here, that touches the wild side has been reported somewhere before, except that the writers have clarified some instances, and filled in a few gaps in history through the eyes of the man who lived it. Names have not been changed to protect the innocent as we feel the passage of time has dulled any impact on those long departed and the people mentioned in this book were far from innocent.

This pictorial biography covers the life of Ray "Swede" Fernstrom, from his early childhood in Sweden to his first days with his precious camera, to New England, New York, around the world, his wild days in Hollywood, where his camera recorded unbelievable footage.

The authors have backed up events with photographs from Swede's private collection; most never seen before and from a time long past, such as the photo of Walt Disney's Mickey and Minnie Mouse dolls that were in his private office in the old Burbank studio in 1933, the only photo of its kind. Allegedly, even the Disney archives cannot produce one.

A foreword is supposed to describe the person or situation you will read about, but in the author's case, this was a very difficult task, as Ray "Swede" Fernstrom was a unique individual. Most of us try to live a fairly organized, normal existence. We are sent or go to college and are trained in a profession that gives stability to ourselves and our families, and taught to live in what is described as a pattern acceptable to society. Just about everyone we know lives and prevails somewhere within these acceptable guidelines.

But there are a rare few that live today, or have lived, with the idea that these guidelines are chains around them. They eventually shed themselves of these shackles, and now uninhibited with the nuisance of a conscience, they soar through their stay on this earth, completely fearless in a way that you and I will never understand.

Ray "Swede" Fernstrom was just such a person, and as his life story unfolds before you, maybe we can gain a bit of valuable insight into this most rare and unusual man.

Perhaps, it all started when his wise, old father, Emil, told him in a thick, Swedish accent, "Raymond, always remember one thing. God gave you life to enjoy, and if you don't learn how, He will take it away from you." And enjoy, Ray did! He had a faith that all the fun and thrills life had to offer were his. He could do anything, with no fear to hinder him. Swede tried to explain this to Russ, his oldest son and co-author of this book, saying, "Russ, this is my belief, and it has never let me down." On another occasion, after observances of Russ everyday routines, which Russ enjoyed, Swede told him, "You know, I think I've lived too much. I've lived too much. I've done more in one lifetime than most people could possibly do in three." After he committed his memoirs to paper, the authors agreed.

Russ Fernstrom

Acknowledgment

Only by chance has this book been compiled and written.

Ray "Swede" Fernstrom married three times in his life. All three wives are alive as of this writing and none speak to each other, of course.

Russell is the second child and first son by Ray's first wife, "Jerry" and was his favorite. Ray used to say, "Russ is more like a brother to me than a son." The two could discuss their mutual love of aircraft, memories of the past, the war years and much more.

It was Russ who urged and prodded Ray to write his memoirs, way back in the '60s.

After "Swede" died, we chased his memories.

He had lived his last fifteen some odd years, in our town. But, even though we had a key to his apartment, we never touched it. Everything, we knew, belonged to his third wife Evelyn and she claimed it all.

It was about a year after Ray died that Russ received a phone call from Evelyn. She wanted to know if there was anything of Ray's notes and pictures we might want, as she was going to throw out all the old musty stuff in his old suitcase. Russ said, "Evelyn, all I want are all the old pictures and things before you met him."

She handed over to us a small, well-worn suitcase with a myriad of worldly stickers pasted all over it. The contents of that suitcase contained most of the material that you shall now read and view. We really thank Evelyn for that. A great piece of history could have been lost forever.

Ray's sister, Acky, contributed immensely to his biography, by filling in the very early years, through correspondence between she and her brother.

Our heartfelt thanks go to both of these women whom Ray loved dearly . . .

Beverly Fernstrom

CHAPTER ONE
Family Background
Lidkoping, Sweden 1874-1890

Lydia Emelia Jacobson was fifteen years old and a tall, slender, pretty brunette when she attended her mother's wake. She had lost her father only three months before, and her five-year-old brother had also been killed earlier in a tragic accident, while her beloved Conrad, her confidant and closest brother, had succumbed to a heart ailment at the age of twenty-four. He had dove into icy waters to save a drowning friend and developed a weak heart from the incident.

Lydia shook herself from the tragic memories and forced her brain to perform the duties at hand. "Yes, thank you so much. You are all so kind. Yes, I'll finish school here, then go to America with my oldest brother Gustave." But who will look after all the graves? she wondered. And what will become of Emil, my love? He had promised Conrad he would look after her for the rest of her life. How could he if she was half a continent away?

Gustave watched her with a careful eye. He was only twenty-five himself, and now Lydia's only family figure. They were the only surviving offspring of the Count and Countess Ivar Von Unger of Germany, who had come to Sweden then changed their names to Jacobson for some reason that shall be forever lost in history. The only clue is that Ivar, Lydia's father, had been very wealthy and had a huge manor in Germany but a horrible gambling habit. Lydia later admitted that it broke the family's heart when he lost everything. Maybe he had taken the only avenue open to him. In America the name would again be changed to Jackson.

The Countess now lay in a new grave beside her husband and sons, while Lydia looked out the window of her home at the winding mountain roads she had known so well, past the grocer, and down toward the *gaveriet*, a brook.

Will there be brooks in America? she asked herself. How will I learn a new language? She sighed and returned to her school books. Soon she would finish her education, and Gustave, "Gus," had already purchased huge trunks, one for each room, ready to be packed. How in the world could one stuff a whole room into a trunk?

She was loathe to go to America and leave her homeland, but if Gus went, she must surely go along. Emil, born Gustaf Emil Fernstrom, in Sala, Sweden on 26 January 1876, had decided to make the trip with them in order to be near Lydia. He was determined to fulfill Conrad's deathbed request and watch out for her. Besides, she had a strong hold on his heart strings. Emil's family heritage of leather tanners dated back to 400 A.D. He would have to leave it behind, but he was determined to follow a new avenue of work, the first of his family to do so.

When they arrived in New York, they went directly to Brockton, Massachusetts where Gus had been promised a good position in a Swedish market, as he had experience from Sweden making a special sausage known as *Kock Corce*, a tasty meal when boiled with potatoes and turnips. Emil went to Boston, obtained work in a French restaurant operated by Mr. Paul Duford, and was made head waiter since he knew a great deal about the proper way to serve meals from his homeland. He suffered the problem of the language barrier, which had made it impractical for him to obtain employment elsewhere. The job was an eighteen-hour-a-day one, but Emil never complained. On Sundays, his day off, he journeyed to Brockton to visit Lydia. They attended mass at the Lutheran Church, then sat with the family on the porch and talked.

Lydia's brother, Gus, married an Indian girl called May in 1892, and May's mother and Lydia came to live with them in Brockton, where Gus had purchased a home and stayed until his death at the age of seventy-seven. It was an unhappy time for Lydia, who felt she was being used as an unpaid servant in the household. She learned to speak English, a most difficult task, while she attended to the cooking and cleaning of the vast house, and also cared for each newborn as Gus' family grew.

Emil never asked her to marry him. Time flew by; she was nearly twenty-three and headed for spinsterhood, while he took pains to mention that he was younger than she by one year, and she was an "older woman." One Sunday, while sitting on the front porch, May asked Lydia if she was ever going to get married.

"Yes, of course. I am getting married next October first," she retorted. Emil shot her a sly glance, noting the firm look of determination on her face. When he took his departure that evening, he asked who she was going to marry.

"You, of course; who else?"

Their long life together did indeed begin October first, 1898, with a ceremony in Bridgewater, Massachusetts. During the vows, Emil's tongue slipped a bit, and instead of "I do," he said "Ya," then grinned, gave her a wink, and corrected himself. They made a fine couple, with Lydia and her thick, dark hair in a fashionable upsweep, tiny waist revealed by the creamy lace wedding gown, standing close to Emil, who was dressed in a black suit, back straight, ready to begin a new life as a married man, wherever the twisted roads of life would take them, through whatever hardships fate might deal them in the next seventy years, hand in hand.

They honeymooned at Niagara Falls, New York. While there, they met Mr. Andrew Carnegie, the steel magnate, who offered Emil a position at the Carnegie Golf Club, which he took. The struggling couple took a one-room furnished flat. Both went to work to save money in hopes of buying some furniture of their own. Lydia worked as an upstairs maid for three elderly spinster ladies, who advised her that she would have to clean their three bedrooms and baths everyday. She awakened them each morning with a quiet rap on each of their doors, detesting the work. She had not told them she was married and had to sleep in a tiny, unheated attic room, which left Emil alone. She considered the old bags a royal pain in the arse, as she told Emil.

On her day off, she shopped for food and clothing, and once in a while Emil indulged himself by buying a small gift for his bride. This put Lydia in a huff, but deep down she adored him for his thoughtfulness. But one time, she stood agape at his offering.

"It's for our first home, Lydia," he told her. Nestled within a pretty box lined with tissue paper were six tiny cocoa cups with a pitcher to match. The set had come from Germany, and was delicately painted with white roses on a soft green background. Tears welled in her eyes as she threw her arms around his neck and kissed him.

"Oh, Emil, I love you so much!" Years later, she would give the cups to her favorite grandson and his bride after serving so many of her welcome friends hot chocolate. The pitcher finally cracked beyond repair and now, forty years later, sits with its precious cups on a shelf in the authors' home, a silent reminder of an era past.

When Lydia discovered she was pregnant, she heaved a sigh of relief, took to an easy chair, and immediately quit her job. Within months, the couple returned to Boston, then Cambridge, where they found an apartment near one of their Swedish friends. Here, Lydia really began to enjoy life, while she and Emil watched her tummy swell, and knew the firstborn would be a boy.

During the ninth month, Lydia finished a romantic French novel whose hero was named Raymond, and she decided at that moment that would be her son's name—Raymond Gustaf Ivar Fernstrom. Gustaf, after the Crown Prince of Sweden and Ivar after Lydia's father. Fernstrom, of course, was the Viking clan's designation of those who did the tanning of leather, which required rushing streams. *Fern* means far off or distant, and *strom* is stream or rapids, thus, distant streams.

When Lydia's time came, Emil hurried down the street and over the Saint Charles Bridge to fetch Dr. Hoger of Boston, and on 25 February 1900, Raymond G. I. Fernstrom was born. He was a hefty, healthy baby who weighed twelve pounds and six ounces.

For a while, the little family was content, but Emil had a burning desire to return to Sweden to spend the rest of his life in his homeland. Lydia was not anxious to make the move, but after much convincing the trip was planned. Little Raymond was about three and a half years old.

Once again, Emil dragged out the trunks.

A going-away party was planned for the Fernstroms. (Emil and Lydia loved parties to the end of their days.) Scandinavians have their own customs and drinks. First, there is the akvavit, 150-proof straight potato alcohol with different flavors depending on the area—Sweden, Denmark, Norway, or Finland. It is served ice cold in tall, stemmed V-shaped crystal goblets which hold a healthy ounce. It is not sipped; it's bottoms up all the way. Yet, not without ceremony. First, one holds the glass in front of the third vest button, then calls out the name of the person to be toasted, and when recognized, shouts, "*Skäl*," and both drink to the dregs. Then comes the chaser, which is a bit of smorgasbord. Every piece of herring, anchovy, meatball, etcetera is one bite, fork-size. For after 150-proof akvavit tears down ones throat, there is an automatic gesture invented by *Nordeners*, north men, which is that of "spear a herring and soothe the throat!" or a meatball, et al. The ceremony goes something like this: Whoever doesn't take the whole doesn't get the second done, the *halven* (half one) or third, fourth and on. When all the toasts are out of the way, there is singing, with glasses filled again. Other foods consist of fish with white wine, meat with red wine, champagne with desserts, and brandy with coffee. Usually, another room or salon is provided for hearty conversations, laughing, and dancing, followed by cognac and Vichy water, called Grog. But no one gets drunk—too much food.

Little Raymond slept during the celebration, and awakened early with no parents around. He crawled over the bed rails, peeked in at Lydia and Emil, and saw they were asleep. He decided he was hungry and thirsty, so he proceeded to the living room where he finished off the remains of the party.

Lydia was first up and started down the hall where she spied Raymond in the living room. He was hanging onto the wall, trying to make it to the bathroom, staggering like an old man. "Emil," Lydia shouted, "Come here quick! What's the matter with the boy?"

Emil arrived, rumpled from sleep, saying, "Oh, for Christ sake, the kid's drunk!" He began to laugh.

"He's going to die!" screamed Lydia, with her usual optimism.

"Naw, put him to bed, and he'll sleep it off," explained Emil, who was more experienced in these affairs. As one can readily realize, Ray's friendship with happy spirits began at a very tender age.

The family sailed for Sweden a few days later.

They arrived in Stockholm, rented a small place, found a nursemaid for Raymond, and sought employment. The old Rydberg Hotel hired them both. Lydia was a stewardess, Emil a steward. They met many famous Swedes at the hotel while listening for opportunities to better themselves.

Finally, they located the Hotel Gastis for sale to the far north in Krokom, Jemtland, near the Arctic Circle and only a few hundred yards from a little red railroad station—the hub of the entire countryside. It sounded like a good business venture, with first- and third-class restaurants catering to a large clientele of railroad workers and those better paid. The Swedish Army held maneuvers in the area in winter and summer, while traveling salespeople traded horses there in order to reach outlying hamlets. Lydia and Emil made arrangements and moved to Krokom.

One day, Lydia was hurrying across the railroad bridge, fenced with fancy ironwork that revealed the tracks below. Just as she reached the middle, a locomotive raced beneath, belching black smoke and startling her. But little Raymond watched with utter fascination. She and the child, who was bundled heavily against the cold, were making their way to the law office to sign the final papers on the hotel as well as all the loan documents drawn up against the investment. It was Olga's morning off and while she would have gladly relinquished her time to care for little Raymond, Lydia did not ask for fear that an explanation was due. It was her secret to keep for as long as she could, for she was carrying not just one child. Raymond was in her arms but another was in her belly. Emil must not know until all was settled with the hotel. Thank God, she thought, she wasn't carrying this baby way out in front as she had Raymond. It must be a girl. By letting out some of the pleats on her two heaviest woolen dresses, she was able to conceal her condition until the fourth month. In due time she would tell him, but not now when he had so many other worries trying to get the hotel open and on a paying basis.

The immediate business behind her, Lydia stopped at the *grosshand-laren*, which was supposed to be a grocery store but was stuffed with an assortment of every conceivable household need. Mr. Johansson greeted her, a warm smile on his face, eager to take the order from this pretty, young wife of Emil Fernstrom, a name so well-known in northern Sweden. The list grew as Lydia mentally went over every square inch of the hotel. Carpet beaters, curtain stretchers, lots and lots of starch, stove black, white wash for the fences, moth balls. The tally grew and so did the bill.

"Do you mind if I charge this, Mr. Johansson? Our money is a little slow in arriving from America," she fibbed.

"Of course not, Mrs. Fernstrom; just sign here."

She had bought a little extra time not only for herself, but for Emil as well.

Lydia fairly flew back to the hotel, with Raymond skipping behind her. Tomorrow she would hire some local help and really tackle the run-down hotel. That night she let out her corset a notch.

Emil worried that the pump house would run dry because Lydia was using so much water. Extra clothes lines were strung behind the building holding not only carpets, but feather ticks as well. Bubbling furiously on the wood-fed kitchen stoves were the copper boilers filled with bed linens, napkins and towels. Buckets and buckets of starch were needed for the curtains and pillow cases and gallons of hot water would be used for scrubbing floors and woodwork. Lydia went through every cedar chest and linen closet, putting little packets of lavender scents between the freshly laundered sheets. Weeks and weeks of hard work passed and at last the doors were flung open for business. Emil and Lydia together cooked the first lavish menu, hiring young girls with ready knowledge of proper manners to serve the excellent food. It was a huge success and a number of guests did indeed spend the night in the well-scrubbed rooms.

Emil tucked the hotel ledger under his arm and gathered the kitchen bills together to be taken to their rooms that first night to be itemized. Lydia snatched them away in mock anger, explaining that she was perfectly capable of handling the books. She knew that now was the time to tell him of the impending addition to the family and heaven knows he did not need the knowledge of their debts.

A little cognac was needed to warm the chilled bones in the unheated private rooms. Lydia had frugally cut off the heat weeks before. Quickly they got into their heavy night clothes and slipped under the down ticks.

"Emil, I can't sleep. Would you mind getting us another small glass of cognac?"

Jesus, why can't she go to sleep, he wondered, we have finally got the damn place opened; I'm dead tired and now she can't sleep!

"Emil?"

He shoved the warmth of the coverings away and stepped onto the icy floor.

Two more shots of the warming liquor were poured and handing one to her, Emil again went to bed.

"Emil, are you still awake? There is something I must tell you."

"Go to sleep Lydia; you can tell me all your secrets tomorrow."

"Hold me close, my darling."

He gave her a squeeze and waited. It was so cozy and quiet in bed. Heavy fingers tugged at his eyelids.

"Emil?"

His ears were half asleep, but he rolled over towards her. Blurting it out in one long planned sentence, the news came out loud and clear that they were in financial trouble. "I'm pregnant Emil, and I am certain it will be a girl. She is due in January and I feel just fine, really I do. There is no need for me to stop working in the hotel. Olga's sister Alma can be the nursemaid for the new baby."

"Jesus." Emil lay very still and would not spend the night sleeping but instead planning the future. A week later Emil sailed alone to America and his old job at the Louis Cafe.

It was Christmas time all over the world. Although heavy with child, Lydia insisted on supervising the final decoration of the hotel and the grand tree which stood in the foyer. Seldom did she venture from the private rooms, since Olga reported every detail at day's end. What a gem she was! Quietly she read and re-read Emil's letters.

Emil was doing fine in Boston, working in a very lucrative position at the Louis Cafe. The extra money certainly helped! Every cent of it went to reduce the burdensome debts. Emil was in charge of the private dining rooms on the second floor where he met many important people—senators, doctors and governors, who patronized the cafe. They liked the privacy Emil bestowed upon them. Never once did he ever reveal any names or who their companions were, since some came with someone other than their own mates. Emil respected their privacy and the customers were most grateful.

Lydia tucked the beloved letters away and ventured down the stairs into the vast hallway, swept in darkness, past the servants' quarters and beyond Olga's room. There were a few things to be done on the Christmas tree to enchant Raymond on his first holiday in Sweden. After she had placed the last candle on the tree to be lit early in the morning, she slipped Emil's wonderful gift to his son under the tree. To be sure, Raymond would love it! What else but a marvelous wind-up train set, with locomotive, all the cars and caboose, tracks and signals, flags, lanterns, all carefully packed in the Christmas box. Rubbing her back in pain and loneliness, Lydia returned to her lonely bed.

It was a cold and snowy day in January, on the sixteenth of the month that Gunhild Emelia was born. For her entire life she would be called Gunnie.

Recollections of a Boy in Sweden

In his old age, Ray recalled the choo-choo train that belched smoke as it came faster and closer. As they reached the center of the bridge, he said, the train dashed under them, and he vividly remembered the cup and saucer stack atop the boiler as the smoke enveloped both of them, forcing their eyes closed. Cinders and odors enraptured his senses, filling his mind with excitement. He loved trains from then on.

He also recalled another locomotive he had seen when he was about twelve years old, while traveling with his parents and stopping at a Norwegian mountain train station, en route from Sweden to Trondhjem, Norway. "From there, we were to travel by boat to England. Then across from Hull to Liverpool by train, and on the Atlantic to Boston on the Cunard liner *Cymric*, said Raymond. "How strange the names we 7 remember from that far back. There were two great ocean liners, the *Cymric* and the *Saxonia*. One a White Star liner, the other a Cunard."

He was being led back to examine, to him, a mountainous giant, and saw that it was a shiny, international locomotive with three huge drive wheels, one of which had no center flange to keep it on the track. This troubled him. But time, people, and experience taught him later that the sharp curves on that line could not accommodate locomotives with the necessary total of six drive wheels unless the center ones were unflanged. That, he said later, was one of the biggest lessons of his life, proving the necessity of compromise in cases of such requirement. The strength, traction, and weight remained, but greater flexibility without loss of efficiency was gained to carry the load.

During that same trip on board the train, as it moved slowly higher into the mountains and toward the sea, he saw the *Riksgransen*, a wide cut swathed away to the horizon, with armies drawn up on both sides ready for combat. His father explained that they (Raymond and Emil) were crossing the Swedish-Norwegian frontier. The armies were there because Norway wanted its freedom and self rule from Sweden and they were there ready to fight for it. The Swedish Army was also there because they were ordered, but good wise old King Oscar of Sweden, who had been ruling both countries, had very sagely decided that there was no sense in brother killing brother over each other's homeland, so he had advised the Norwegians to go and find their own king and rule themselves if that's what they really wanted. Thereafter, both armies got together and had a party to be remembered. The two countries lived in peace from that day on. Later, Raymond wondered if the King had learned a lesson from our own Civil War.

Raymond Fernstrom's fondest, most exciting, and happiest recollections were of his youth, growing up in the land of the midnight sun. He loved everything. Things seemed to happen to him, or in which he could at least participate, observe, or taste. He remembered Krokom as a beautiful and delightful little town, picturesque and busy. It was not more than half a mile from the great gorge, at the bottom of which crashed the rapids of Indalsalven. The railroad approached from Ostersund and Stockholm on the south, over a tremendous steel bridge. Just across the bridge and off to the east was the huge Hissmofors Paper Mills with the sweet smell of pulp wood.

———— >=•=< ————

Raymond recalls:

There, too, we used to go for steam baths; a fine adventure, sweating and switching ourselves with birch twigs after dipping them in the water. Thereafter, thoroughly pore-cleaned, we ran out in the snow and rolled about nude. Then in

One of the oldest actual photographs in the Fernstrom Archives. To the right of the two standing ladies who worked for our family stands Proud Emil, the "Saint," and his wonderful woman Lydia. Seated on the rail is Gunhild, and beside Lydia is a very young Raymond. Picture is on the porch of the little Hotel "Gastis" in Krokom, Sweden.

for a fast, cold shower and towel rub, before donning skis for the long glide home over the tiny swinging bridge.

Our shoemaker was just that, a shoemaker. He had no shoes for us, other than the ones he made right there for our feet. Heavy and useful they were, too. I can remember to this day the wonderful aroma of the leathers and glues he used, the smells of the leather thongs, the Lapp boots, and other goods he manufactured before my fascinated childish eyes. The shoes were square-toed and crude, but the most comfortable I ever wore. I didn't get these hammer toes from them. I acquired them from the stylish shoes my mother insisted on later when I had to wear Little Lord Fauntleroy suits with those damned, tight, pointed patent leather slippers, a velvet broad-brimmed hat, Buster Brown collars, and sissy bow ties. God, I'm glad that era is past!

We had a majery (dairy), where the girls ran around in wooden shoes. Ah! The sweet aromas there of fresh milk, cheeses, girls, and the general air of Swedish cleanliness, which still lingers in my mind.

Johansson was our grosshandlaren (grocer). His store had enough stuff in it to make any drugstore or Sears envious even today. Oh, the fond memories there; the colors, variety, smells, and the interesting people, especially Folke Johansson. Folke was a kid my age, and we became best pals. He was Mr. Johansson's youngest boy. We stood together against all competition from the older boys, including those two sons of the station master's, Sten and Ake Bloomberg. They had come to our town from Stockholm, and now lived on the second floor of the colorful railway station. All the rest of the kids in town hated these superior characters.

Of all the men in Krokom, their father, the station master, was the most imposing. Mr. Bloomberg, dressed in white trousers, blue coat with brass buttons, and white uniform cap and gloves, would appear on the platform of the station just before trains were to arrive, then stride out erectly and stand on the edge of the platform, two flags in hand, one green, the other red. Beyond him, behind the platform, stood a kiosk which opened at train time. There, the best tasting hot chocolate in the world could be bought, along with newspapers and magazines from Stockholm.

As the train came across the bridge, the engineer would give forth with three high shrill blasts on his whistle, and our town would assemble to either see the train stop or roar on through. It would barrel along past the slaughterhouse, lumber mill, then over the crossing where the gates were down, with the watchman waving his red flag. It raced past the sidetracked lumber cars with their logs for the paper mill, then either stopped with a hiss of steam and a screech of brakes or dashed northward past us, as we stood in awe and wonderment at its beauty.

If it stopped, we would run along the international cars gazing up at the people from other worlds, waving and smiling with our plum red faces. Red they always were from spring to spring, for the winters sometimes got as cold as fifty-four below zero, Fahrenheit.

In winter, the locomotives had tremendous red plows in front of them, and they arrived in a cloud of white snow-fog. Nowhere since have I seen any engine to compare with the monstrous beauty of a Swedish Railways locomotive—big, black, and brassy, with green and red trimmings, polished like jewels, and smelling of smoke, oil, and steam, silhouetted against the frozen white beauty of Swedish winter.

We played with the little Lapp kids when they came into town, and they really taught us how to dress for winter. Thereafter, we all looked like Lapp kids during the cold months from October to May. Lots of loose fitting, light, windproof clothes and reindeer skins. Our winter boots were Lapp, with skins turned fur side in, loose woolen socks, two pairs, and woolen tight knit underwear, which I hated. Wool was too scratchy, so I wore some loose cotton ones. When I grew up, I swore never to wear wool close to my body. (The Swedish woolens even itched through my cotton underwear.) Our pants were water, cold, and wear-proof, almost like iron trousers, they were so tightly woven. At the top of our Lapp boots, which turned up at the toes, we wrapped colorful Lapp binders to keep the snow from getting in between the pants and boots. The ends of the wrappers had colored woolen balls that dangled and bounced as we skied or ran. In Krokom, we grew up from five years old on, on either horses in summer or skis in the winter.

My father Emil had horses. They were a tiny breed that one sees today all over Scandinavia, Greenland, and Icelandic lands; rugged little giants, with long hair that hung with icicles through the long, below-zero winters, and shod with spiked shoes for walking on ice. For even the snow froze into a bed of crystals, so cold that sled runners screamed as they traversed the silver terrain.

Ray and Gunhild in Sweden circa 1906.

Our hotel was a small one when I saw it years later, but as a child it seemed tremendous. The little red schoolhouse with white trim sat on a hill, with ski racks outside, an outhouse, and a one-room interior with a corridor for hanging clothes. Much of the teachings were from beautiful lithographs. Geography was my favorite subject, and with the colorful lithographs I traveled the world in my imagination. My love for adventure and vivid color was formed there and has never left me. In the summer, the roads were dirt and graded, though very primitive, with deep ditches on both sides for water runoff. It was down one of these roads from out of town that I saw a most amazing apparition. So profoundly did it affect me that one of the greatest love affairs of my young life began.

A gigantic, blazing, red and brass Blitzen-Benz motorcar came roaring toward me, then stopped at our hotel. A man from out of this world, Hjoran Ollson, jumped down from the high driver's seat dressed in a leather coat, pants, boots, helmet, and gauntlets. He caught my eyes of wonder and invited me to climb up on the seat. I sat there, enthralled, my hands on the enormous steering wheel, much to the envy of Sten, Ake, Folke, and a few mangy Lapp kids. Finally, my father joined us. It seems he and Ollson were good friends and were about to embark on another jaunt with Pa's other lifetime pal, the train engineer Roytersvard.

After a few words with my father, I was invited for a ride and pleaded to let all my friends join us, even though I knew the rest of us would have to be deloused when we got home after sitting so close to the Lapp kids.

What a ride! Screams of laughter rang through the hills and dales, with everyone turning out to see us. I don't know if anyone there had ever seen an automobile before, for it was 1905 and there weren't many, especially that far back in the Swedish wooded wilderness.

The road that led past our hotel, the grocer, and the creamery descended toward the garveriet, the brook. The garveriet had a tanning plant. Emil was the first Fernstrom to break away from this occupation since the Viking days.

The Vikings had not all been sailors or fighters. Each clan had its own occupation, too, living on a strip that ran through what is today Sweden, Norway, and Denmark. Earlier they had been known as Goths and Visigoths, which is why today we have Gothenburg and Gottland, names recalled from the Viking days. They were restless warriors, travelers, plundering sailors, and land robbers. They fought eastward through the land we call Russia and conquered the people, giving them the Viking laws which later developed into English common law then our law in America. The Vikings ran most of the world, and their favorite plunder was women. Swedish Vikings sailed up the Seine in Gaul and settled it as Normandy. Then Rolf, a Viking's son became William the Conqueror. It was the Goths and their henchmen who overthrew the Roman Empire.

A strange new network of communication developed. Families split to the far corners of the earth, but managed to communicate with their clans through other Vikings who returned with their loot after conquests. Where the name Krokom came from has been a mystery. The closest translation could be hook-around, or bent hook.

The little bridge that crossed the stream by the tannery took one to the road beyond, which now climbed a hill on the way to Rodon Church far off in the hills. Many tiny towns lay in all directions from Krokom, the rail center for all the hilly area. The nearest city was Ostersund, a lovely place half a day's travel by train to the south.

Farther north on the railroad were the winter mountain resorts of Gallivara and its mountain of pure iron ore. The ore was extracted from Kirrunnavara Mountain and used to make the famous Swedish steel. Farther on, winding its way eastward, the railroad track leads over and through the mountains to the sea at Trondhjem, Norway. Here, the North Sea was and is crossed by ships to England.

Raymond states: It amazes me, as I write, that I can recall not only incidents, people, trains, odors of my childhood, but even the flavor of foods. The feel of Northern winters, the nip on my nose, frost in my eyes, and the smell of winter in my nostrils, the wool on my body. Frost forms on my scarf as I breathe the air and mist of twenty-five degrees below zero.

Our Hotel Gastis was a post station. The yard was usually filled with carriages in summer and sleighs in winter. Travelers and salesmen dropped off the train, stayed overnight, then left for the next town and post station hotel, where our sleigh or carriage pulled by a horse would be liveried and a fresh one hired, ours to return with the next traveler coming our way.

Mother's prayers taught me from as far back as I can remember that if I hung onto the simple faith, and I have, it all adds up to, "Wherever in the world I travel, there stands my luck—in God's hands. Luck comes, luck goes, the one God loves, to him luck goes. Amen." It works, but only with simple, blind, positive acceptance of God's best will for me. This is my entire religion.

Lydia and Emil journeyed back and forth between Krokom, Sweden and Brockton, Massachusetts at least three times before their family was completed. Astrid Lydia Christina was conceived in Sweden, but born in Massachusetts on 30 June 1906. She was a fragile child. The fourth baby was almost born aboard the ship on yet another return to the Americas. Carl Emil clocked in on 27 October 1910, a very difficult birth during which Emil almost lost his precious wife. Astrid was called Acky, Gunhild became known as Gunnie, and Raymond and Carl were known by their proper names.

Emil and Lydia had realized a large profit from the sale of the Hotel Gastis in Sweden and set about looking for a suitable home. The decision had been finally made to settle in America, as so many of their close friends had done for the tremendous opportunities.

The homestead was found in the country in the little Massachusetts town of Sharon. It was a gorgeous mansion on twenty-four acres, and affectionately called *Sharon*. The house contained twelve rooms and three bathrooms, but water had to be obtained from a pump house a quarter of a mile away.

Author's Note: Although the acreage has dwindled over the years the proud old estate still stands to this day.

Of all the children, Raymond was the most difficult, always into mischief and busy doing something every minute. One account of his childhood has him hanging himself by his tongue! He was at the top rung of a ladder pounding nails into the barn, when he slipped and caught his tongue on a large nail. He screamed and bled as he hung there waiting for help. Emil shoved a ladder under

The estate Sharon.

him, and carefully removed his son from his impalement, then proceeded to beat the bejesus out of him with his belt for being so stupid. In later years, Ray loved to show off his scar wherever and whenever he could gain attention.

At thirteen years of age, he looked for a job and found one in Everett at the Crown Theater, which featured a prominent film each week, five vaudeville acts, a short, and a newsreel. First he was a candy boy, then an usher, and when he became manager he was permitted to wear a woolen uniform with dark blue braids on the shoulders. He thought himself a big shot in his fancy uniform of Swedish colors. By the time he was fourteen, he was promoted to assistant projectionist. Theater was already in his blood.

When he completed high school, Emil and Lydia steered him in what they thought was the right direction. "Raymond," Emil instructed, "I have a close friend in the knitting industry. It may be a wonderful opportunity for you."

"Yes, Pa."

It was boring, learning the knitting machines, but he did it for his parents. Finally, Lydia and Emil paid for samples for Raymond to show on his first selling job in Upper New York. He hated this so much he promptly sold all of them for cash, then bought his first camera, a Wilart. When he brought it home with the great news of his intended career, Emil was dumbfounded and Lydia almost fainted. But the boy had matured fast, and his mind was set.

A young Swede with camera, circa 1926.

CHAPTER TWO

The Kings and Swede

"I'm young. I have my own life to live," Raymond wanted to shout, according to his memoirs. Instead, he sat down and made a complete inventory—one fine camera, a few hundred dollars in the bank, the ability to speak Swedish as well as English, and most importantly, the lessons learned while a projectionist at the Crown Theater, particularly the newsreels and how they were shot, cut, and put together. He made copious notes, and acquired enough knowledge to qualify as a newsreel cameraman. When the *Boston Fox* newsman had two subjects to cover on the same day, he was given one of them. But this wasn't enough. One night while in bed, he carefully laid out his plan—get a job and prove himself to his parents. Sleep finally came, and an idea was hatched.

Early the next morning, he dressed carefully and headed for Boston to spend a few of his precious dollars on stationery and envelopes embossed with his name and address. He began writing to every American newsreel representative in New York, foreign steamship lines, and railroads in Europe.

The mailbox rewarded him with an offer to cover northern Europe on a freelance basis. He ran, waving the letter above his head. "Ma, Pa, I've got it! An offer!" He read the letter aloud, then to himself over and over again. He would be supplied with plenty of raw stock, film negative, as well as stationery with a new letterhead showing his foreign address in Stockholm, Sweden. One dollar per foot would be paid for film used in a newsreel, Kinograms, and the balance returned to him. *Author's note: Kinograms later became Universal Newsreels.*

The Swedish line also offered free passage across the Atlantic in return for a filmed record of the trip. In addition, free rail transportation was given all over Europe by various railroads.

Emil grabbed his son and gave him one of his famous bear hugs, saying, "Lydia, get the trunks out of the attic. We have to get the boy packed."

Lydia spun on her slender heel, and dashed about, sweat on her brow, as she carefully mended and ironed white shirts, collars, and trousers. Suits were cleaned and brushed. Time was important. Raymond was to sail in one week.

They made their way by carriage to New York, by way of the old Boston Post Road to see their son off. As they waved to their son, whose face appeared among the varied colored streamers aboard the ship, Lydia whispered to Emil, "He is so young." She felt as all mothers do when their sons grow up.

However, Raymond was anything but a child and found his way around the ship quite easily, gleaning faint memories from other trips as a boy. His passage was booked first class.

The first shots Raymond "Swede" Fernstrom made as a newsreelman were sent to New York, then returned to him developed but not used. Undaunted, he sold them to the Swedish-American line, who ordered more prints for their New York and other offices. He'd made his first dollars or Kronor.

It was a fine day in Stockholm when he emerged from his newly rented room located in an old inn downtown. He didn't know where to begin first, shot film with a frenzy, then shipped it back to New York almost every day. Money and film dwindled, while room and eating bills grew. But eventually, his efforts paid off.

The Swedish-American line delivered fifty thousand feet of fresh film, plus checks covering stories he had submitted. Northern Europe was virgin territory for American newsreels, a novelty, and novelty was news—not spot news, but feature material for theaters, newspapers, etcetera. The world was his plum. Filler materials were greatly needed in those days, and here was the man to supply it.

Raymond Gustaf Ivar Fernstrom must have cut quite a figure to his fellow Swedish newsmen, for he knew no rules of courtesy. If he wanted a picture, he went after it. His belief was that if something interested him, it would certainly be interesting to America. Action was the name of the game, and he shot it all. Swedish firemen on duty, mass gymnastics, swimming races, down the North Sea to the Baltic. He shipped them all to New York, along with captions to muster as much sales pitch as he could. Everything seemed to sell.

The local newsmen became jealous and started kidding him, for they saw nothing novel in what he shot. But they enjoyed his food and drank his liquor while laughing at him.

He chased from story to story, learning all the while. They called him "Yank" and "Swede," but they could call him "son-of-a-bitch" for all he cared because he was working and making money—lots of it.

The train gave a last puff of smoke and left the station in a roar. Swede sat contentedly in first class, on a seat that ran from the side windows to the corridor along the side of the European train, gazing at his camera, magazine case, and tripod resting on the baggage rack across from him and above the men seated on the other long couch. He shivered a little in pride as he read his name properly embellished on each case. It was obvious he was well-traveled.

A distinguished gentleman sitting next to Swede was also studying the equipment and remarked in Swedish, "Are you Swedish or are you American?" Raymond explained who and what he was. "But your American newsreels don't come over here until more than four months after your stories are received, and by then most are old hat to us," the stranger responded.

An idea was born. Swede hadn't thought his material was of interest to the European countries, only New York.

"In the manner with which you seek material," the man continued, "and the way you cover these stories, you should find great appeal elsewhere. Do you understand that you see our countries through American eyes with a fresh new viewpoint?" The man speaking was Raoul Le Mat, an American of French extraction, who was self-employed and owned Metro-Goldwyn-Mayer Film Distribution which covered eleven Northern European countries. He had no newsreels or short subjects and needed Raymond.

They poured the cognac and became very talkative. Raoul devised an excellent plan for himself and Swede. Why not let him develop Ray's negatives in Stockholm, make prints for New York, and serve the European market first? Ray would make double the money, Raoul Le Mat would be considered a genius, and New York would never know the difference. Furthermore, Ray would be given an office supplied with the prettiest secretary Raoul could find. That did it. The deal was struck.

The romantic, as he called himself, skipped through his rather dusty office. The windows needed a wash, he noted, but otherwise the place was nice. And as promised the gorgeous new secretary was there to assist him in every way. He felt like a big man with plenty of money and always an idea that was purposeful. He picked at everyone's brains, listened, learned, and bought a lot of drinks.

One day he was asked if he'd read the evening papers concerning the King's moose hunt in Vermland Province with the Danish King. "Hell no!" God, he thought. What a story! Two kings. However, he did not know the press was *forbjudet* (forbidden). His competitors drank to his ignorance as he thanked them for the tip, then set off for Majestatsbrot, Sweden, where not only cameramen but angels feared to tread.

The lovely little railroad station in Vermland was quiet. Swede stood there, one camera hung on a shoulder, the combination magazine and tripod over the other, his hand clutching a little box containing a clean shirt, a pair of socks, toothbrush, and other small personal items. He had been told where the royal coaches would arrive and would be stationed on the siding. In Sweden, there is no night during the summer and he could see clearly at five in the morning when the two lavish coaches, one red, the other a shiny light blue, arrived across the platform from where he stood in admiration. The blue one, the Swedish King's, bore a golden coat of arms, while the second was embellished with the royal coat of arms of the Danish King from Denmark. A white graveled path graced with a little white picket fence led to the cars.

Where are the other cameramen and the press? Swede wondered. He stationed his camera on a vantage point, waited, then set the lens to stop. Swede ordinarily had nerves of steel, but on this day he was on edge. He snuffed out yet another cigarette, further annoyed by an old man drifting around the area then staring at him and his camera, but kept his eyes glued to the two coaches for signs of life.

"So you are from New York?" the old guy asked.

Swede swore. Why me? "Yes," he answered courteously, "I am an American." He hoped the stranger would go away without fouling his chances of getting pictures of the kings.

"But you speak Swedish," the old man persisted.

Goddammit. "Yes," he answered irritated. "My mother and father were born here."

The old man warmed up to Swede, asking where his parents were born.

Jesus, who needs this? Swede swore to himself again, then spat out the wanted information that his mother was born in Lidkoping and his father came from Sala. "And now would you please leave me alone?" He shrugged off the intruder, checked his gear, and kept a watchful eye on the intended scoop, his alone since no other camera was in sight.

"Are you going on the moose hunt?"

"I hope so," Raymond answered. Will this guy ever leave?

"Oh, that would be fine," the old man said kindly. "We would love to have you."

Raymond spun, looked the old geezer in the eyes, then saw the poor man was clad in a well worn hunting coat. Blue eyes danced, as the stranger announced, "I am the King Gustaf of Sweden."

"In that old coat?" Raymond blurted.

"Yes," the King said, smiling gently. "I've had this favorite hunting jacket for fourteen years." He offered Swede a cigarette. Mouth hanging, Swede accepted, noticing the royal crest of gold on the old man's bosom. But instead of smoking the precious offering, he shoved it into his pocket.

"Why do you do that?" the King inquired.

"My parents would never believe this happened, unless I had proof, sir—eh, Your Majesty, Your Highness, Sire."

"Oh, smoke it," he persisted. "I'll give you a carton of them for your parents in America."

Swede felt milky of leg, but nonetheless became bolder and asked if he could take a close-up of His Majesty.

"Certainly!"

My God, Ray thought, wait until the guys hear this tale. He clicked away, until another tall gentlemen in hunting clothes joined them. The

King of Denmark! Ray's head throbbed as he made two close-ups of his first sight of royalty, still the reigning thrones of Europe.

The Danish King eyed the box Swede carried. "What is this?"

"Your Majesty," Swede answered, bowing, "this is the eyes of the world."

"Fine," King Christian of Denmark remarked. "What do you want me to do?"

"Well, you can take off your hat and nod, if you like," Ray told him. And thereafter, in every scene Raymond made, the good king would doff his hat and nod.

That morning, after each king had shot his moose, a little farm house was commandeered for lunch. Bertil Norberg, the *hov forografer* (royal photographer) took all the pictures, recording the occasion in still photographs.

Raymond wondered aloud, "Why are there no other photographers present, including the Swedish newsreel cameramen from Stockholm?"

"They are not allowed," Bertil explained. "They thought they were putting you on the spot when they sent you down here."

"Well, those so-and-so's," muttered Raymond.

"You're in the clear now," the royal photographer added. "Nobody can say anything, as long as the King gave his permission. Of course, those newsmen in Stockholm won't like you very much."

"I don't care, as long as my company buys lots of footage!"

Suddenly, the Danish King stuck his head out the window. "Where is that damned Yankee cameraman?" he roared.

"Here, Your Majesty."

"Come in here!"

Raymond entered as the King explained, "Now I want you to settle something for us! Which is the best, Swedish akvavit or Danish akvavit?" He pointed to a seat. "Come sit down between us." Raymond sat. First the Swedish then the Danish akvavit; ice cold and potent. "*Skäl!*" both kings yelled with each drink, until Swede was ready to topple.

"They are both the same high quality," slurred Raymond diplomatically, burping, unkempt hair tumbling in his uncooperative eyes.

"Reward him!" bellowed the Swedish King. A beautiful white box bearing the coat of arms, full of the King's special private, royal cigarettes was handed to him. Raymond asked for an autograph. Then, not to be outdone, the Danish King offered a lovely red box of his own cigarettes. Mind boggling, not only from the booze, but from his experience as well, Raymond backed out through the door, taking shots, and covering scenes of the entire entourage.

He had shot about eight hundred feet of film, and Mr. Le Mat used every frame of it. In New York, it was made into a special documentary featurette. During the hunting party, Bertil and Raymond had exchanged notes, then Bertil was summoned to take more pictures, and Raymond was caught in them. Naturally, he received vast publicity and criticism in the European press, but his name was spelled correctly.

Picture taken by Bertil Norberg: Royal Swedish Photographer.

It was this photograph that "Swede" Fernstrom presented to his peers at the American Society of Cinematographers. They questioned him as to why it merited being considered for entrance into their sacred "Hall of Fame?" Ray replied that the guy behind the camera is now Gustaf VI Adolph, the King of Sweden. Swede and the photograph were immediately inducted. The Picture proudly hangs there today.

Royal Recklessness and Reindeer

After the moose hunt exclusive, Swede was the envy of every news cameraman in Scandinavia. The practical joke had backfired. The American press reproduced many stills and ran them in newspapers throughout America and Canada. Le Mat made a special film of all the footage, which was a full documentary, and made a massive amount of prints to be shown all over Europe.

Swede's income rose tremendously. The New York bosses loved the royalty and nobility angle and yelled by cable for more—anything about counts, barons, castles, kings, princes, or princesses. Swede used his royal contacts to the optimum, much to the dismay of his cohorts who couldn't even approach them. An American with a movie camera and the eye of the American public, Ray cashed in on every opportunity.

Swede learned to dress, and did they dress in Europe! Morning clothes, sports clothes, business clothes. Tuxedos were referred to as smoking jackets. Formal dress was tails, white tie, top hat, cane, overcoat, white gloves, and a monocle. Ray became quite the actor, playing the part to the hilt, sometimes changing clothes as many as seven times in one day.

Then, one afternoon as Ray sat watching one of his prints with Le Mat, his gorgeous secretary slid quietly onto the seat next to him in the dark projection theater and waited. In the darkness, while the projector flickered, his hand naturally fell to her smooth, supple legs. Swede was born to be a lover as well as a cameraman and couldn't wait for the film to end. When the lights came on, they bid Le Mat adieu, went straight to Ray's office, locked the door, and used the couch for what it was designed.

Finally she murmured, "This is not what I came to the theater for—this time."

"What then, sweet Svenska Flika?" Ray inquired tenderly.

"There's a man in uniform waiting for you in the reception room," she answered contentedly.

Swede went out wondering if it was a Swedish cop. No, it was a chauffeur, dressed in the most gorgeous uniform Ray had ever seen. He suggested that Ray had undoubtedly rented automobiles very often, and to that Ray agreed. Did Ray have his own car and chauffeur? he asked.

"No."

"Would you like to see my car?" Next to cameras and cuties, cars were Ray's life. The chauffeur explained in careful Swedish that he and his car were for hire. So Ray went out to have a look. It stood at the curb, a tremendous large, long, impressive French-built V-8, De Deon Boute Laundeaulette, in all its gleaming splendor. It was a duel convertible, actually one for the driver and one for the rear occupants. The back seats were regally cushioned into couch-like affairs, with folding seats behind the chauffeur's compartment. A telephone connected the resplendent owner in the rear with the driver.

Swede immediately imagined his camera set up and fastened down on the roof for high shots and facing back at the highway from the rear tonneau when the folding top was down. He shot his secretary a wicked wink as together they envisioned the future with anticipation. Room enough for love and rest as the miles rolled by. There was a pull-down curtain between the chauffeur and the rear compartment. This magnificent motor car was definitely built in France!

Would Swede like to engage him and his comfortable monster? the young man hesitated and pondered. "I'll even carry all your gear," he added.

It was agreed. Elsa and Ray folded up the new office for the day and spun slowly through the colorful Swedish countryside toward a lovely hotel in Uppsala. A lunch basket had been packed full of Scandinavian cookies and goodies, and there was a cooler crammed full of akvavit, cognac, soda water, wines, and champagne to be served on a small folding table.

The owner of the car, now assistant cameraman and chauffeur, would do many jobs for the price of one, and he also had a girl. They took her along as well. They had phoned ahead, and engaged two beautiful suites, which would be ready when the foursome arrived. And the party began in Stockholm, the capital.

It carried on through several Swedish provinces as Ray searched for subjects for his camera, which was always as close as his first wrist watch or secretary. Fortunately, the secretary had warned Hank, the chauffeur, to take along plenty of clothes, as no one knew where the crazy Yankee would take them. So everyone was prepared.

Once they even rented a speedboat to visit the many beautiful islands of the Archipelago that stretches from Stockholm many miles out into the Gulf of Bothnia in the Baltic Sea. It came in handy for Swedish boat races of all kinds.

As the days flew by, in work-fun and play-fun, Ray's income continued to grow. The rate of exchange from dollars to Kronor was ever in his favor. One dollar bought about five dollars worth of Swedish goods, and he lived like a millionaire but still put aside money for a rainy day.

In 1925, Ray went nearly to the North Pole on a special assignment cabled from New York. Roald Amundson and Lincoln Ellsworth were reported lost at the North Pole with their two Dornier-Wals seaplanes. These were special aircraft with twin Rolls-Royce engines, one pulling, the other pushing, and mounted atop the wing. The Norwegian Navy was sending a relief expedition with two navy seaplanes on the deck of their cargo ship the *Ingertre*. Aboard were two newspapermen, one from London, the other from Paris, an American from a newspaper syndicate, and three flyers. Lieutenant Lutzow-Holm, Lieutenant Styhr, and a flight lieutenant, seaplane designer later to become world famous, Bernt Balchen, and all the Norwegian air service.

It was an adventurous group full of life and experience. Two better storytellers never lived than the two newspapermen. The one from London had limericks by the yard, which kept everyone laughing from Oslo to Spitzbergen. The other told stories of Paris that had the audience unbelieving, yet enthralled. Everyone has had some experience with man-woman relationships, but from Paris came stories that tested imaginations. Evidently, the normal procedures had become jaded to the insatiable girls and boys of Paris.

The group eventually arrived in Advent Bay, Spitzbergen, where the open water in the bay gave them the chance to hoist the two seaplanes overboard. Balchen had already ran up the engines on deck, and with seaplanes propellers turning, the crews and Ray's camera were swung down onto the icy cold water. This was the first time Swede had ever mounted a movie camera in an airplane, but with Balchen's help it was secured. They taxied away into the Arctic morning. During April and the summer months, there was only daylight in the land of the midnight sun.

Lieutenant Styhr was at the controls of one seaplane with Balchen and his binoculars as observer, while Ray served the same purpose in the aft cockpit behind Lieutenant Lutzow-Holm. The two planes flew over the glaciers toward Kings Bay farther north. As they came in over Kings Bay, something smacked Ray in the head and he was pinned back against the cockpit. The camera had broken loose. He banged his fist on the cockpit for help. Lutzow-Holm finally got the message that Ray was in trouble and landed smoothly on the bay, where the other plane joined them.

Swede with camera mounted in airplane, from the rescue of Amundsen and Ellsworth in 1925.

Together they dismounted the camera, then flew back to the mother ship at Advent Bay. On the next flight, Ray's lesson was learned, so the camera was properly bolted in, instead of roped.

After several flights in search over the polar ice and on their way back from the Pole to Kings Bay, they flew low and finally spotted the Arctic explorers. When all were safe, they told of having to make one Dornier-Wals seaplane ready for flight by combining parts from the other.

The next day, Ray got his pictures as they took off for Advent Bay, circling, giving him terrific angles. But Ray and his pilot got carried away, and

23

while banking a little too sharply, they crashed. The accident wasn't serious and Swede laughed it off, for he had gotten his precious pictures. But later he realized he had sustained a back injury which was to plague him the rest of his life.

Swede shipped the film to New York from Trondhjem, Norway, then entrained for Stockholm and his secretary. More and more of Ray's newsreel stories showed up on the American screens, and the competition became interested in his virgin territory. Russell Muth showed up from Berlin. He was staff man there for the Fox office. As an old newsreel veteran, he felt Swede was some sort of crazy nut, neophyte, and Johnny-come-lately, and he began lording it over him like a Samson, which amused Ray no end, his ego unblemished. He was full of confidence, as youth is when gaining a little experience. Russ became a constant challenge to the young Swedish-American, but Swede was intelligent enough to study Russ. Whatever Russ did picture-wise, Ray picked his brain, experience, and attitude. Whatever he could apply to himself and his work, he adopted. But he was selective. Sometimes he liked certain things Russ did, while others he dropped, as he had his own technique developing. They covered quite a number of stories together.

For the first time in over 150 years, the Swedish King and Queen were to visit their island in Gotland, which was another reason for Russ to show up in the frozen north. Russ and Swede drank their way on a little overnight steamer to Visby, the old Hanseatic port of the island of Gotland.

The royal destroyer arrived, and the two newsmen covered the first day's activities, with Russ cashing in on Swede's previous contacts with the royal family and staff, as well as the navy and army brass. But the next morning when the royal couple were scheduled to review the native defense forces, Russ' bragging perfection hit a snag. On the way out to the field, Ray asked him if in his egotistical perfection he had ever forgotten the crank to his camera.

"Never ever!" he bragged. "I always carry it here, in this—in this— pocket. Goddamn, turn around, I left it back at the hotel!" From that day on, Ray felt better and had learned. He made a bracket for the side of his camera and tripod cranks, which fit onto the camera itself, so as not to ever have that happen to him.

Russ may have been a German-American, the arrogant type, but he was rather more friendly than average. The Stockholm competition were happy to greet him, hoping he would take the edge off Ray's success in their homeland, trusting that a second interloper would cause his downfall. In spite of this, Ray suggested to Russ that they jointly cover a reindeer separation up North, in the area where Swede had spent and loved his early childhood.

Lapps count their wealth not by Kronor, but in the reindeer they own. During the winter, the animals join, en masse, from all herds, traveling in search of moss and lichen for food. In the early spring, which is still more winter and colder than elsewhere in the world, the owners surround the herds, wearing short, wide Lapp skis, and separate the thousands from their own herds by lassoing the leaders, who are marked by nicks in their ears.

Russ and the local city slicker newsmen were all enthused by Ray's suggestion. Russ saw only a good feature news story, while the city boys, too soft for the harsh climate up North, were only too eager for the two of them to hang themselves in the cold where it was too rough for even movie cameras to turn. Neither they nor Russ Muth knew that here Ray had been taught well how to survive in those conditions by no other than the Lapps!

After several days and nights by train, they arrived at Gallivera, rented a sleigh drawn by reindeer with a Lapp for a driver, and set out early in the morning in the biting cold to shoot movies. Ray's mind kept recalling a funny incident on the train as they traveled North. Russ had checked his wallet and expense ledger, then asked, "Hey, Swede, do you mind if we take a smoking compartment instead of a sleeper?" He was a thrifty guy who wanted to make a buck on his Fox expense account.

"Yeah, that's okay with me," Swede agreed doubtfully, hoping the overnight trip would turn into a disaster and teach the arrogant, tight, know-it-all bastard a good lesson.

They found the smoking compartment not too uncomfortable, with two long seats facing each other, providing a bed of sorts. But smoking compartments were open to all first-class passengers, with the door never locked, and as Russ and Swede stretched out on the benches, another passenger entered. Courtesy demanded that they now share a bench to give the unwanted intruder a seat. The two newsmen sat hunched in their corners, while the other man stretched out, arms splayed, and fell sound asleep. Ray, too, slipped into a deep snooze, and during the night, eventually pushed Russ to the floor. Huddled and cold, Russ tapped and tapped on Ray's forehead until he was awake.

"We've got to get rid of this guy," Russ whispered, desperately.

"Sure," snorted Ray. "I'll open the door, and you shove him out." Whereupon Russ grabbed the sleeping man, pushed him through, his German temper flaring, and locked it tight.

The next morning, Russ remarked to Swede, "I'll never travel second-class again."

"You betcha," Ray replied, with a shit-ass grin on his face.

Thousands of reindeer galloped round and round in the deep, hard-crusted snow, while the warmed camera ground away. Russ began to freeze and yell. Even the potent akvavit couldn't seem to warm him up. His feet were killing him. He had not listened to Swede's advice to buy Lapp reindeer boots, pants, and parka. Nor had he picked up the fur-lined Lapp gloves Swede had suggested. All the arrogant German could say was, "I know what I am doing!" He thought Swedes were dumber

Swede knew how to dress for the cold.

than Germans, and had a thing to learn the hard way. Swede thought, do Germans ever learn?

Back in town after a hard day's work, two house-maids rubbed Russ' feet and ears with snow from a bucket until the circulation returned to his frost-bitten ears, feet, hands, and ankles. They kept pouring the Lapps' favorite beverage down his stubborn gullet, which was made up of hot, black coffee half filled with 150-proof Swedish *renat brannvin* (burn-wine), the most potent akvavit in Scandinavia. Germans are stubborn, but Swedes can be worse.

When it was all over, all Ray's friendly competitor wanted to do was head home to Berlin and get the hell out of Sweden, leaving Ray to his happy devices in his friendly country! *Ja! Ja! Jah!*

A Danish Picnic, a Dutchman, and Sweden's Pride

On the delightful rail trip back to Stockholm from Lapland, Ray took note of the little town in the northern province of Jemtland and the tiny hamlet of Krokom with such happy memories. He saw the shining, smiling, red faces of the children with some Lapp kids watching him and knew their feelings.

En route, the temptation was irresistible to accept an invitation to Paris for a short vacation. He had been informed by cable that his New York boss would like to meet him, which meant a few days away from his camera, secretary, and a few other damsels as well. So he locked away his camera in Raoul Le Mat's private vault, in his own private and reserved compartment, and took the train to Malmo, then boarded a Netherlands-built Junkers Tri-motor airplane to Amsterdam, Holland, and away he flew.

A short while later, the plane developed engine trouble and the pilot was forced to land skillfully in a farmer's pasture somewhere in Denmark. It was the funniest forced landing Ray had ever seen, and he had been in his share of them. They were in the middle of a brilliant green field, where the pilots went to work immediately on the engine while the passengers milled about in the warm sunshine and lolled on the lush green pasture.

Then a funny thing happened. The Danes began to arrive. They came from all directions. A truck came with iced beer, which sold out fast to the thirsty passengers. Women brought baskets of food, sandwiches, akvavit, salads, and fruit, making the pasture into a giant airborne picnic.

The carnival atmosphere turned an accident into a party, as everyone was having a ball. Soon the pilots joined the drinking and eating, then announced that it was okay to take off when everyone was ready. No one seemed in the least bit of a hurry. But soon the women began to clean up the mess, and everyone pitched in to clear the field and take-off strip of debris. Airborne, the passengers waved to the grand people. What a great experience, Ray thought. Couldn't have been better if it was planned.

Again, they headed southward and in short order landed in Hamburg, Germany. Swede had made arrangements to fly to Paris by way of Amsterdam, with a short layover in Hamburg. He found a charming cafe with a verandah overlooking the airfield, where he sipped cognac and munched a heavy German sandwich. He had learned in Sweden that to drink is to eat, chasing each draft with a hunk of food for a long and cheerful existence. A fine lesson American imbibers should emulate for good health and longevity.

He was joined by a tall friendly Dutchman who informed Ray that he was his only passenger to Paris in a single-engine Fokker, due to the fact that he was flying alone and the cabin would be filled with mail. He sat down and joined Ray in a bit of cognac. After a few more drinks, he informed Ray that he could fly with him in the cockpit if he wished. You bet!

It was a high-winged Fokker, Dutch wonder, with an open cockpit, and only a windshield between them and the roaring Maiback engine. They drank, flew, and yacked. Finally, they landed in Amsterdam, unloaded some mail and picked up more, while Swede remained the only passenger. They loaded more fuel and cognac, then took off for Paris. Once in the air and a few more cognacs later, the Dutchman yelled, "Want to see the battlefields in France?"

"Sure," Swede hollered back.

Ray was fascinated as they soared over the landscape. Meanwhile, he passed a few more bottles of cognac to the pilot, joining him sip by sip. Both were feeling pretty good when they landed at Le Bourge Field over an hour late. Ray practically fell from the cockpit, down to the spot where Lindbergh would land a few years later. He was relieved to learn that an international breakfast was planned at the Fontaine Blue. His eyes were playing tricks on him—too much cognac!

The party was joined by his editor, a real stuffed shirt. Everyone agreed that the man needed a night on the town in Paris at the Red Mill, 27 the Cafe of the Dead Rat, where he became ill. For the cafe was lighted by a weird illumination of Cooper-Hewitt purple tubes, which cast fantastic shadows over the coffins where the drinks were set up. Customers banged on them for drinks with human leg bones. They added cognac to his choice of weak wine every time he looked away, so he became plastered for the first time in his life. Nothing much more than a good time was accomplished in Paris, and the editor was happy to leave the others to their enjoyment. But all good times had to end. Heavy heads had to clear and eyes had to sharpen, too. For there was a wire from Le Mat back in Stockholm: "Return for something important that I am sure you will like."

Ray bade his new found friends adieu and set out by plane to Sweden.

Le Mat really was working on something interesting, a trip to New York and back on the maiden voyage of the Swedish-American line's sleek, advanced liner—a giant, new motorship—the original MS *Gripsholm*.

Le Mat owned the largest theater in Stockholm, except for the one belonging to the Swedish film industry who also had the largest movie studio in Northern Europe, of which there were quite a few.

Raoul wanted something exclusive and original in a feature-length movie. He had contacted the line with a proposition to make a complete documentary of the new *Gripsholm's* maiden voyage from her home port Gothenburg, Sweden to New York and return, arriving back in Sweden for the traditional Christmas celebration, which begins December thirteenth with Lucia Day and runs well into the first month of the new year.

La Mat had outlined and laid out a script and plan for Ray, and his enthusiasm grew with his recitation of the typed outline. The passenger list on the trip from Sweden was to include the country's richest and most influential people, to which on the return trip would be added the same in Swedish-Americans. Some of them had not seen their native Sweden since they had left her in their youth.

Swede visualized great potential for a really dramatic production filled with human interest stories. His enthusiasm increased even more by the fact that he now had a new negative film, panchromatic, which is sensitive to all colors, instead of the old orthochromatic blue sensitive negative. Now, he would have the chance to expand his storytelling from short newsreel yarns into a full-length story, blending human angles into the development of man's great love of sea and ships.

The *Gripsholm*, Swedish built, was the first ocean liner equipped with the new diesel engines so highly engineered and now on her maiden voyage.

Ray followed his gear up the gangplank mid confetti and colored paper streamers thrown from the top of the pier and the already boarded passengers. As the ship's band played Swedish and American music, tears flowed from the half-drunk passengers, as well as those saying fond adieus, all of which was recorded by the intrepid cameraman. Slowly, the gangplanks rose, waving followed, then the release of cables, and the gradual receding of the huge liner from the pier. Ray panned the crowd, then up to the beautiful city of Gothenburg and the heights above her— the towers, monuments, and fortresses from olden days, Sweden. He experienced much the same tug at his heart strings as the crowd of Swedes felt, but with an additional elation at the prospect of going home to the good old USA.

On this trip he never relaxed, never stopped working. For the first time, Ray had lights to shoot interiors, as well as deck-side pictures. It was a wonderful, exhilarating voyage.

Once docked in New York, he headed straight for Sharon, Massachusetts. He longed to see Ma and Pa, his two sisters Acky and Gunnie, and kid brother Carl. What stories he had to relate!

Ma rushed around her enormous kitchen, cooking all his favorite meals, and carefully inspecting the soiled laundry. With loving hands, she washed, dried, and ironed the shirts and brushed his suits. It was good to see her Raymond again. The nine days before the *Gripsholm* sailed had passed quickly. But Ray, on the other hand, was anxious to return to the ship and continue his adventurous life, for he could handle the quiet at home on the farm for only about one day.

An Epic Film and Jerry

Back on the *Gripsholm*, Ray heard the warning bugle. It was a short time to cocktails, dinner, coffee, and after-dinner drinks. He dashed off to put away his gear then dress for dinner, even though few did the first night out. But he was a romantic bachelor on the prowl and wanted to compete with the less-prepared gents who had not yet received their luggage from the baggage rooms. Swede was at his best when trying to impress the ladies. He could be a mild, suave, diplomatic man one minute, then suddenly switch to an exciting, utterly devastating rogue the next. In addition to his meticulous dress, he had learned the magic lure that movie making had on women. "Would you like to be in a movie?" That line was a great opener in those days. He was making a feature film for Europe, especially Sweden. "You'll see yourself on the screen soon after we dock."

He cased the dining room for possibles. Naturally with his photographic mind he had selected a few beforehand and he sought them out. Were they in first or second-class? he wondered. He had permission to cover the entire ship while making the production for newsreels, so began his search in first-class in the dining salon.

Ray usually preferred brunettes but was stopped in his tracks by a gorgeous blonde on the arm of an older, tall, serious, and distinguished looking gentleman. "Is she his wife, daughter, or mistress?" Ray asked the purser.

"She is his daughter," he responded, then added, "Her father is a multimillionaire New York importer." Swede listened as he kept his eye on the ravishingly beautiful girl. "Her father, Hans Lagerloef, has sixteen ships plying the seas with his wood pulp products."

He gathered courage, approached their table, bowed from the waist in his best Swedish manner, then presented himself in Swedish to the father. He then requested with over-emphatic suavity the pleasure of a dance with the lovely young lady. Her father cleared his throat with annoyance, then introduced his daughter Mabel with wary reluctance. "I'd love to," she replied in English.

It was infatuation at first sight, but courting had its problems and obstructions in the form of a very stubborn, opinionated, thick-headed father. Then one evening after dinner, he said to Ray, "Come, let us walk on deck. I want to talk to you. I am taking this trip to Sweden with my daughter for a very definite reason," he said coldly and calmly. "She wanted to marry my chauffeur! But I paid him off with six thousand dollars and shipped the bore off to Cuba."

A stunned Ray felt like leaving, but the man was a challenge and now he had become accustomed to taking things as they came. The courtship continued with no holds barred on the father's or Ray's part. But Swede also had to concentrate on his work, for they were getting closer to Sweden each day.

On the last day at sea, Ray set up the camera at daybreak. Already people were gathering at the forward rails on every deck straining for a first glimpse of their native homeland, some after fifty years in America. This was real human interest stuff, with dramatic close-ups of all those pathetic, tear-stained visages as the first faint outline of the Swedish coastline came into view. He used camera lap dissolves, and brought the coast ever closer, larger, more impressive, while close-ups were cut in on many of the people, recording their reactions.

Before he knew it, his job was completed to the last passengers as they disembarked to meet fond embraces with families waiting on the pier. Together the flags of Sweden and America waved gently in the breeze, and Ray made a final fade-out with his dissolving shutter. Well pleased, he patted the trusty wonder box and put it to bed.

Swede looked for his girl and discovered she and her father had left the ship early while he was performing the final filming. But he had enough contacts with the line and the officers to learn that the Lagerloefs were registered at the Palace Hotel in Gothenburg. He phoned from the ship immediately and luckily found Mabel, or "Jerry" as he liked to call her, alone in the suite. They made a date for dinner, then Ray went to work unloading the reels of film from his camera magazines, taped it all in cans, then shipped it off to Le Mat in Stockholm.

Jerry's shrewd father outwitted Ray, and swept his daughter off to Stockholm. Disappointed, Ray phoned Le Mat's office in the same city and asked a friend there to check all the hotels for reservations in the name of Lagerloef, then set out in pursuit of the blonde.

Ray found Le Mat deliriously pleased with the new footage. The man had set the whole crew feverishly working throughout the night, cutting, splicing, and editing, then the entire film was tinted on the color sensitive negative, and a truly elaborate documentary was the final result.

Naturally, a huge party was thrown with a banner prominently displayed which said, "Welcome Back, Swede." An orchestra played, while drinks and hors d'oeuvres were set out on a long linen-covered table. Flags of both countries were displayed proudly mid tears, laughter, dancing, and lots of hand shaking.

Then the lights dimmed and a special preview was shown of Ray's efforts and Le Mat's brilliant accomplishments. He had had a musical score specially written which the orchestra now played as all watched, enthralled. The final scenes were shown, the picture faded to its finale, and there was a hush in the audience as the lights were slowly turned up.

There wasn't a dry eye in the house, as everyone applauded and cheered. It was truly a beautiful documentary. The entire viewing group of dignitaries and invited guests were filled with tremendous pride. Swede rose and gave a thankful speech to all his co-workers for their delightful and thoughtful assistance in the making of the new classic, which became a huge success all over the world.

When Ray finished his speech, he was handed a note. Jerry was staying at the Strand. He phoned the hotel trying to get in touch with her, and finally made contact. She told him she would slip out under some pretense with her mother's help. He hadn't known Jerry's mother had made the trip. Jerry explained that she had never once left the state room until they slipped off the ship.

Ray sent a friend to fetch Jerry, afraid her father might shoot him and ruin the reunion. Soon he led her in to join the party, and realized she was more beautiful than he had remembered. She meant a lot more to him than her old man's dough. His determination grew to win her from him. He was not in love yet, but the pursuit had its compensations. He loved the chase.

During her stay, which was not to be long in Sweden, they had a chance to see enough of each other for their relationship to matter sincerely. But her father was a stamp collector, and a young agent of his in Stockholm was after the same young daughter. Sharpened by fresh competition, Swede used every recourse at his command. As a matter of cold fact, he extended himself quite daringly, to the point that when the young competitor asked her to attend the gala New Year's Eve party at the Royal Grand Hotel Ballroom, he found that Ray, through the good graces of the King's brother Prince Carl, had already asked her to sit at his table. She would be seated next to the Crown Prince and Princess. Other guests included a Russian Prince and Princess. He had beat the bum at his own game, and of course the old man couldn't avoid letting his daughter attend such a royal invitation. Her father did not know that Ray had better contacts with royalty than his lousy stamp collector friend, regardless of how much dough he might have.

It was the greatest party Ray ever attended, much like a later fabulously staged Technicolor movie production in Hollywood and shot in vivid color, the gowns, chest ribbons, decorations on silk cords, and colorful Swedish uniforms. It lasted far into the new year, and as morning slowly emerged, the party broke up into smaller groups who disappeared, some to homes, others to suites or rooms in the hotel, as did Jerry and Ray. They were happy for a while with champagne and song, but soon both realized that love had taken over. In the early dawn of that marvelous new year, he made love to her and realized they would marry. He returned her to the hotel by taxi and saw little more of her before she returned to New York.

Ray and Jerry corresponded regularly, and she fully took over his mind. This was a new experience for him. Other girls had no appeal and now he was back to work. Le Mat was organizing the big show, the premier of the picture-length film of the round trip journey of the *Gripsholm's* maiden voyage. There was great pride in their own Swedish-American line, and it was the first ocean liner built to their own design and new ideas. Also, the film would show more about Sweden and Swedes.

The MS *Gripsholm* went on to become world famous through war and peace and ended her days sailing the Seven Seas as a US Army transport known as the *John Erickson*. The new liner *Stockholm* was involved in the collision with the Italian liner *Andrea Doria* which sent the Italian ship to the bottom of the Atlantic. Swedish liners were built with much stronger hulls to cope with the icy conditions of the northern seas.

Two Loves Beckon

Ray was beginning to tire of Sweden. An unfamiliar feeling of homesickness settled upon him. He hungered to be with Jerry again. One day Le Mat gave him the information that the Crown Prince and Princess were planning a trip aboard the *Gripsholm* to visit New Sweden, Delaware, USA, where a gala anniversary was being planned.

Ray set to work on ideas and contacts and in the end sold Le Mat, the Swedish government, the Crown, and his office in New York on a series of newsreel stories showing the royal couple visiting various sections of Old Sweden, skiing and motoring over through the scenic wonders and fine roads. The idea grew and furthered Swede's plan to get home. He was invited on the voyage in the household of the Crown Prince's entourage, an American among Swedish royalty, and arrived in

New York with a goodly group of stories of the royal couple aboard the ocean liner. Le Mat's film was packaged for the return trip aboard the *Gripsholm*. Still aboard, for there were swarms of American newspaper and newsreel men waiting on shore, Ray bade the royal couple and family adieu, with his heartfelt thanks for all they had done for him. His job was finished. His attention was now cast dockward, where he finally spotted Jerry and her mother.

Somehow they had eluded the old man, and his car and chauffeur Watson awaited. Naturally, Ray had forgotten that Jerry's father had great business interests he had to attend to and this was a work day. Hans was on some reception committee for the royal couple's visit. As a result, Swede had Jerry, her mother, and the chauffeur all to himself, his good luck continuing.

They had lunch together, and afterward Swede boarded a train for Sharon to visit his parents and family and make plans for the future. He had received a promise from Jerry's mother that she could come and meet his family. She would drive up with two of her best friends and friends of the family, Eddie and Gibby.

It was great to be home again, and Ray filled his family with story after story of his many exciting adventures, while they poured over the many photographs he'd brought back with him.

It was the middle of the 1920s, and while Europe retained her dignity and charm, America was in the throes of one of her most famous decades, the Roaring Twenties! From Chicago to the East, shootings, murders, booze, and speakeasies abounded. Not again until the 1960s would this country again lose control. Then the downfall would be the result of drugs and drug dealers, which would effect everyone, enveloping the very young of our land. Children would sometimes be abandoned on the streets as their parents drifted through a drug hazed world. Violence, murders, freeway shootings, etcetera, would continue, history repeating itself as pathetic babies were born, shaking with addiction from the womb.

Each morning when Ray awakened in his old room, it surprised him that Lydia had kept everything in place just as he had left it. He felt comfortable, almost boyish again.

At breakfast, a few days after his arrival, he made his important announcement. "Ma and Pa, I'm going to get married!"

Silence.

"Well, I met this gorgeous gal on the *Gripsholm*. Her name is Mabel Lagerloef."

"Do you mean the daughter of Hans Lagerloef?" Emil's mouth fell open.

"Yeah, that's her."

Emil and Lydia exchanged glances, brows furrowed. Then Emil asked Raymond if he was aware of the family's importance.

Ray winked. "Of course."

"Is the bride any relation to Selma Lagerlof, the famous Swedish writer and Nobel Prize winner in literature?" his mother asked. Ray told her that Mabel's father was second cousin to Selma, upon which Lydia puffed up in pride. What a fine match, she thought.

Author's note: Selma Lagerlöf [Lagerloef], novelist, received the Nobel Prize in Swedish literature in 1909. The prize was awarded for her Story of Gösta Berling, which appeared in 1891 in Stockholm and exceeded the Miracles of Anti Christ and the Wonderful Adventures of Nils, fairy tales of Swedish folklore. One story was of a fireplace and family, and allegedly John F. Kennedy and Jackie had included a passage of her sayings on their Christmas cards for 1963, a month before JFK's assassination. In 1914, Selma Lagerloef was also elected to the Swedish Academy.

Emil was not so sure. "Have you spoken to her father about your intentions?" he asked dubiously.

"Well yes, Pa, I have. The guy's a real pompous jerk. He didn't exactly jump for joy at the thought of me marrying his precious daughter. We don't get along very well," Ray admitted, adding, "He requested a year's wait before the nuptial vows be exchanged, and I agreed."

Emil strongly advised him to honor the promise! "Don't upset him enough to disown her on your account and cut her out of his rich will."

Ray had a healthy pocket full of large bank drafts and travelers checks, and he cared little about his future father-in-law's millions, but promised Emil he would heed the advice.

Mabel Lenz Lagerloef was a perfect example and product of the Roaring Twenties—rich heiress to a fortune, spoiled, beautiful, highly educated, accustomed to servants. She had never washed a dish in her life and was as loose and wild as Ray. She was the golden girl born with a silver spoon in her mouth.

Emil and Lydia rushed around for days preparing for her visit. Only the finest linen and china would grace the luncheon table. Lydia cooked her heart out, while Emil and Raymond shoveled the driveway and steps of newly fallen snow.

Jerry was delivered by her friends, who waved a cheery hello and good-bye. Then Ray escorted her into the house. Emil and Lydia were impressed by her loveliness and enchanted with her happy, vivacious personality. Yes, it is a fine match, Lydia thought to herself. They make a grand looking couple.

Through his mother's eyes, Raymond was the perfect son, handsome, talented, and successful. But actually, he was a self-educated cameraman who would go to any lengths to promote and better himself, no matter who was injured along the way. He was ruthless and selfish, with little or no moral standards. He'd jump in bed with any gal willing as long as she was a doll, be it a friend's wife or a pick-up from a bar. His dangerous dark moods were never displayed to his parents, but friends and associates knew of them. But he had one thing going for him; he could be charming, dashing, and the women loved him. He was also a genius with camera and color. However, about the only thing Mabel and Ray had in common was their love of fast cars, fast times, parties—lots and lots of wild parties—and, of course, their true love for each other.

Once I asked him, "Dad, what are the most important things in your life?" Swiftly, without a second's hesitation, he replied, "Cameras, cuties, and cars, and in that order."

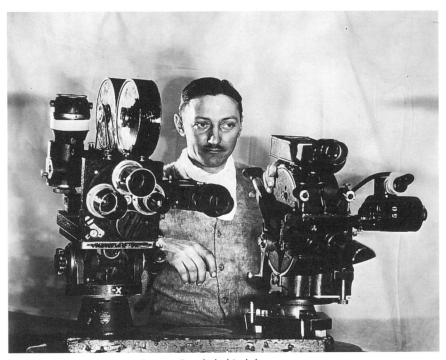

A suave Swede behind the cameras.

CHAPTER THREE
A Natural: Swede,
A Camera, and Hollywood

Hollywood had more attraction for Ray than Sharon, Massachusetts, New York, or anywhere else at that time. Hollywood and marriage—those were his plans. His dad, the charming Emil, had many friends during his life, and one of them owned a fleet of tankers that traveled from New York to California. So to save money, Emil asked his cohort if Ray could go along on a run.

When Ray arrived in New York, he learned that Jerry would never be permitted to come to Hollywood to see him. So before he left on 15 November 1926, he and Jerry ran off to City Hall and were married in New York City. Thereafter he sailed alone on their honeymoon night from Linden, New Jersey for Hollywood, California.

The next day, the skipper of the ship asked Swede if he wanted to sign on, instead of experiencing a boring trip as super cargo. This sounded good, so he signed the articles, was given a card, and was immediately put to work cleaning the captain's cabin. He shined the brass on the companionway, and served the officers' mess.

They made an uneventful trip through the Panama Canal and arrived in San Pedro, port of Los Angeles, where the skipper, Larsen, asked if Ray wanted to ship out again. "Never," Ray replied. Once was enough. Larsen thanked him for a job well done, paid him off, and added a tip of forty dollars.

The big red cars of Pacific Railways took him to the Elks' Club in Los Angeles, where he registered for a bed. Early the next day he was served a glass of orange juice and coffee. A great introduction to California, Swede thought, as he gazed out the window, down at beautiful Westlake Park and the Hollywood traffic going west on Wilshire Boulevard, work uppermost in his mind.

He took another hop on the red car after reading in the newspaper that Paramount Studios was looking for a cameraman. They needed an Akeley assistant. He had never used an Akeley camera before but was rather intrigued with the idea of learning about one.

Author's note: Those cameras were and are today the very best for the utilization of telephoto lenses. A gearing arrangement ending in a little whirring flywheel steadies panning and tilting.

Ray soon learned from perfectionist John W. Boyle how to properly load the complex magazines, which held only two hundred feet of film but could be changed rapidly, making them the best newsreel cameras ever designed. In studio work, he discovered they were used as specialties; each cameraman was an Akeley specialist.

While the first camera crew shot with normal or medium lenses, the Akeley boys used six-, eight-, or twelve-inch telephoto lenses to follow the action. Swede immediately decided to become an expert in the use of the Akeley, practicing every time he got near one, and John was a fine instructor. They even made a coupling device for a second camera atop the Akeley, so they could get the same scenes with two different focal length lenses.

Ray's first assignment with his Akeley was with John on a film called *The Rookies*, and Swede really was one. A captive balloon was used, and scenes were needed from the ring above the basket carrying the rookies. The work turned out to be quite exciting, as wind tumbled the craft all over the sky, but he got his pictures and another job, which turned out to be a better position, with Metro-Goldwyn-Mayer in Culver City.

Historic photograph taken in 1927 of "Swede's" short stint with MGM Studios. This picture shows the arrival at the Studio in Culver City, California. There have been many changes in 70 years at MGM.

Two months passed, and Ray was in the position to send for his wife. Jerry had kept their marriage a secret, but the dreaded hour had come.

37

She gathered every bit of courage she could muster, then tapped quietly on the closed door to her father's private quarters.

"Yes, who is it?" Hans bellowed.

"It's me, Papa," she said, trying to steady her voice. "I'd like to have a little talk with you."

"Of course, my dear. Come in, come in." He was working with his stamps, a magnifying glass close at hand, along with a tall tumbler of iced bourbon in ready reach.

Despite her carefully planned speech, the words blurted out. "Papa, Raymond and I are married. We have been for two months."

A purple rage swept the Colonel's face. "That bastard! He promised me you'd wait a year!" He raged on and on, then, "Go! Go! Live with that horse's ass, but never expect a penny from me, not now—not ever! As of this minute, you are disinherited." (He kept his word during the years to come.)

Ray's wife came West from New York, bringing him best wishes from her mother and news of what her father had said. "You made your bed, now lie in it!" And they did, in a little apartment called Studio Arms across from Paramount. Later they moved to Metro to a little duplex on Madison Street, within walking distance of Metro-Goldwyn-Mayer studios.

At MGM, Ray had to learn about Bell and Howell cameras and the new Mitchells, the standard for studios all over the globe, then and now. His balloon scenes from the Paramount Akeley camera were considered excellent, and he was assigned scenes from high in the rigging of a square-rigged old sailing vessel used at Catalina Island for the epic *Captain Salvation*. One star, he recalled, was Theodore Roberts.

They assigned Ray to class shots at the studio with Ray Binger, who taught him well. Sets were built through the first floors, while the rest of the scenes were painted on glass in front of the camera. From there, they graduated to miniatures in front of another secured camera.

Ray & character actor on the bridge of the good ship "Santa Clara," off Catalina Island while filming "Captain Salvation."

During the filming of *The Student Prince*, starring Ramon Novarro and Norma Shearer, Swede learned to shoot traveling matte scenes, and this only increased his avid interest in cinematography.

Author's note: Ramon Novarro was one of the great heart throbs of the twenties and thirties and an admirer of Rudolph Valentino, the lady killer of all times.

Rudy had given Ramon a large penis symbol, signed by him and cherished by Novarro, who kept it in a place of honor on a shelf over his bed. Two brothers in from Chicago, thinking Ramon had a lot of money hidden in his Hollywood Hills home, chose Halloween night, 31 October 1968, to ransack the old heart throb's house. They proceeded to savagely beat him into unconsciousness. Later it was determined by the L.A. Coroner that Novarro had choked to death on his own blood. The brutal intruders proceeded to completely demolish the house in their frantic search for hidden money, loot and any other valuables in the process of destroying Ramon's lifetime collection of his illustrious career. As a final act of savagery and complete brutality they grabbed the huge phallus he so cherished and proceeded to cram it down the now dead old idol's throat. Ah Hollywood!

Authors note: Because Ray knew Ramon well we feel this is a good spot for a sobering observation. Let's talk about a very mysterious enigma that seems to hang like an ominous dark cloud over Hollywood. A black cloud of impending tragedy. An eerie foreboding cloud, if you will, that has haunted the Tinsel City ever since picture making and the first cameras rolled the first piece of film. From the never solved mysterious death of William Desmond Taylor to the bizarre suicide of Marilyn Monroe, explain it if you can. There is one thing that we know for sure, the list of tragic events that still permeates Hollywood covers much more then we can ever understand. This mystique has enveloped Fantasy Land ever since we can remember and continues on to this very day. It's like a pall of impending tragedy that looms like a specter of things foretold but yet to happen.

Now we know that Ray was not the least bit superstitious and neither are we, but we were all in complete agreement that an evil something hovers around and over Hollywood. Ray would refer to it in his memoirs when Monetta died. [You will read about it later.] Let's refer to this phenomenon as The Hollywood Black Cloud or, better yet for simplicity, as just The Cloud. We were thinking of using the words Hollywood Curse, but a curse is the will of someone in the name of God. We also thought about the word Hollywood Hex, but a Hex is from a witch. Just what do you call this thing that watches Hollywood and all who seek her riches and fame? Our further thoughts on this matter shall remain private, but we do firmly believe, as Swede did, that something very eerie certainly does exist.

We sincerely wish that we had queried Ray a little more on his thoughts and experiences in greater detail about this Cloud, as we now   39 refer to it, but we think we know what he would have said. He would have shucked it off as God's will and moved on, but we won't. If we were to mention all of the Hollywood celebrities who have met tragic ends, it would cover endless pages. We therefore shall refer to The Cloud throughout the book only in reference to people whose paths crossed those of the Swede.

A Telegram and a Decision

It was only a short time after completion of *The Student Prince* for MGM that Swede received a wire from Emanuel Cohen in New York. While in Sweden, Ray had met Sidney R. Kent, an executive of Paramount Pictures, and had inquired why Paramount had no newsreel organization of its own. Kent had thought it a good idea and said he would look into the possibilities and advantages. He gave Swede his word that if and when they ever did, Ray would be offered a job, for Kent was well aware of Ray's talents. Now they were forming one, and the job was offered. Decision time. MGM Pictures or Paramount News?

Author's Note: This decision changed the course of history and that of many lives, including Swede's. Russ [coauthor and son of Ray] asked Ray if he had made the right decision, and Ray admitted that he had thought about where he might have gone had he stayed with MGM. But on the other hand, it changed what the viewing public would see on the Big Screen for years to come. His exact words were, "Russ, if I had stayed with MGM, I'd probably be one of the best known photographers in the world, but I went for the money and excitement. Besides, making feature films is boring."

Joe Johnson, who stuck with Mr. E. Cohen when he left Pathe News to form Paramount News, called Swede at home that night. "Ray, I've read all the correspondence carried on by you and Kent. We'd like you on our team! We'll start you as a staff man and you'll make a hell of a lot more money then a lousy film photographer at our studios or MGM's. We'll give you a liberal expense account, too," Johnson argued.

Swede accepted and soon learned to be an expert at padding the account. He and Jerry celebrated with a bottle of prohibition cherry brandy he had procured and proceeded to kill it with anything but celebration results, as both passed out on the floor.

Swede's first assignment was to be Paramount News' staff man in Seattle, Washington and with an enhanced wallet, it was time for him to think about a new car. They owned an old Moon that Ray had picked up from a friend at MGM, but it was a hunk of junk; the drive shaft had fallen off during a Sunday outing. The car was okay on gas but craved water to the steaming radiator. On a trip to Palm Springs, he had to stop and add water to the boiling monster every few miles. Even their friends had to carry extra water in their cars for the Moon!

It would be a long trip to Seattle, and with Ray's new job as a newsreel camera- man, he would have to get around fast. The couple fell in love with an Essex Speedster, a little green bug with a boat-tail, then off to Seattle and a new beginning.

E. Cohen was orga- nizing Paramount News in New York and the

Ray and Jerry by their infamous "Moon"

rest of the world, but the actual start date for releasing a twice weekly news- reel was quite a time away. Therefore, in his amazing ability to anticipate, he ordered all the staff of newsreel nuts to dream up feature stories, any- thing spectacular or novel. Joe Johnson, his other staff man in Los Angeles, bought a couple of old Jenny airplanes to crash. One had a spring-wound camera shooting all the way down to the smashup.

Ray tried to figure out a situation from Seattle. Since Paramount's emblem was a mountain with stars around it, he dreamed up a mountain climbing story up Mount Rainier, some 14,480 feet high. Neither Ray nor Jerry had ever climbed a mountain, but both thought it was a great idea. Swede had a cutout fabric sign painted that could be rolled up. It had everything the Paramount trademark featured except the mountain. He focused the real Mount Rainier in the cutout hole in the middle and shot it as the introduction to his film about mountain climbing. It was a dupli- cate Paramount logo, but this time the mountain was not a painting. It was the real thing.

They arrived at the Paradise Inn Hotel and waited and waited for a climbing party. In the meantime, they met the guides and photographers, all members of the National Park Guide and Photographers Associations. One night after entertaining them, Ray and Jerry were invited to the guides' and photographers' building. There on the walls were copies of the pictures that the King's personal photographer, Bertil Norberg, had made of Ray with the Kings of Sweden and Denmark years before. There was also a huge jug of applejack, sandwiches, and a roaring open fire in the mammoth fireplace. The party was on.

Swede had drank everything prohibition and Europe had to offer, but it was his first experience with Washington State applejack, which seemed mild after Swedish akvavit. In a drinking bout that lasted into the wee hours, he was the definite loser. But he won an honorary member- ship in the Guides and Photographers Associations.

Early the next morning, after Jerry and Swede had just hit the bunk, they learned a party was going up the mountain. Ray was still sleeping when Jerry threw a bucket of glacial ice water in his face to cure his hiccups and revive him for the long climb.

Ray made it to within forty feet of the summit, then unfurled a smaller version of the Paramount logo he had made for the climb. It waved in the wind as he photographed it against the awesome background. That'll be impressive, he thought. And it was.

Swede and Jerry just before their climb up Mt. Ranier. Anything for a news story. Note the Paramount News camera he had to lug while filled to the brim with Washington State Applejack.

He shot the party with Jerry climbing the last forty feet, where she signed their names on the ledger in the box. Ray always said he didn't know why he gave out so close to the top, but he just couldn't make it that last forty feet. He never did conquer Mount Rainier. It has been said that if he had been drinking akvavit instead of applejack, he'd have run those last yards.

He completed the story, and New York was delighted with it. A few more Seattle feature yarns followed. He had just filmed the first airmail delivery when a wire arrived from E. Cohen, who said he was holding a newsreelmen's convention in New York. Cameramen from all over the world would be there. A newsreelmen's convention, Ray wondered. Who would dare? Only Cohen. He must be as crazy as the men behind the cameras.

Joe Johnson arrived in Chicago to change trains, where they met others on their way to the convention, thus the party started on the Twentieth-Century Limited.

A once-in-a-lifetime gathering was in progress. Never before or since had anyone dared such a collection of wild men of the cameras. They were nutty daredevils; crazy, but could make pictures regardless of the odds. The whole unruly group checked into and took over the entire seventh floor of the Roosevelt Hotel. There were many banquets during speeches by Adolph Zukor, Jesse Lasky, Sidney R. Kent, and Emanuel Cohen, drinks, more food, then out on the town.

The Everglades Nightclub floor show consisted of beautiful dancing girls dressed as birds. Steve Early, later to become President Franklin Delano Roosevelt's press secretary, suggested that a drunken Swede put a little salt on the gals' cute tails. He did, and all hell broke loose. When the group was ushered out, the management demanded and received ninety bucks from each and every one of them for damages.

The grand finale was strictly for the camera staff, with Emanuel Cohen, Al Richard, his assistant, Sidney MacKean, the assignment editor, and Lou Diamond the money man. The table formed a horseshoe, and the entertainment was fit for a king.

The next morning, Cohen and Diamond made the rounds of the rooms to see if anyone was still alive. Ray had roomed with Joe Rucker from the San Francisco office. When Cohen and Diamond opened the door to Ray's room, they found that some dirty prankster had collected every empty whiskey bottle in the joint and dumped them on the floor, leaving the impression they had been emptied by the sleeping roommates, who looked as though they had drank every drop. Rucker reclined on one bed in pajama bottoms and tuxedo top, while Ray wore pajamas over a tangled tuxedo, and one shoe on a sockless foot. Everyone roared with the knowledge of their predicament, and with that the convention was over. Hangovers lasted for days.

When Ray returned to Seattle, another telegram was waiting. E. Cohen was ordering him to join the New York staff. It seemed to Jerry that they were forever moving and living out of boxes and suitcases. She had reduced her once lovely and lavish baggage to a few meager belongings. Just lugging the heavy camera equipment around was rough, and she had marveled that Ray could work such long hours with all that heavy stuff he carried by hand and hanging on his back.

Jerry taped the last box closed, said her good-byes to the Seattle apartment, then heard the familiar car horn—seven short beeps. She pinned a smile on her face and yelled, "Hi Ray, I'm ready."

"That's great, baby, let's go!" They motored across country in their dependable little bug to a more familiar territory, and found a lovely apartment in Weehawken, New Jersey, right on the Hudson River in Jerry's hometown. New York was just across the river, only a short jaunt to Ray's new office.

The view from the Palisades gave them the New York skyline of night and a breathtaking sight of the glittering, ever changing river by day, with giant ocean liners coming and going. They got so they could tell the *Normandie* from the *Queen Mary* by their different deep throated whistles, saying hello and good-bye.

Author's note: The French liner Normandie *would later burn and capsize in the berth where she sits now, while the elegant* Queen *would sit silently, de-gutted, in the Long Beach Harbor in California.*

Ray and Jerry were given two weeks to settle in. He checked out his new office while she unpacked, shopped, and enjoyed visits with her mother when her father was at work. Papa was still in a snit.

On a last Sunday eve after a fine French dinner, Ray took Jerry's hand, pulled her close in a tight embrace, and said, "Well, baby, this is it. We're in the major leagues now."

Newsreels: Speed and the Network

In newsreels, twin brother to the press, speed was of the essence. An event of nationwide interest occurred, and *flash*, the whole world knew about it as soon as the story was transferred over the wires. People not only demanded the news over the radio, the pictures and story in their favorite newspapers, but they also wanted a living record in motion pictures as it actually happened. This demand was satisfied through the newsreels. Behind them stood one hundred and fifty people who were constantly at the beckon call of the never resting, always active syndicate called the press. This comparatively small but select group of men, the newsreelmen, were the power behind the news in the motion picture field. They saw to it at the risk of their lives daily and hourly that we saw world events as they unfolded before our eyes on the giant silver screen.

The newsreel cameraman was in every part of the world, constantly alert and seeking out news. He was always there when it occurred and faithfully recorded it. Speed was (and still is) the newsreelman's greatest benefactor, and accompanied him on all his adventures. Speed was needed to spur him to the scene of action and required to rush his recorded film back to the public. Speed, the newsreelman manipulates through the medium of the airways, the motorcycle, speedboat, the fastest automobile.

Back at the laboratory, speed was king in developing and editing the reel to be shown to the public. All the rapidity humanly possible was exercised in the group of lab technicians who worked fluently, thoroughly, and cooperatively so the film could be shown on the local screen as soon as possible. Even while the newsreelman covered his story, he used speed with complete thoroughness. Haste was not waste in his case, as he was perfectly trained, so acutely keyed up to the situation, so cool and collected that he never failed to get his story.

To lose a story would mean his job, and losing his job would break his heart. The newsreel game was his life's blood—the pulsating, breathtaking thrills of his chosen career. He lived and breathed the very intoxicating spirit of adventure. Behind the archives of newsreel history lies many a tale of daring, humor, and heroics.

People viewed the films, mouths agape in awe, yet knew so little about the splendid, undaunted group of guys who were responsible for their success. When the cameramen met socially they all began to chat at once, with the usual run of stories about interviews with famous personalities like Einstein, Rudyard Kipling, Lindbergh, Amelia Earhart, President Roosevelt, etcetera.

It was the cameraman's duty to instruct the famous people on how to perform in front of the lens. They had to tell them what to say, when to shake hands, bow, take off their hats, or put them on. Ed Herlihy, narrator for the old Universal newsreels, once said, "I always thought the newsreel cameraman was the star of newsreels. He was a self-contained unit; producer, director, and sometimes even actor. He had to get the action of the moment that could never be repeated. He had to do it all, and there was never an excuse for his failure."

Newsreelmen would speak of the permission and cooperation they had to gain from the army or navy through Washington, DC for dirigible and blimp stories, warships in action, or sailing through the Panama Canal. Hardest of all was obtaining permission to cover war maneuvers. Tank stories were brought up in which the audience saw the huge monsters climb up over their heads in the theater. Of course, the cameraman had dug himself a nice little pit to crouch in with his faithful and trusty camera before shooting up at the tank as it rolled over him. Too bad if the tank operator miscalculated and a tread ground into the pit, a self-dug grave, the cameramen called it.

They liked sports and promised themselves someday they'd buy a ticket. How they always managed to get the big plays on film was remarkable. They claim it was training, and they went on hunches. They enjoyed the baseball season openers, with the President throwing out the first ball for luck, the close-ups of the Dean brothers and our own Babe Ruth.

You could find them tucked away most anywhere there was ticker tape and confusion as famous personages were escorted up Broadway. Sometimes you'd find them poised with their heavy cameras in a tiny nook, forty stories up some skyscraper, in the company of some grinning gargoyle. They dared not think of the drop so far below, but kept their minds intent on finding the smiling faces of our heroes in the finder lens. They cranked away intently, vowing to get back to the office first with the scoop.

New York became the center of the newsreel world, the body of the octopus of news. Its giant tentacles reached to the four corners of the globe. There in the home office under the guidance of clever news editors, newsreel organizations were built. The assignment editors ruled supreme. From their desks, they knew practically everything that was news in the world, and had cameramen, staff, or correspondents there on the spot when such news broke.

Staff men were permanently assigned to key cities or big metropolises throughout the world, with correspondents scattered everywhere. People always wonder at the speed in which cameramen arrive at the scene or action. It is done through organization.

In Swede's office, there was a newsreel map of the world, which looked like it had a case of measles. Each red dot signified a cameraman on the job. Every one of them could be reached at any time, day or night, by wire, radio, or telephone. If a man decided to make a move of any sort, he first advised the home office as to where he could be reached immediately.

Direct wires came into the home office from one of several agencies. Everything was read immediately, and if the subject was suitable for a newsreel, the assignment editors got busy with their maps. They dispatched the nearest cameraman to the spot. Sometimes it was possible to buy a newspaper, read the stories, then walk into a local theater and see the events on screen.

———>=o=<———

Swede wrote:

The public's thirst for up-to-the-minute exciting events on film was insatiable. Every magazine and newspaper in the world was studied for oddities and novelty entertainment value, in addition to the so-called spot news. This type was also called feature news and included stunts, human interest stories, and spectacles. Without them, no newsreel could fill a reel twice a week. Because every three days a thousand feet of film was released from New York, one might conclude that the newsreels had a tremendous photo staff. True enough, but only about sixty of them were salaried men or staff. The balance were correspondents or freelance men, who were paid so much per foot of film accepted by the newsreels.

Sometimes an amateur photographer on a trip or cruise, with his small movie camera, was fortunate enough to record a sinking ship. (Example: *The Vestrous*.) This film was frantically bid for by the different reels, who offered high prices by way of cable or radio. This was usually shot on the narrow 16 mm film, and the newsreel that bought it from the lucky photographer blew it up to standard theater 35 mm.

The result was a rather grainy picture on screen, and was used only in an emergency, like being the only record of a hot news story.

Few people in the movie audience realized the time, film effort, and money that was spent to entertain them for a brief ten minutes on the big screen. Each cameraman shot about two thousand feet every week. When you consider the staff of sixty or more, you begin to realize the tremendous amount of negative film consumed.

Remember, only two thousand feet were used to make up the two weekly issues released by all the newsreels. Only the hottest news, the most perfect photography, and the best features ever reached the screen. Imagine for a second the heartaches suffered by the newsreelman, when after a week's work on a staged story, it was thrown in the can. Perhaps just because some other staff man had a better subject, or a competitor's film reached New York first. If it happened again, you got a thorough ass-chewing from the editor besides.

Many of the big stories that broke around New York were covered by the entire photo staff. Only those angles that looked the best were used, and you felt pretty damned good and mighty proud to see your shots appear with all that potent competition.

On such days, the staff delivered their film to the lab, then collected in the negative projection room, and sat in orchestra seats. The editors were on the thrown [sic] in the rear. When a desirable scene flashed on the screen, a button was pushed, and a bell rang in the projection booth. The projectionist immediately marked the scene on the negative as it passed to a huge holding basket. The basket then went to the cutting room, where the selected scenes were removed from the rest and cemented together.

This was what you saw on the screen. The cuts of all the big stories were saved in the library or morgue with the theater negative after prints were made.

One final screening and off to the theaters, sometimes within an hour of the actual shooting. The diversification of a newsreelman's assignments and the scope of his activities were colossal. He had to be familiar with the coverage of all sports, from cricket to horse racing. He knew all the proper technical terms used in reference on his dope sheet, by which he kept track of his scenes. Who was being photographed, and what for. The dope sheets were turned in with the negative for reference by the editor.

A newsreelman had to be able to shoot from any plane, balloon, dirigible, or even a glider, if the assignment called for it. He was a good photographer at sea, whether or not he was a good sailor. The picture always came first, the nausea second. He stifled fear, walked girders of skyscrapers, climbed cables of bridges, or shot while strapped to the minute hand of the Colgate clock. It was all in his day's work. He always followed orders implicitly, regardless of how long and hard he had already worked or how dangerous the assignment was. But most of all, the industrious cameraman had to have a strong back.

There were many newsreel companies of the era, but five were really recognized as the leaders. They were, and not in order, Warner Pathe News, News of the Day MGM, Universal Newsreels, Fox Movietone News, and of course, the new kid on the block the eyes, and later the eyes and ears of the world, Paramount News. Just to mention a couple of others, RCA, Vitaphone, and Hearst International Newsreel. Ironically, Hearst was the last to survive.

No newsreel would be complete without the great announcers and their characteristic voices: Ed Herlihy, Harry Von Zell, Graham McNamee, and, of course, Lowell Thomas and his famous sign-off, 'So long.' And the rich bass tones of the voice of the weekly feature, The March of Time, Westbrook Van Vorhis.　47

The motion picture newsreels ran from 1911 to 1967, and succumbed to television news.

PLAZA 7-4120

HEARST METROTONE NEWS, INC.

NEWS OF THE DAY

450 WEST 56TH STREET
NEW YORK 19, N. Y.

August 7, 1967

Dear Ray:

Enjoyed your piece about the two Scandinavian Kings in July's American Cinematographer. Did they ever give you a moose steak after the hunt?

Haven't seen you since war days, when you were at Hal Roach's bughouse. I took over the Twentieth Air Force Unit with General Rosey O'Donnell, and stayed with it until we dropped the big one on Hiroshima - just twenty-two years ago. How time flies.

What are you doing these days? About the only old timers I see are Jess Kizis, who works for us, and Jim Lillis, who has just retired. Norman Alley is still with us and he is more or less retired from shooting. Sort of manages things. George Westbrook, a Paramount soundman is also with us. Write me, ask me, and I'll see if I can account for those you once knew in the happy honest to goodness newsreel days of yore. They were good.

My daughter teaches in San Francisco these days; so I may get out and say hello to you once 'na while. Keep the faith.

I run the desk here and dont get out too much, save on special jobs. But I keep my card active. Max Klein is with us. Had he started at Paramount when you were still with them? We took over most of Paramount, Pathe and Fox Movietonews personnel as they folded. Young Eddie Reek is a cameraman with us, too. My God, it is thirty-nine years this month that I started with Movietonews and Johnny Tondra. So we are both in the same boat career-wise. But I try to stay young. And I am sure you do.

Once again, it was nice reading about you, and do drop a line.

Sincerely,

Chic Peden

A Metro-Goldwyn-Mayer Release

A letter to Swede in later years, from friend Chic Peden. With the advent of television news, newsreels became obsolete.

Dear Ray:

      Glad to hear from you. First, we stopped our newsreel as of November 30, this year. Instead, we do government color work, a very successful school reel which shows all over the country, Voice of America and TV commercials. So we keep plugging.

      Norman Alley still represents us on the coast, and now I'll try to tell you about those you inquired about. Max Klein became make up editor of Paramount News just before the war. So you could have missed him. He wrote before then. He is a short guy, about five feet; but works like hell. He shares assignment duties with me. DeSiena is dead, so is Bartone. Dupont works for TV News, Mingalone is retired, Freddy Fordham is retired. Santone does very well in production, Hutt seems to be retired. Can't find out. Jim Lillis is retired, and also very sick.

      Bobby Denton still in Washington for Paramount Pictures. Bob Donohue senior just died. Rody Green, Whipple, Leo Rossi, and Varges have all retired. Teddy Rickman still shoots a good sports picture, and Jess Kizis is with us. Just did a wonderful color job on Spellman's funeral. Eddie Reek junior also works for us.

      Jack Painter, Delgado retired from Fox when they folded. Al Gold passed away. So did Neil Sullivan of Pathe. And Roy Kluver, our man in San Francisco passed on. Bockhorst died in a fire accident. And of course you knew that Johnny Tondra died.

      That's about the whole sad list. Phil Coolidge still works in Boston, The rest passed on. Any others all went into TV. Many soundmen became TV Video men.

      I'm still on the same wife you met many years ago. My daughter teaches college in San Francisco. She is a brain and a good one.

      I could stop but still like the call of films, and now and then go out on stories just to keep my hand in. Live in Connecticut in a fine old house, and spend my spare time growing Iris.

      Yes, we knew the best newsreel days. They will never return. TV news is too demanding - too many stories a day and too many "crisis". Every story seems to be the big one Which is a lot of crap. They put out specials on three alarm fires.

      I see General Rosey O'Donnell now and then. He was my CG at Saipan when I commanded the IIth Combat Camera Unit. I rode on many raids with him because he liked newsreel men. He was a friend of Gloria Hatrick who's old man headed up Hearst Metrtone News. She is married to Jimmy Stewart out there. I worked on Ed Murrow's See It Now until it folded. we were farmed out to CBS for that one. Never see any of the war days crowd, save the men in my own unit, who are all god friends.

      Drop a line again sometime. There aren't too many of us left around and its good to hear. If I get out that way I'll look you up, and we'll bend a pretzel.

                Bestest,

                Chic Peden

These letters echo the death knoll of the Newsreel Era. Very historic.

CHAPTER FOUR

Pure Swede

The following was taken from Raymond "Swede" Fernstrom's memoirs:

I tried not to let the butterflies in my stomach get the better of me. New York and the big time—Paramount News. As I headed across the river on the ferry, I had a little time to assess my new job. New York would bring busy days and nights, for Paramount had just started hitting the twice-a-week pace, which meant get out and get 'em. Pictures, spot news, on-the-spot, hot news. That's why I'm here, I thought. My job will be to get the pictures, then to the lab fast, and on the screen on Broadway. I was as excited as hell at the challenge.

The ferry docked on the Forty-second Street side of the Big Apple. New York was an awesome sight. My office was a block over and just up the street at 544 West Forty-third Street, in line with our little apartment across the river. But the ferries and later the Lincoln Tunnel would make the job of getting to work easier, as I was to learn quickly.

After all the formal stuff, I was briefed again on my duties and alerted to the awareness of our competitor's challenge to squelch us. For it was getting hotter and hotter, and we were pouring more and more dough into that competition. The word was out with them to scoop or exclusive us. Who were these upstarts, Paramount? What did they know about newsreels?

Emanuel Cohen and most of his staff in the office and behind the cameras had left Pathe to start Paramount. Now he was out to establish us as *tops*. Top of the mountain, top of the world. Paramount, first on the screen with the news. If we were an hour ahead of the competition, it was a *beat*. If they were after the same hot story and we got it ahead of them, or they not get it at all, or the story was old hat, it was a *scoop*. And now, good people, you'll meet what to me were the wildest bunch of daredevils in the world—the Paramount News cameramen.

I knew I had to prove myself to me, E. Cohen, my father-in-law, and especially my colleagues of the camera. All knew about my mountain climb, so they sicked the tough assignments on me; the ones they wanted to dodge. If it was a two or three-man assignment, I always got the dirty end of the stick. Take a dare? You bet! For I was always nutty enough to go. When it was a really tough and dangerous coverage, the word was, "Give it to the crazy Swede. He'll do anything." This is how I got most of the air assignments, for most of the guys shied away from the stunt flying. I was promised a minimum of sixteen flights a week, and at twenty-five dollars a flight, they had their man. Right down my alley.

As mentioned before, speed was becoming God. There was so much competition that anything faster or newer our boss got it for us, and hang the expense. Our competitors were well entrenched, organized, rich, and fighting us. We *had* to be good to survive. We *had* to be first to steal the market; knock the others out of the box. This is what I was up against when I became known as ruthless.

In the beginning, I used a De Brie camera which carried magazines with four hundred feet of 35 mm film, but the changing of the lenses and reloading of film was too slow for our work, especially on spot news when speedy action was essential. So we all switched to the Akeleys; light, fast, and efficient, with the ability to pan, tilt to extremes, up, down, and move steadily on gear and flywheel gyro effect. They could even hold twelve-inch lenses evenly while in motion.

They were round cameras with doors on the right side that also held the eyepiece. Our two-hundred-foot magazine could be removed and replaced quickly. In those days, we had to crank our cameras and could speed up or slow down the action by winding our cranks accordingly. Also to give us more mobility, we carried a hand camera, either a De Vry or an Eyemo.

The De Vry was a box-like affair, easy to set on the road and let cars, airplanes, or whatever travel by or fly over it. It was spring wound, held one hundred feet of film, and could run forty-five feet before running down. On these, we always used a wide angle 25 mm lens.

The Eyemo could only be used when viewing from the hand, for it was too rounded off for setting on the ground or runway. But a great hand camera.

Our usual load was made up of three pieces, sometimes four, when we carried our hand cameras. The Akeley case would hold the camera, a wide angle lens, two two-inch, one four-inch, and a six-inch and twelve-inch telephoto. A magazine was in the camera loaded, and a shirt, underwear, handkerchiefs, socks, toothbrush, razor, etcetera. Other wearing apparel could be stuffed between the strapped legs of the tripod. The magazine case held five loaded Akeley magazines, so they were ready for an assignment at a second's notice. Sometimes we took a typewriter, but seldom. We learned to hand print our captions.

If we were lucky enough, we drove our own cars, which meant padding the expense account. Mine was the most expensive car to drive, ever! Naturally, since I had so many assignments to Curtiss-Roosevelt Field for flying stories, I used my car more than most other newsreel men around New York. They moved around town quicker by cab or subway. The field or combined airfields were out in Mineola, Long Island, so naturally I attended every auto show to select my beloved automobiles.

When our little green Essex Speedster wore out, I bought an Erskine, built by Studebaker. We soon discovered it rode too hard for my pregnant wife on those days I had off, weekends. So I bought an Auburn, boat-tailed Speedster right off the showroom floor, while the then-mayor of New York, Jimmie Walker, was admiring it. God, what a beautiful automobile! She was cream and black, with black leather upholstery. It could do close to a hundred miles per hour, and in perfect tune probably more—an unheard-of speed at that time. I once made it

Swede and Jerry with their Auburn "Boattail" Speedster. Ray reportedly bought it off the showroom floor from under the nose of Mayor Jimmy Walker. Newsreelmen had to be the fastest.

from New York to my home town of Sharon, Massachusetts in four hours and ten minutes. It and the green bug became well known around the air fields.

News breaks at all hours of the night or day seven days a week, so we were always in touch with the office. Woe to the guy who couldn't be reached when a story broke.

Our office had a direct set of teletypes from the Associated Press, manned twenty-four hours a day. A story would break, a fire, plane crash, flood somewhere, then the phone call, "Get there!" Our assignment editor was an old newspaper reporter, who had been bitten by the newsreel bug. A rough, tough, sarcastic bastard, six foot tall, Scotch-Irish, or at least filled with it—whiskey, I mean. "I'd never hire a gentleman who didn't drink," he'd say. "No imagination."

I'll never forget "Mac" Sidney MacKean. One time, I had fourteen teeth pulled at one sitting, and returned to his office. "What's the matter with you, Swede?" he asked.

"Aw jus ha foooteen teef pooled!"

"Fourteen? God, man! Here, take a shot of this and go home to bed with the bottle. When that Novocain wears off, you'll feel like a streetcar ran over you!" and he ordered me home at once. I did as told, passed out blissfully, and woke up the next morning feeling great.

The Little Colonel, E. Cohen's assistant chief editor, was Al Richard. A real old-timer in the picture and newsreel business. He was a great guy, and every time Cohen fired me, Al would hire me right back. Our chief film cutter was Bill Parks, and he'd give us holy hell if the captions we sent in with our film weren't complete, in sequence, or not detailed specifically. In later years, before he passed beyond the screen, he ran my old pal Walt Disney's Mickey Mouse Newsreels.

We had a truly international group of cameramen on the New York staff. Henry De Siena, Turkey Neck Bartone, Lou Hunt, Big Romantic and Daring Doug DuPont, Ludwig Geiskop and a tricky and able Italian, Al Mingalone. It was this dude, a slim, daring, able, and agile newsreelman, who taught me how to walk steadily while shooting a hand-held camera.

One of the first exciting assignments I had in New York was with Bartone. "Let the Swede come along to help me?" he asked Mac. And off we went to do a skyscraper story, which meant there was nothing but structural steel of the new New Yorker Hotel.

Turkey Neck wanted to show me the old thrill stuff about workers fitting gird- ers, throwing red-hot rivets, catching them in buckets, riveting, and finally eating lunch. Of course, all these scenes were to be shot from above, showing nothing but space and New York below, and scaring the hell out of the audience.

We went up in the construction elevator which seemed to have elastic bands that pulled us shakily skyward. Up, up, we went, very fast, then to a sudden, bouncing stop, forty-eight floors up. Space! Up, to get the shots we needed.

The foreman riveted a couple of girders in place above the spots Bartone had selected, then laid a few planks for us to walk over, miles up in the sky. Bartone shot the stuff from the platform, and gave me the girder walk job, alone—out over the action below! I got some swell stuff, with Bartone yelling orders from the safety of his platform perch.

I started back, Akeley on my shoulder, holding the folded tripod legs, trying for all my worth to balance the outfit for easy carriage. A few steps, then I made the horrible mistake of looking down. For the first time in my life, I froze! I could- n't move a muscle. Then a voice hollered, "Come here, you son of a bitch before I throw this goddamned hammer at you. MARCH!" All eyes were on that crazy nut in the middle of a girder, walking a path no more than two feet wide, forty- eight stories up. I made it.

We dropped our film off at the lab then took off for Luigi's speakeasy and a few stabilizing belts.

Henry De Siena was another Italian who tricked me into a few stunts. One was a painting job aboard the SS *Leviathan*, then our largest American ocean liner. My job was to be a cinch he said. "Just bring along your Eyemo hand cam- era. All you've got to shoot are the hand-held shots with the one-inch lens. Easy," he said, and off we went to Hoboken, New Jersey. But from the ferry, I could see where the ship painting was going on, high in the rigging above the giant liner. So now I knew the job. De Siena would stay on deck while I climbed up the rig- ging and shot the stuff from above the painters, sitting in their bosun's chairs, whose brushes were hard at work on cables, crossbars, and space. And that ship was high out of the water!

I started up the foremast, climbing to the top, with my camera strap over my shoulder, the camera dangling at my side. As I climbed, I realized the ladder was leaning back because the mast was tilting slightly. I was about to reach the first crossbar and platform when I saw I would have to climb through a hole to get up on it. I arrived at the final rung and reached up to hold on. But my arm slipped through the strap and the damned camera grabbed me around the neck, hang- ing. Ordinarily, this wouldn't be much of a choke, but with the tilt of the ladder and the camera swinging, my Adam's apple got wedged and I was gasping for air.

There was Henry, far below, yelling at me to hurry up. I could have killed him had I been below, and it looked like I might get there a lot faster than I had expected. Getting mad gave me that extra strength I needed, and I pulled myself up through the opening.

I shot the scenes, then gingerly scrambled back down and off to a damned good Italian lunch, with gobs of wine they dubbed Dago Red.

One might think stunts like this are crazy, but they made spectacular viewing on the screen. However, sometimes we overdid the stunts. This brings to mind one nutty one that Lou Hutt dreamed up with a goddamned blimp! It was to be about a guy taking a bath in a bathtub, slung under the blimp as it passed over New York skyscrapers. My job was to capture the people looking up, while my assistant threw whipped cream in their faces, simulating soap suds falling from the man in the sky. Silly? Yes. But silly enough to evoke, "What will they think of next?" And think we did, always dreaming up new exciting material for our newsreel addicts.

So were the guys in other areas. Jake Coolidge and his son Phil, our men in Boston, were a couple of New England Yankees, and most of their stuff concerned ships and the sea. One story in particular, I'll never forget. They dreamed up a yarn about a storm at sea, with the famous Gloucester schooner the *Columbia*, that once raced the Nova Scotia champ, the *Bluenose*.

Jake had arranged and paid for rigging the ship with all the canvas she could carry, even to the higher extension of sail on added top masts, his idea being to sail her into a nor'easter, with gale force enough to put the deckhouse under water. On the deck, he strapped a nest of old New England rowing skiffs to be washed overboard, which would add to the action.

Willard Vanderveer and I had been assigned to Gloucester to help out on different camera angles. Jake was to hand-hold the Eyemo and roam, Phil in the stern with the Akeley, and me on the bow, of course, with Van on a coast guard cutter shooting long shots of the whole mess.

Captain Ben Pine, the famous skipper of the *Columbia*, would handle the ship for us with a Gloucester crew. We explained what we wanted and were met with a lot of skepticism, down-east style. They looked at Captain Pine as if he were nuts to even think of doing this. They knew nothing about crazy movie guys and their pictures, and cared less.

Away we sailed, Phil and I taking Eyemo shots from the bowsprit, as the old *Columbia* heeled over to starboard. We were doing cut-in shots for the film snippers when Jake asked me to walk the sail with the Eyemo. Walking the sail is quite easy when a ship like the *Columbia* is under full sail, heeled way over on her side. One merely goes hand over hand up the rope, hanging from the upper boom above the center of the sail. I made a few shots, shooting back at the deck. But then Jake, with his crazy sense of humor, had Captain Pine head her into the wind, and there I hung, swinging out over the water. I almost let go of the rope, but the Captain brought her over to heel again and I made it.

We waited days for the storm to come, and finally it did. The decks went awash, while we all ground away on our cameras. The sky grew darker, and we adjusted by opening our lenses. On and on we went, while the schooner heeled farther and farther over. Cascades of water blasted the decks. Then the skiffs went overboard in the middle of Jake's scene. He thought this was beautiful. Then slowly the deckhouse began to take water, much to Jake's delight. A sky full of sail caught the gale full force. In the bow, shooting aft, I got all the action, while Phil, in the stern, got the same from his angle.

The ship went lower and lower, over on her side, until with a resounding crash a top sail snapped and flew away. This caused some guy on the deck to feel we were all nuts, so he grabbed an ax, chopped the mainsail stay, and away she swung into the briny. Now all hell broke loose. Captain Pine headed her into the wind, sails flapping. I was still in the bow area with the job chain flying around me, grinding away with my camera and soaked to the skin.

Swede hanging on the bowsprit of the Schooner "Columbia." Circa 1925.

Finally, Captain Pine brought the schooner slowly, steadily, and carefully around, and maneuvered toward a point back to Gloucester, under the one remaining sail.

It was one hell of a picture; a terrific feature of the sea in calm and fury. Paramount and the public cheered. I'd loved to have read Jake's expense account on that one.

After Charles Lindbergh's successful solo to Paris from Curtiss-Roosevelt Field, the other contestants kept at it. Rene Fonk crashed on takeoff, which all the reels covered. Then Admiral Byrd flew out in his rare GAC Balchen, and some other guys (I can't recall their names) tried it. Ruth Elder made an attempt, and I followed her and her pilot out to sea, but they landed in the drink. Some made it over, while others failed.

The airfields were regular hangouts for many newsreelmen, newspaper photographers, and reporters, who are famous people today. Just to credit a few; Tommy Pryor, editor of *Hollywood Variety*, Damon Runyon, Walter Winchell, and Martin Mooney, a Hollywood writer and producer.

When there were quiet times on the field we could be found at the end of Curtiss, close to Roosevelt at Hangar Thirteen, a speakeasy, or out on other assignments.

This time it was the Republican Convention in Kansas City. Al Richard had made hotel reservations for us ahead of time, and all the gang arrived from New York—Ludvig Geiskop, the two Frenchmen, Italians Bartone, and Al Mingalone, and I. Joe Murphy soon joined us, a still photographer with the *Kansas City Star*. We got all the front rooms facing the street and another hotel, which made Richard feel he had done a fine job.

But we soon found out that all the rooms across the corridor contained the finest collection of Missouri whores, and all superbly capable of every known sexual preference. Al was a true newsreelman, but he had reservations from which none of the rest of us suffered. He was timid with broads, not much of a sexual athlete or researcher, and was horrified when he found out the girls' occupations. But it delighted the crew, and he was stuck with the situation he had connived, as no other rooms could be found in Kansas City.

The fun was on! The great convention was thoroughly covered and film flown back to New York, but my memory is of much more fascinating adventures, and I don't mean politics.

E. Cohen, as the boss always signed his name, offered many prizes to stimulate a bunch of guys already alert to their jobs. Loot came easy if we got what he wanted, and this time it was the arrival of Hugo Eckner in a flight from Europe in his crazy Graf Zeppelin.

Lou Hutt and I were to fly two Ireland amphibians from the field in Mineola and meet the Zeppelin over New York. She had been buffeted in a storm and had lost part of the stabilizer on her tail. News flashes said it was in tatters. Cohen offered a hundred bucks bonus to Lou or I, whichever of us would fly closest to the damaged vane, which was huge.

We intercepted her over Staten Island, as she was headed for Manhattan Island. Lou figured on flying above to get close, but my pilot and I had a different idea. We planned to head right for her nose, then dive close under her belly, so I could shoot up and see daylight through the torn fin. And so it went, pass after pass, while old Eckner, hanging out of his command gondola window, shook a clenched, Teutonic fist at us. We got close, all right. Our prop nearly ripped the fabric from the airship's rudder as it flapped at us.

We landed the amphibians on the Hudson River where a speedboat picked us up, and the film was on Broadway before Eckner could dock his Graf Zeppelin at the Lakehurst naval air hanger over in New Jersey. Hutt and I were assisted by the rest of the gang in spending the prize money at Luigi's, which was now our second office. Total cost: two hundred fifty dollars.

Zeppelins bring to mind too many stories to relate at this point. Too many balloons are boring, and balloons they are; a bunch of them surrounded by an aluminum cigar-shaped body, with gondolas and engines just hanging there. But, wonderful! Their size always held me in awe. We had some of them in the US Navy as well. The *Shenandoah*, the *Los Angeles*, the *Macon*, the *Akron*, but the *Los Angeles*, which was German built as restitution for World War I, is the subject of this yarn.

She was a gorgeous airship, and the only one to survive of all the prior names mentioned. After the era ended and her useful days were over, she was dismantled. It was on the *Los Angeles* that I made my first Zeppelin flight, at Lakehurst air base hanger, which was built for Zeps and blimps. Those monsters of the air only took off in the cool calm of the morning and landed only in the evening, often not until the next dawning.

The takeoff was indescribable; smooth, quiet, slow, gentle, comforting and serene. A magic carpet, much like an astronaut must feel in space. On the *Los Angeles*, bags were filled with helium, not hydrogen which was to be the cause of the *Hindenburg* holocaust. Helium is nonflammable, and the only supply known was in the United States. At that time, we would not share our helium with the Germans because of their war maneuvers.

We were not to land until early next morning, so we had hours of sailing through the skies of the eastern United States. On and up we went into the beautiful moonlit night. Then late as I walked the companionway back to my berth with a delicious martini in hand, I happened to look up at a ladder that seemed to reach to the heavens. Way up there, I would be able to see the moonlit sky with its fleecy clouds slowly drifting by, much as modern astronauts see things from their spaceships. The impulse was irresistible.

I started up the aluminum ladder, martini in hand, slowly, higher and higher. Higher yet, I went. Hundreds of rungs, it seemed. Not a sound. No one to stop me, as most aboard were asleep. Finally, I reached the top and peered out over a sea of silver airship, bending away from me toward the bow and rising heavenward back toward the stern. To this day the scene remains the most magical sight this old Swede ever has been graced to see. The view was exhilarating.

Clouds of all shapes passed and skirted around and over the bulging, shimmering silver hulk. Then I turned back toward the direction we were sailing. Below me, twinkling in the early moonlight, lay the skyline of New York City, bathed in a glorious silver glow that sent chills up my spine. I couldn't resist climbing to the edge and sitting on top of the hatch, with my heels still on the ladder, gazing and wondering in complete awe and enchantment. Why was I so privileged to view such a wondrous sight on my silver carpet? A humble feeling of facing God and the universe bathed my body.

Okay. When speaking of Zeppelins, let's talk about the biggest news story of them all—the *Hindenburg*, a tale that still haunts any newsman when the name is mentioned. Where in the blankety-blank were all the newsmen?

My wife, Jerry, our baby Barbara, and I were still stationed in New York, but at that later time I was no longer a newsreelman. I was shooting *Popular Science* and *Unusual Occupations* for Paramount Pictures. I'll explain later.

The newsreelmen, still my buddies, were partying again. They had been alerted to the famous *Hindenburg's* time of arrival, but none were aware that she had encountered a threatening thunder and lightening storm with tremendous tail winds that shoved her far ahead of her schedule.

The liquor flowed and yarns were exchanged. All the guys had commandeered a hotel at our old hang-out near Lakehurst, just a short hop from the air base. Everyone had been on dirigible alerts before and the wait was very often boring and tedious, so all the gang had brought their wives and girlfriends and were having a grand old time when the call came from the editor that the ship was ahead of schedule. They sobered immediately, and the entire troupe of newsreelmen grabbed their cameras and dashed off to Lakehurst, leaving behind wives, cards, booze, and burning cigarettes.

The wives and girlfriends sat stunned listening to the terrible news being broadcast over the radio, and everyone realized that their men were not there. This horrible disaster, probably the greatest of all time, would not be covered. Some were relieved, as they did not want to see what they were hearing over the air waves.

The men arrived too late. One lone cameraman had inadvertently recorded history, and we all recall the narration. When there is talk about newsreel spectaculars, someone always says, "Oh, you photographed the *Hindenburg* disaster?" No, I did not photograph it. You can't be everywhere at the same time. However, in the news business we had as fast a grapevine as anyone.

Shortly before the *Hindenburg* disaster, the dirigibles were always coming and going, all the way back to the *Shenandoah*. Even my mother-in-law, Clara Lagerloef, had crossed the Atlantic on the *Hindenburg*, a couple of voyages before the ship blew. *Author's note: A picture postcard from the Hindenburg may be found in the next photo section.* I had warned her about the dangers of hydrogen, but she was German and had faith in their engineering.

Every takeoff and landing by the *Hindenburg* caused a cameraman to be sent to photograph it, always with the thought in mind that something would happen. But nothing did.

Before the disaster, two newsreel editors were sitting in a bar and made a pact. If one of their cameramen got something big on film that the others didn't, they would make copies immediately and share it with the other newsreels. This way, they could have the other cameramen on other stories. And when the *Hindenburg* blew up on 6 May 1937, there was one guy with a camera set up. As the airship approached, he started the camera, then went to get a cup of coffee, and wasn't on the field. His camera ground away, but *he* was not there.

When the *Hindenburg* blew, he saw the flash in the window, realized what was happening, called his boss, and told him. Due to the pact, which was honored, everyone got a copy.

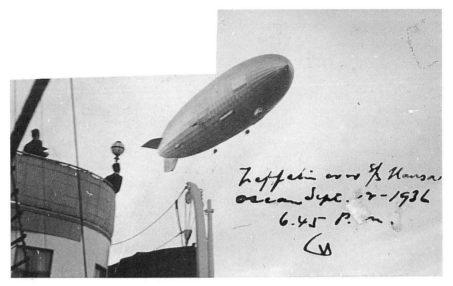

This is the postcard sent to our family from Jerry's mother Clara from the ill-fated "Hindenburg" a couple of trips before the disaster. One of Jerry's church members admired the famous stamp, so Jerry clipped it for him. The date, in Clara's handwriting, reads Sept. 12, 1936.

What this did to newsreels will never be told. Not one of them was there! Not one! It was the biggest story of all, and no one talks about it. A lot of my buddies lost their jobs over it.

News kept happening, or we cooked some up. Secrecy was important so our competitors wouldn't get wind of our stories. If they did, we postponed it. But usually, we let the reel (newsreelman) that got wise to us come along if he kept our idea from the other reels, which rather cooled our ardor about the subject, but still made good film.

Then, there were activities at Madison Square Garden, annual routine stuff, and this we were told to do differently, better, more novel, new camera angles, anything to make it more newsworthy, and I got the job of shooting the six-day bike race. I went over to study them, for every other guy from the reels had covered them for years.

I studied angles I knew had been used before, then sat back, hands behind my head, and gazed out, then down, finally up—up, way up to the ceiling, seemingly miles above me, wondering. Could I get an Akeley up there, directly over the track, looking down with a twelve-inch lens? How to get enough exposure. Russell Birdwell!

I called Russ, and he recalled for me that he was the only cameraman on the scene, and a Hearst man, when Lindbergh took off for Paris. The others were all drunk back at the hotel. Russ was later renown for handling public relations on Gone With the Wind, the Howard Hughes exploits on The Outlaw, and Alamo, etcetera. He gave me tips I needed to get clear pictures from that height.

Back at the Garden, I found the building boss and he directed me on how to climb up onto the steel rafters. I crawled along, until I guessed where the center of the oval bike track was located, where I proceeded to punch a hole in the 59 board ceiling. Then I moved along, figuring the exact spot for the Akeley camera in order to shoot straight down, which would be fastened to a girder with a newly devised mount.

Back at the office, I conferred on film speed and gauged that by hypersensitizing the negative and keeping it on dry ice, I could have enough exposure speed to take care of the less light through the telephoto lens. Next the mount, and our machinist made that in an hour. Now it was my job to shoot straight down at the racers in long shots, medium, and close-ups. My assistant would cover the floor shots.

The result was stupendous. Today, as I watch the *Jackie Gleason Show* and the great scenes looking down at the Taylor dancers, the Esther Williams water shots, which switch back to overhead then aimed straight down, and made so famous by Busby Berkely in the '30s and '40s, I hark back in my memory to that dusty drag up into the rafters above the bike racers at old Madison Square Garden back in 1927, and I wonder where they got their inspiration. New?

The view from the rafter makes me think of another crazy stunt staged on the huge Colgate clock in New York. I had nothing to do with that one, but it was certainly typical of the feature stunts we dreamed up in those super exciting days of nuttery.

I can't recall which group of Paramount squirrels did that one; DuPont, Bartone, Mingalone, De Siena, but I know the details. They did long shots of the clock, various angles, closer and closer, then scenes from above. Then someone thought of shots from the giant minute hand. One guy was strapped to it at the hour and went thirty minutes with the hand camera, shooting angles until the half hour, on his head with thousands of people looking up at the screwball.

At this point, one might wonder how I got sixteen flights a week to reach my weekly loot quota. Practically every newsreeler had established scenes to set the locale, and surroundings. So as we had been assigned to Curtiss-Roosevelt Fields, we sat around playing cards, reading, or shooting craps. A story would break, the phone would ring, and off we'd fly, each with his own reel. Often our reel would get wind of a story staged by another, and my job was to fly there, bust in on their story, get the air stuff, then land nearby and crash in on their party.

Sometimes it was a tank formation yarn at night with movie flares. In that case, I'd have to pad my expense account and help pay for the flares. It worked both ways. All of us at the field were suspicious of each other if anyone went near a plane with a camera. But by ruses, many a competitor flew off on a wild goose chase, and sometimes just to get in flight time. Once, we laid smoke screens from the air from a bomber while the French ship *Ile de France* sailed through it as we made air shots, and one of the guys aboard made scenes from the ship as she traveled across the Atlantic. Did he get a free trip? No. For he, his camera, and film were picked up by a navy blimp and brought home so the film could hit Broadway fast.

We landed blimps, army and navy ones, on trains while moving, and on ocean liners sometimes far out at sea a day after they'd sailed, and brought mail and newspapers aboard. The blimp landing crew was aboard the ship on a large wooden platform where they caught the lines from the airship, dragged her down, and held her until we got our pictures. Thereafter, we couldn't take the crew on board, as they would add too much weight, only our cameraman and all his equipment could go. So the blimp crew, whether army, navy, or Goodyear, enjoyed a round trip to Europe and back at our expense, just to get a good exclusive newsreel story.

Often, we flew out to cover floods, ships on fire or in distress, or a crash. This brings to mind how Lou Hutt lost his right hand pointing finger years earlier. He sat straddling the engine cowling, ahead of the pilot, on an old World War I training Jenny, shooting back at the pilot and a wing walker, who was to approach them so Lou and cameramen in other Jennies could get all kinds of shots at various angles of the whole show.

Lou became excited and angry at the pilot for not getting ahead of the formation, which was required for the job, and pointed to where he wanted the plane to go. He pointed right into the prop, which obediently flung his finger away. He got the pictures anyway.

Lou was the same one who pulled President Franklin Delano Roosevelt to the floor of his car during an assassination attempt in Florida when Mayor Cermack of Chicago was shot. His actions saved the President's life, which made the grateful leader a friend of newsreel cameramen.

I have had back problems and arthritis since I was a young man at Huntington Prep School and rowed on the racing crew in eight oar shells on the Charles River in Boston. But later in my New York newsreel days, I jarred it a bit farther.

The navy was commissioning a new aircraft carrier, the original *Saratoga*, down at old Point Comfort, Hampton Roads, Virginia at the Newport navy base and airfield. My assignment was air shots, and I was to meet the Fighting Fifth Squadron and their planes, Voight-Corsairs single-seaters. But they had one plane with two cockpits, one behind the pilot's for me.

At Hampton Roads, I received the message as to what was wanted. This was to be the first time the squadron would actually land and takeoff at sea with the new carrier. All prior training had been in simulators on the ground, including gear to stop the planes while landing, so they wouldn't go over the bow and into the sea.

We had a couple of days to get ready. My cockpit was large enough, the camera mount perfected so I could shoot directly back, or pan and tilt to either side. For this job, I took a De Brie, which holds four hundred feet of film instead of the Akeley's two hundred. I didn't want to try reloading in the air in an open cockpit, due to the unknown speed of the Corsairs. The navy knew how fast they flew, but I didn't. I was left to find out the hard way.

I strapped a spare magazine aboard, and was ready for the big day. Early the next morning, weather perfect, camera mounted, I was informed I had to dress to navy requirements; parachute and restraining harness over a Mae West life jacket, then squeeze into the plane. I dressed as required, then worked my body into the open cockpit, feeling like a sardine, jammed so tight I could hardly turn, and looking like a big gob of ice cream sprouting out of a cone.

I gave my pilot the okay slap on the windscreen and we blasted off. My allocated film went through nicely on our first leading shots of the formation. Then the wide-angle lens took in the whole flock as we flew low over the speeding *Sara* and her destroyer escort, ready to pick up any pilots that wanted to drink some of the Atlantic. Then came the landing shots. We flew down low over the deck, followed by the first plane to land so I could get shots of this historic first.

Finally, I ran out of film. But we had men on decks with cranks winding. We circled until it was our turn to land, with me standing halfway out of the cockpit, but locked in tight. We approached, but were waved off, made another circle, sideslipped, leveled off, glided, then cut the engine, and bang! Yank! I felt my spinal vertebrae play a xylophone solo up my back as we stopped dead. There I stood, stuck.

An hour later, with a fresh load of film, all of us were on the tail of the deck. Props revved, me in the lead, to make the first ever of those scenes you have watched so many times since in war pictures, with the planes landing or taking off from a carrier.

Our following plane was allowed to takeoff close behind, and my crank turned out an awe inspiring shot as we flew off, tailed by the next Fighting Fifth Corsair, who quickly got into perfect position above our tail so we could see the others taking off, and we all climbed heavenward.

I flew back to Mineola, and soon Broadway saw the navy's latest wonder and our pictures. I had also brought the film the other men had shot after the navy flew them to me on land.

We had an exclusive on this one because we had asked permission with knowledge of the impending event from inside sources. We had our own secret service set up. Our guys had lots of old friends, and our men in Washington had more, plus tips, and a way of not letting secrets slip out to our competition.

The Seaplane

Sikorsky had just built a giant flying boat, which was to be used on a planned airline to South America. It was tentatively called The New York-Buenos Aires Airline.

Author's note: The early airlines had ambitious routes to conquer—Puerto Rico, the Canal Zone, Caribbean, and South America. To do this, a new type of aircraft was needed, one that had greater range and could get along without prepared runways. They turned to Sikorsky Aircraft for a plane to meet the specifications. The craft that resulted was the Sikorsky Amphibian S-Thirty-eight, which turned out to be a beautiful machine, with its twin 425-horse power engines, carrying 10,480 pounds of plane, crew, and passengers at a speed of 105 mph. As an amphibian, it could operate on land and sea, with a three-hundred-mile range. It helped open up more than eleven thousand miles of air routes in the Caribbean. Eventually, the airline bought thirty of these airplanes. The S-Forty, which joined the fleet in 1931, was the first commercial four-engine flying boat, and offered a new standard of luxury to the air traveler. In 1934, the Sikorsky S-Forty-two, shown in the following photo, was put into service. It was America's first true transoceanic transport and an outstanding achievement in aircraft design for the time.

I was assigned to make air shots of the aircraft flying over New York on her first test flights and the ground scenes of her christening, the *Habana*. Behind the

Swede flew on the maiden voyage of the S-38 Sikorski Giant flying boat from New York to Havana. It was the forerunner of the Clipper ships and Pan American Airways. Shown is the later version, the S-42.

scenes, our office was conniving for me to go along on the first flight to Argentina. This was not to be an exclusive, for the new line had a sharp press and public relations man who figured the cost could best be justified by making it a press flight.

The day came and photographers, reporters, and a select group of newsreelmen congregated. We took off from Long Island Sound, Port Washington. Destination Havana, Cuba.

Havana was quite a spot in those days, the old Siboney Hotel, Sloppy Joe's, the Cunard Bar, and a new lifelong friend, the owner Raoul Sanchez.

Naturally, with an excellent public relations man running the show, we all got the ground shots we wanted of the flying boat landing and taking off. Then the parties started, for weather held us up in Havana, much to everyone's delight. We were guests at the Tropical Gardens, which had everything one could wish for—girls, gambling, good food, drinks, and more girls who were international beauties.

Dear readers, Bacardi, the distillery with such hospitality, sent direct from the Bacardi family, case upon case of Carta Blanca, Carta Elixer, and Carta Oro to our hotel rooms. Enough for a load for every guy on the trip.

The weather cleared, but when the pilots tried to take Sikorsky's amphibian flying beauty away from Havana, she couldn't get on the step, that is, break the waves. The load was too heavy. So the merry passengers went ashore, lugging cases of liquor, and proceeded to drink the plane lighter. Then off we went to Rio.

Years later, I met the daughter of the publicity man for that airline. I was shooting a Chevrolet film for television, and we stopped off at a Malibu Beach bar, en route to Hollywood. She and I ordered a rum cocktail, and I began to relate my experiences in Havana—the flight, the flying boat, the Bacardi, and the wonderful job the public relations man had done. It was then she told me he was her father and that airline we pioneers had filmed became the sire of other flying boats, which they called clippers. At this time of writing, the airline is known as Pan Agra, or Pan American, and flies the entire globe with much experience, part of which we shared.

Long Island has been the birthplace of many new developments, inventions, and newsworthy events. From the Sheepshead Bay auto races after the birth of automobiles, to the first Sikorsky helicopter. But my experience with the whirling wings began while shooting a different type of bird, the autogyro. This was an entirely different toy of which we could cook up stories. And, of course, the manufacturers cooperated for publicity in newsreels.

When five of the autogyros were ready, we staged a formation flight. The gyros used conventional propellers to pull rotating vanes to hold them up instead of fixed wings. They were a striking sight over the White House, Lincoln Memorial, across the Reflection Pool, then above the Capitol in Washington, DC. The gyros were a very safe craft, able to rotate down should the engine fail, since there was no power sent through the whirling wings. They operated strictly from the air flow created by the forward pull of the conventional propeller, or down to a safe landing merely with the rush of air created by the falling craft. On take-off, their short roll down the runway before becoming airborne argued well for their future. But now they have passed into history. However, they added to the newsreel library. I loved them, and the only reason I can figure for their vanishing is that the helicopter proved technically superior.

The mention of film libraries brings to mind a young man named Sherman Grinberg. He has offices today at Columbia Pictures Studios in Hollywood, and has collected all the newsreel libraries under his wing into the largest film library in the world. Most of the picture stories I have related here can be found in his vaults in New York, including my early Kinograms material.

Poor Hi Lutz. He was with International Newsreel. "Oh, my rheumatism," was his cry. So we called him Bellyacher Lutz. One winter, one assignment from my boss was to take the train to Niagara Falls and make ground and air shots of the fancy spectacle in icy garb, an assignment I cherished because it was there that the camera bug had really bitten me in the selling days.

I ran into Lutz at Grand Central Station. Suspiciously, we asked each other, 'Where the hell are *you* going?' Since Niagara in winter was one of those annuals, we decided to travel together. There was no escape. Ordinarily, we cooperated more or less but still tried to top each other in composition, angles, or ideas. But on deals like this we stuck together like leeches to be sure the score stayed even, or holy hell would come from the boss.

First and foremost, we were both good newsreelmen. Each shot had to hit the target; there were no re-takes in the newsreel game. We were an unscrupulous bunch, keenly competitive, but beyond all requirements, everyone of us had a good sense of humor. We were fun-loving, excellent expense-account padders with unending ideas to make them look legitimate. Furthermore, all of us were con men and promoters. This was amply demonstrated at Niagara Falls.

On the way to the new Niagara Hotel, Lutz admonished me to play it cool and let him do the bit with the manager, which he did neatly and got us free rooms, a good supply of Vat Sixty-nine Scotch, and free meals, of which I ate little. We drank toasts to each other, the manager, Niagara Falls, winter, and the grand scenes we were about to take.

I called the airfield trying to promote a plane and pilot, but for that we had to charter, the cost of which we split, then padded our accounts by adding hotel charges. We fooled no one, but it was fun.

The trip was all set for the next morning—first the aerial photography. We both had Akeley cameras, but poor Hi Lutz was too drunk to get out of bed. He had awakened before me and went right to the Vat Sixty-nine, which was no way to fly over the falls as low as I had planned. Naturally, our Akeley magazines fitted any Akeley camera, which Hi knew, so he cried, "Oh! My rheumatism."

"Rummy-tism, you mean, you stinker," I yelled back at my bedded buddy.

"You'll have to cover for me," he pleaded. "Take my mags."

Before I left the room, I had to buy him more booze. He said it was the only cure for his aches. He gave me two twenty-dollar bills, one of which I used for liquor and brought the other one back, figuring that was enough drink to keep him until I returned.

This meant I'd have to risk two flights. Every pass down the river and into the gorge below the falls would have to be made twice, one for me and again with Hi's mags. I did it gladly so the bastard wouldn't lose his job.

One low pass over the falls in an airplane with it dropping off was tough enough, but twice was really tough. The pilot must have thought I was very stupid to miss so many shots. He didn't know what I was doing, as he had his hands full with the plane. He flew low, time and time again. Double different angles, across the falls, American and Canadian, over the hotel to get it into the foreground under us, as had been promised the manager. I wondered if Hi would have done that, but I was happy he wasn't along. He was a heavy character, and the stunts were safer with a one-man load and much less confusing to the pilot. Finally, we got the ground shots, then back to the hotel to gather up Hi and entrain for New York.

When I gave Lutz his magazine case, he said, "Bet you made all the good shots for yourself and the lousy ones for me." Then he accused me of swiping his twenty bucks. It wasn't until I ran into him months later that he apologized. He had found it inside his overcoat pocket.

Poor Hi. No one could help but feel sorry for him. He had the sad, suffering face of a bloodhound, for he always looked sick. Years later he was doing a story in a hospital, which had to do with X-rays and was curious about them. An operator asked if he had ever had X-rays taken, and he said no. He felt fine, except for his rheumatism. The doctor gave him a free one of his chest. When the film was placed on the viewing box, two doctors were called to study the plate, as did Hi. He was asked how he felt.

"Fine," he said. "Why?"

"You have tuberculosis of both lungs!"

Hi blanched. "Not rheumatism after all?" He died shortly after.

I was given the assignment to cover the annual Miss America Beauty Pageant in Atlantic City. I realized I would enjoy the change from the aerial stuff, and photographing lovely women was just my style. I loved them in front of my camera as long as they were gorgeous. The pageant's annual nature called for new and different angles to give a new look to the girls.

I emptied my glass of good bootleg booze, then gazed downward, wondering how a direct upward shot would look with the girls walking across thick plate glass. The girls were in bathing suits, and got as big a kick out of the photography as I did. They walked well enough to give the scenes class. Naturally, my competitors wanted to borrow the heavy glass, but who the hell gives away innovations to the competition? Especially when I had figured another use for it. I prepared a reverse action scene, using the Eyemo and shooting upside down, then posed a series of single beauties, one at a time before the perpendicular glass. Each stood still, then as my aide poured oil from a trough down the glass until it was almost opaque, I instructed each girl to walk backward slowly. They did it perfectly with a little practice. When the scenes were screened, the opaqueness raised like a curtain, and revealed each lovely little doll. The boss gave me a bonus which all the gang knew about, and it was swilled down at Luigi's in one night.

Beauty can be fun, and I always wanted to be an artist, a painter, pastels, oil, anything to create beautiful composition of form, light, and color. But I was always too impatient, although I loved studying art museums wherever I found them. I always remembered what Abraham Lincoln said, "I'll study and prepare myself, and someday my chance will come." Rarely was there an opportunity in the fast pace of newsreels to compose scenes artistically or to light with the touch of the masters. But once in a while I could obtain gratifying results with only photo floods or outdoors with movie flares.

One icy morning, while sitting with the assignment editor, "Mac" MacKean, he looked up and asked if I thought I could shoot a well-known subject differently than it had ever been photographed before, by other reels or even our gang? What brought that up? I wondered. Evidently, it was something he had seen me do on another story. I never found out.

Then he asked me what I could do on Niagara Falls that would be different? I told him we had already done Niagara for that winter.

"Yes, I know," he said. The competition had also covered it enough to kill that yarn for a year, and he didn't know I had shot it, too, for old Lutz! "I've got to get something novel," he went on, "an exclusive so different it would be an entirely new picture of the Falls in winter."

That was a challenge! I asked him if I could have the afternoon off for a little study and think session.

"Go ahead. But I want you to catch a train tonight!"

I took a cab to the Metropolitan Museum of Art, where I could always find inspiration; not at a speakeasy, as one might think. We were always stone cold sober when it came to work; there was a time to play and a time to work.

Ideas came to me at the museum as I walked, gazing at the works of creative geniuses, and I sketched out a whole new format which would make a new story of Niagara and the Falls in a winter mood, the shadows of winter night, art, composition; only the subject matter would be changed.

It was bitter cold at the Falls, clear and lovely, but freezing. That was what would make the difference. Lots of icicles.

My cab driver, who I chartered for the day, kept warm with bootleg whiskey while I used Rembrandt lighting, Coret and Millet compositions, back light through hanging icicles, frozen trees of arty shapes, ice, the Falls, frozen honeymooners. My cab driver and I became artier and artier. The more we tried to keep warm with alcohol antifreeze, the fancier I became. Finally, I had exhausted every angle and scene on the American side. But we stood there, looking at the International Bridge.

66   "Let's go over to the Canadian side," I suggested.

He looked at me rather enthusiastic and artistic now and offered the opinion that I couldn't do what I'd done here. "They don't have the trees with long hanging icicles on the Canadian Ridge side."

"Why not take a branch with us?" I offered.

"No, the heater in the cab would melt the ice."

"Then shut the goddamned thing off!" I yelled. "Open up all the windows." He did.

Everyone has always known not to cut the tree branches in the Falls area, but the gin we had consumed made us forget the prohibition, both of them. We must have been a sight, for when we reached the Canadian side of the bridge, it showed on the faces of the customs and immigration men.

"What have we here?" they asked. My cabby explained the sort of nut he had in the back seat, holding the branch with its delightfully beautiful icicles intact, sticking out three feet on each side of the cab's open windows. What could they do but wave us on?

The trees on their side were too far from the Falls, which caused the mist that fell on the branches, then froze, and made the icicles. We put up scenes in our pictures that were truly creative, giving us our artistic triumph.

E. Cohen gave me a generous bonus for that one, as he was truly impressed with the beauty. But this time I asked Lou Diamond to mail the check to me so the gang wouldn't drink it up.

Our head cutter complimented me on my artwork, but I caught hell for the lousy captions. I guess he understood the situation. After all, the pictures were the most important, and I didn't tell him that I couldn't write with my hands half frozen and full of tree branch and icicles.

Lou Hutt asked me to join him on a story of the early preparations for spring activities at Coney Island's giant amusement park, where they were testing engines and motors, painting brighter colors, and checking out all the famous popular rides.

Our big feature would be the giant Ferris wheel. I went up, and from its heights could see the empty Long Beach in winter's last despair. Round and round I rode in the swinging cage, the Akeley my only companion, Lou on the ground. Up and down, then ugh! Something happened. The wheel jerked to a stop. I yelled down. "What in hell happened?"

Men worked feverishly, but to no avail. I was at the top, no rope, and evening drawing on. "I'm coming up with a rope," Lou yelled. Up, up, up, he climbed, a light line tied to his waist, until eventually I saw his hand and pulled him into the open door of the big cage. He had crawled up through the cross pieces of the wheel on one side. They were at up and down angles, so one can imagine how his feet must have felt, after pushing his body upward. Both of us pulled at the light line and at last a heavier one appeared, which we tied around the camera, mags, and tripod. Then came the slow, painful descent, down to blessed mother earth.

Mount Rainier had been nothing compared to that adventure. We tried to tell the gang at the office the next day, but only received sarcasm. "Aw, you guys are always dramatizing everything. So what! Sympathy is next to shit in the dictionary," one of them blurted.

Lindbergh's solo flight from New York to Paris stimulated everyone's imagination in flying, including women. First, it was Ruth Elder. Then a princess supposedly was going to fly from England to Canada. Bill Winston, one of the Curtiss Flying Service's best pilots and I were ordered to fly to Ottawa to shoot the arrival.

We took off in a Curtiss Oriole, a round, wooden-bodied affair, reputed to be very fast. After a great flight, we arrived above Ottawa, but neither of us knew where their Lindbergh Field was located. Evening came on us and our gas was low, so Bill decided to put down in a farmer's pasture. He touched down nicely, but the Oriole decided to roll on and on, bouncing and weaving until we ended up in a manure pile. The trip sure stank, and no princess arrived either. We gave up the idea.

But this isn't the way it was with a tall, slender Lindbergh-type of girl. Our man Jake in Boston, the boss, the Little Colonel, E. Cohen, and George Palmer Putnam, publisher from New York, were all in cahoots. I believe Putnam had bought her plane; a Fokker single-engine job, equipped with pontoons and piloted by Slim Gordon.

I had been assigned to help Jake cover the takeoff from Boston, and saw her for the first time on the tug we rented when we brought her out to her moored seaplane. She was a tall, quiet girl.

We shot the taxiing and takeoff, which was the first and last time I saw her, except in pictures. At another time, I shot a flight of hers when she flew alone, but I was in another plane, in which I could only see her head above the cockpit. She went on to greater and farther flights from there into eternity.

The flight we photographed in Boston was kept a secret from our competitors, and we scored a complete scoop. The tall, silent lady was none other than Lady Lindy, or Amelia Earhart. *Author's note: Sherm Grinberg has the film.*

Curtiss supplied us with all our charter planes, except Ireland amphibians, boats with wings and wheels that could land on water or airfields, a different kind of plane. Nevertheless, nearly every known type of aircraft could be found at Curtiss-Roosevelt Field. Fairchilds, Curtiss, Sikorsky, amphibians, French-built Loening amphibs, Ireland amphibs, Orioles, Curtiss Hawks, Wacos, Stearmans, Fokkers, Ford Tri-motors, Bellancas, and Stinsons, most long forgotten, but all the forerunners of today's jets, with pilots that flew by the seat of their pants.

Today, as I watch color movies on television of astronauts floating in the air, it reminds me of our earlier reach for the sky. Airplanes were our only spacecraft, but newer engines were being developed daily with more and more horsepower. Radial air-cooled motors replaced the water-cooled OX-Fives, Curtiss C-Sixes, and Hispano Suissas. Improvements went on and on.

I used to peck out ideas on the typewriter while sitting around the service office at Curtiss-Roosevelt Fields. Sometimes when things got slow, we would actually shoot short films of the stories we dreamed up, and many times they were used as feature news. The following story shows the ends to which we would go while awaiting calls and assignments.

Early one morning we equipped our cameras with the new infrared film and filter, which was extremely contrasting, cut atmosphere and haze amazingly, but was so dense we couldn't see through it. We had taken photo and lab tests with it to find out our exposure levels. Our boss wanted a few scenes of Manhattan

Island from the highest altitude we could reach, exposing as much of New York state and New Jersey as possible. The higher we went, the more newsworthy our film would be.

Bill Weston and I were ready for new thrills, with a cabin-fuselaged Fairchild that contained a four-hundred-horsepower Pratt & Whitney engine, as we flew higher and higher, reaching for our ceiling. At about twenty thousand feet, the ship began to shake from the struggle. Bill established a smooth ceiling, steady so I could shoot high stuff. Our gas load was diminishing, but we attained more height as I shot the pictures, demanding we go higher yet. Up we went, until he feared we would run out of fuel. Finally, it was time to slide back to Long Island and the welcome field.

The final edited newsreel created its own sensational news value. It was astoundingly different, with beautiful shots, and the viewing audience was aghast.

It was about this time that Jerry was five months pregnant with our first child, which she preferred to have at home in Sharon, Massachusetts in the fresh air of the country, instead of in a hospital in the mad metropolitan area of New York with its insane newsreel people. So I drove her there one delightful autumn evening. Emil and Lydia were very happy about the occasion.

Flyers, aircraft, distant flights, anything pertaining to airships of any nature, and breaking or setting records was big news. Lindbergh had caused the fever that had swept the world. More and more, farther and farther, and always faster. The next big anticipated story would be who would be the first to duplicate Lindbergh's flight, but this time east to west, from Europe to the continental United States, North America, where there were more cameras waiting.

Paramount News, the eyes of the world, wasn't a year old on the screen, but we had made significant inroads into the competition's theater accounts. We struggled to increase our circulation, reaching for every chance to improve, expand our facilities, capture stories and hence the theater business. Money, of course, was no hindrance, but news could not be bought until it happened. Then it did.

My assignment was to fly to Montreal, Canada where a flood had occurred. I covered it by air, shipped back the film, then threw a party for my pilot and some delightful people we had met at the Mount Royal Hotel. It was in full swing when a telegram arrived from E. Cohen. Two of our staff men in Germany, Stindt and Stoll, had been following the activities of a pair of fliers there.

The pilots, Baron Von Huenfeld and Captain Koehl, had been preparing a Junkers airplane for a mysterious flight and had added additional fuel tanks to it. This led the two newsreelmen to surmise that an attempt would be made to fly the Atlantic, which could bust into a big news story if they made it across.

The two pilots flew to Ballmorel Field, Ireland, which assured our men of their intent, and added Major Fitzmaurice to their crew. Cameras and men were on full twenty-four-hour alert. I received a wire that read: "Remain Montreal, view possibility German fliers flying Atlantic. Landing somewhere Canada. E. Cohen."

I immediately got Cohen on the phone, and requested expense money. He wired a lot. The party was over; back to business. Then another wire arrived: "Alert. Fliers en route. E. Cohen."

Now it started. That alert was followed by a news explosion that has not been equaled since. There was a prolonged buildup of suspense, dangers, silence, imagination, delays, and extremely bad weather. All the elements needed for writers to build up the frustrations of a modern world. The two pilots were trying to reach the vastness of an unknown area without communications, where only an airplane could go.

Our news should have broken shortly. "They made it!" But where? Where were the fliers and plane? Finally, somehow, word reached the outside world. They were on Greenly Island. Where in hell is Greenly Island? We found it on the map. It was on the coast of Labrador, Straits of Belle Isle. It had a lighthouse. Maybe the keeper had a short-wave radio transmitter. In the excitement and the anxiety, I never found out. But news travels fast, even by carrier pigeon.

How could we get there? Who had a plane? I made a series of phone calls to all parts of Canada, Maine, New York, and found there were only two Fairchilds equipped with skis and owned by a little outfit in Quebec called Canadian Transcontinental Airways. A company with a large name but only two planes!

The aircraft were located at Lake Saint Agnes, quite a distance from Quebec. The only way to get there was via train, which was made up of a short haul with two cars and a broken down steam engine.

When I arrived, I found the Fairchilds were cabin jobs with radial Pratt & Whitney 423-horsepower engines. Newsmen of all kinds had arrived at the Chateau Frontenac, including friends and competitors. And with the heightening tensions, friends became enemies and ruthless competition began in deadly earnest. But I found a guy to confide in, for in our frustrations a companion was needed.

Eddie Jackson was a still photographer, a real old trooper, wise in the ways of cut-throat competition. Everyone was trying to get those planes, so he and I decided to pool our mental resources in an effort to get both of them. We decided that he should go to Lake Saint Agnes and try to get us aboard at least one.

News arrived that Duke Schiller, the famous Canadian pilot had already taken off with one of the planes on a rescue effort over ice and snow, a thousand miles from the lake to a tiny spot in the middle of the Straits of Belle Isle. There went half our chances. Pouf! The possibilities of finding the area were slim. It was a frozen sea with a little lighthouse in the middle, on a lone, unheard-of arctic dot.

Every minute more and more newsmen, photographers, and newsreelmen arrived with every chartered plane or train, giving us the nervous twitters. Eddie and I were no competition to each other. His stills were for newspapers and my reels for theaters, which made our pact reasonable, and the only way to protect each other's interest was to be in two places—the lake where the lone remaining plane was located, and Quebec where I would remain. My thinking was to find the guy that owned the airline, made the decisions, and controlled the aircraft.

He ran his business from his home, which I finally located. By now he had clammed up and gone into hiding from the swarm of news hawks, vultures, eagles, and rabble that had descended on Quebec. It cost me real dough to see the frail Frenchman, but he had good cognac and was very gracious. Once I wormed my way into his confidence and hideaway, I hoped he would be pleased to have one friend for company. However, I was as much a friend as a rattlesnake because by that time life itself had paled when compared to the big scoop that was in every newsman's imagination.

My first job was to call the boss from the phone hanging on the wall. When I entered the Frenchman's home, I wanted to rush for communication with my boss, but became as cagey and calm as possible. I turned on my best charm for that plane and phone, saying my job was at stake and my wife was expecting a baby at any moment, trying to gain his sympathy.

I got New York on the phone. "Keep someone on your end from now on. By all means!" I instructed. "I have a slim chance of getting the only transportation available. Wire me ten thousand dollars at this address, fast. I'll be right back, don't go away." I returned to the old Frenchman.

"Swede," he said, after much prodding, "Hearst has bought and confirmed one seat in that plane, which has room for only four passengers, in addition to the pilot and mechanic." Then he added that the other three seats were bought and confirmed, except for one that Pathe Newsreel had purchased but had not yet confirmed by wire, for five thousand dollars. Daily News had one seat. That meant Eddie Jackson was in. Associated Press of Canada had the other, confirmed. I had one chance—Pathe's seat. I rushed back to the phone.

"Mr. Cohen, get every son-of-a-bitch and girl to wire me here, hundreds of telegrams. Tie up the wire service! Pathe hasn't confirmed the last seat on the plane. I'll do the rest. Get 'em going as fast as you can!" Now I went to work, pleading with my new French friend. I laid five thousand on the table, asking, begging. How long would I have to suffer this torture? Where is Pathe, anyway? Why wasn't someone here for them, like I am for Paramount?

Finally, the doorbell rang. I ran to answer it. He tried to stop me, but I told him to pour us a drink. The telegraph messenger handed me a bunch of telegrams. I ripped one open. It was a confirmation from Paramount News, which I stuck in my pocket. He opened all the others; all from Paramount. I asked to use his typewriter, and wrote out a contract as best I could, in duplicate.

Then a thought struck me. How would we fly over two thousand miles of wilderness, snow, ice, and open sea without gasoline? I asked him about that.

"Oh, we have gasoline cached all the way to Labrador, for we are trying to get an airmail route flying up the coast in the spring." It was now April.

"How much do you have stashed all the way?" He told me. "I'll buy it, every last drop!" But he was too smart for me.

"Not until you have a seat on the plane."

"How long are you going to make me wait for Pathe?" I questioned. He finally agreed on six o'clock P.M. It was now five-fifteen, and the telegrams kept arriving. I gladly obliged at the door, shoving telegrams under rugs, seat cushions, behind the piano, anywhere I saw a chance.

Six o'clock arrived, and we shook hands. I signed, he signed, then we both swigged a well-earned drink. I wrote another contract, handed it to him, and with a sly smile on his face, he sold me every drop of gasoline the company owned that was cached or at Lake Saint Agnes, which thwarted any and all competition.

The Frenchman phoned for a train to the lake, chartered the locomotive and one passenger car, and I made him go with me to make sure there were no hitches, because he owned the whole setup and gave the orders.

71

When I got off the train, I knew Pathe's man would be there, so I hired a few lumberjacks for bodyguards, for no one in our business at that time took any chances. The four I hired were mean, tough hombres, and I paid them twenty bucks each; ten now, ten when I boarded the plane. "Watch me, my equipment, and my film," which during those hectic hours had been sent from New York by way of a chartered plane Cohen had kept as a standby in Quebec.

No wilder gang ever assembled than that at the lake airport on the ice for one lone ski-equipped Fairchild. Romeo Vachon, our pilot, was a fine, tough guy who could easily have been a lumberjack. He had steel-blue eyes and an easy grace about him that was reassuring. He had flown the wastelands many times, and it showed on his face. He wore an amused "what's all the excitement about" expression. "Yes, I think I can find the way," he assured us. And I felt better.

Among the early morning crowd, angered and frustrated competitors watched as two newspaper men, one still photographer, and one newsreelman climbed aboard. I was glad I had given my bodyguards the ten spots, as they had loyally elbowed everyone out of the way while I lugged my camera to the Fairchild.

Fairchild Model 71 of the type Swede and Vachon flew to Greenly Island on the big "Scoop." It was fitted with skis for the venture.

He skimmed fast and smooth over the ice and snow of Lake Saint Agnes as we took off into the wild unknown. Thanks to the Almighty, none of us knew what lay ahead. We no sooner reached the correct altitude when the air got rougher than hell. "What's up?" I asked Romeo.

"Oh, this is normal. It'll be like this quite often," he explained. As I returned to my seat, I noticed the two reporters. They looked green. So I whispered to Eddie, if one can whisper in a noisy Fairchild. "Eddie, let's talk those two bastards off the plane when we land if there's a place for them to stay." They were air sick. Eddie and I had the stomachs of goats and did not feel the trip, but their illness would be a way to get rid of them.

"I'll ask Romeo," he volunteered.

Romeo had planned our first overnight at a place called Seven Islands. He said there would be a dog sled there to meet us when those on the ground spotted the plane over the village. There was also a Hudson's Bay store, accommodations, and a telegraph operator. This would be the last civilization before we reached our destination, Labrador and Greenly Island.

At the first opportunity, Eddie asked the two green-faced reporters if they would like some greasy pork for a snack. The looks on their faces told all. I think they wanted to die, so we suggested they stay at Seven Islands, as we good guys would bring them back the story. We reminded them that we had three more days of rough air ahead, and they agreed to our suggestion. What would they write about anyway? We could bring back all the stories they needed. Eddie explained that he had been a newspaper reporter before becoming a still photographer and promised them the world; human interest, sidelines, the works. No need for them to go on. Stay at Seven Islands. We fed them sickening suggestions of food, like the one about the guy who had the strongest stomach in a contest. The chap won at breakfast when he ate a mouthful of oatmeal, puked it up into his dish, and went on eating it. That did it! The two reporters couldn't wait to get off the plane, and wouldn't think of flying another mile with us crazy bastards.

Romeo Vachon slipped the plane, then leveled off for a smooth landing. "All hands to work," he yelled, and he meant *labor*. First, we had to fold up the hinged wings, then drain the oil from the engine, dig deep holes in the ice for tie-downs, tie her down, cover the engine with a canvas hood, unload our stuff, and then came the dog teams. Pilot, mechanic, cans of oil, luggage, and three of us on one sled, three on the other. I stayed with Romeo and the mechanic, for Romeo was a thoroughly experienced bush mail pilot, with plenty of rough weather and terrain flying time. *Author's note: In later years, Romeo Vachon became the Dominion Air Minister of Canada.* George Oulett was the mechanic, a capable, willing, man of twenty-one years.

Vachon knew what we were doing to the reporters and was happy to lose their weight in the plane. He even helped out by offering information that the air was seldom as calm as we had experienced. That encouraged our dead-weight passengers to do their reporting from a nice warm haven on Seven Islands. Then I whispered to Romeo to fill them in on the hazards ahead. He told of the bad weather, fog, and rough air, with the only refuge being scant Indian villages, etcetera. The reporters spoke with the sled drivers and the store keeper at the Hudson Bay Company and were further filled with the horrors of the vast snow country that lay ahead up north. If we had heard the yarns spun or read the news accounts these two excellent reporters sent out to the world during the days and nights we were gone before our return to pick them up, we wouldn't have gone on the flight either, and that includes Vachon, for imagination is far worse than factual experiences.

While we were at Seven Islands, Duke Shiller's plane arrived from Greenly Island with the Irishman, Major Fitzmaurice. They had come to help the Breman and rescue the stranded fliers, and needed fuel to get to Lake Saint Agnes. This, of course, would completely ruin me, and wreck all of Paramount News' chances for the biggest scoop of them all. This would have been okay with me, except for the previous arrival of my arch enemy, Tommy Hogan, in a nifty little Waco plane.

Since the birth of Paramount News, our keenest, most resentful and competitive newsreel had been Pathe News (sees all, knows all), and of all the thorns in my side, Tommy Hogan was number one. And I know it was mutual. If the two reels were competitors, we two guys made it a personal feud. Feud, hell—a god-damned war!

When our boss formed Paramount News he took Pathe people with him, which included all but Tommy Hogan, whom he had left behind. Tommy was jealous because we got more salary. Now, here he came, crashing my free-reign party, and arriving with his old flying buddy Bob Fogg. Bob was a New England pilot of great ability, daring, and experience.

"You in charge of this exclusive story, Swede?" he asked. His "exclusive story" sounded like the hiss of a diamond back rattler, the son-of-a-bitch! We both shot the arrival of Shiller's plane with our Akeleys, then the exodus from our sister ship, and I shuddered with fear that all were aboard. Thank God, only Duke, the Major, and the Duke's mechanic had arrived. The stranded pilots had opted to stay with the Bremen.

We completed the coverage jointly, for now he had cut into my cake. Somehow I had to get the film back to Lake Saint Agnes and thwart Tommy. I knew he was scheming to screw me, too. But I held the aces—gasoline.

Fogg tried to get Vachon to give him gas, but Vachon explained that I owned all the fuel. Score one. Vachon told me Fogg had decided to use casing head gas which he could purchase at the Hudson Bay store. But Romeo told him he wouldn't fly fifty miles without burning up his valves and crashing. Tommy pleaded with me to give him gas.

"Give you gas to kill my story? Hell no! You bastard!" I thought if I gave them gas they would fly north, but Tommy wanted no more. He swore that he, Fogg, Duke, and the Major would head for Lake Saint Agnes, and agreed to take my film with them if I'd give them the gas to fly the two planes south for the sake of the German pilots' lives. I weighed the values. Fitzmaurice was not the story; the Breman and the fliers were, and that was another day's flight north to Labrador, and they couldn't follow. So I agreed.

So, they all flew south, Tommy and Fogg in the Waco and Duke, the Major, and the mechanic and my film in the Fairchild. But unknown to me, Duke also was an old buddy of Tommy's, and he faked a forced landing which allowed Tommy to get to Lake Saint Agnes first with his film and a *beat* of my Seven Islands coverage. The slimy bunch of bastards. *I* would never do anything like that! I can imagine the reaction at Paramount News headquarters. I'm glad I was in the icy wastelands and knew naught thereof.

Early the next day, Romeo and George were up heating the engine oil while we ate. Then everyone got onto the sleds. A changed appearance had taken place with the four or us who were to fly. I had bought a parka, heavy matching wool pants, a pair of mukluks, big flying boots, a beret, a huge knife and holster, and sun goggles and used film tape to make slits across the latter to prevent snow blindness. Eddie was dressed in equally dramatic fashion.

This was all old hat to Vachon and Oulett, "Away, dogs. Mush!" After the sled ride to the plane, the preparatory work began in earnest. First we loaded the gear aboard, removed the engine hood, and proceeded to heat the engine with two blow torches. Then the warm oil was poured in, and the engine started. While the plane warmed, we unfolded the wings, and locked them into place. Then Vachon replaced the mechanic, who sat in the pilot's seat revving the engine while the rest of us tried to break the airplane skis from the ice. Once that was accomplished, Vachon taxied in circles, smoothing the crusty ice and the bottom of the skis for takeoff. Then we all climbed aboard and waved good-bye to the reporters who had so gallantly lightened the plane's load. But it wasn't long before we felt they were the lucky ones, as we were enveloped in heavy fog.

Vachon flew high then low searching for a way out. He didn't want to crash, so out to sea he headed, trying in vain to get out of the mess. We spent hour after hour in the thick heavy fog. Suddenly, a bank seemed to open up. Eddie felt his rosary, which had been blessed by the Pope, and believed his prayers had been answered. Our spirits soared. Then, *wham*, into another mess. We flew farther and farther out to sea, climbing to find clear sky. Gas was dangerously low. The only cache within our estimated reach was in a little Indian village called Natashauan. The outlook grew darker. It began to snow. First lightly, then thick and heavy.

Vachon estimated he had gone far enough out to sea to miss any mountains, so he headed landward. If we ran out of gas, we had a better chance on ice than water. Carefully, he began a descent, while all eyes searched ahead. Then a light opened in the blinding snowstorm. A dark patch. "Open water!" shouted Vachon, as the day waned fast, our fuel exhausted. Snow and fog ahead, water below.

Suddenly, the dark patch of water was replaced by the eerie gray of snow covered ice. "We've reached the shore," Vachon called out. A slight clearing, and Romeo decided now was the time to land. But just as we were about to touch down, there was water again. He gunned the Fairchild into a slow turn, and settled into a calculated final approach as the engine quit, committing us to land.

Eddie prayed there would be no more water. Our right ski just missed a large chunk of ice, then miraculously the weather cleared to a magnificent flat field of ice, and we glided toward a perfect landing while Romeo exclaimed, "Look!"

We saw them. Low Indian huts, black as ink against the snow and ice. A few dark spots moved. "Indians!" we shouted. "God bless them!" The plane slid to a well-earned stop. More Indians. We were surrounded. They had heard but could not see us. They had also heard about our flight on the radio, and of course the stories our two intrepid reporters were painting from Seven Islands. It seems they, too, were in the middle of a bad storm, a day's flight back.

Vachon showed us a stick he had used to measure the gas. Not a drop!

"Has anyone got a drink?" I asked. They did, and we drank, then folded the airplane wings, drained the oil, performed the whole routine, then retired to our limited accommodations on a floor. But it was warm, comfortable, and interesting, as it was the kitchen, town meeting hall, and radio listening post. We heard over the airwaves in utter amazement the stories of our flight. It scared the hell out of us, almost as much as the real thing had. But the warm coffee, spiked with antifreeze of course eased our cares.

We had an Indian send-off that topped Lindbergh's from Curtiss-Roosevelt Field. He had one lone reporter, Russ Birdwell, and his crew, while we enjoyed hundreds of wildly cheering Indians, who helped us refuel from my private cache, the Indians aided us with the warm oil, etcetera, and off we went through the day, monotonously, over the mountains, snow fields, huge rocks, until once again we were aware of the dwindling gas supply. And still no Greenly Island.

"We should be there by now," Vachon informed us, not reassuringly. Lower went our gas supply, and the panic flag was flying in our chests once again, when George spotted the two red flags on the ice, then the island with the lighthouse.

Vachon banked and dove, then I spotted the crashed German Junkers plane, the *Bremen*, lying flat, behind a stone hedge near the lighthouse. All was excitement.

"Bank this way, Romeo," I shouted as I shot pictures. "Now, over there, now here, steady," then we landed, sliding fast over the ice marked by the two red flags.

I knew they thought we were there to rescue them instead of just make pictures, and we sure as hell didn't tell them any different. We put on a great show. Eddie and I greeted them with open arms as rescuers. But the whole idea was strictly pictures, our life's blood.

The Germans treated us as if we were guests in their homes in Germany instead of strangers. We took our first series of pictures, then stowed our equipment on a dog sled, and all walked up to the lighthouse keeper's home, where we met our charming hosts. This was a gathering of people from the three corners of the world, together in a strange sort of void. A truly dream world, completely away from the life we knew. A cold, lonely island in an unknown wasteland. So forbidding, but dramatizing how our twentieth century was growing up. Civilization was stretching its fingers into unknown areas of mother earth, like our little group standing there in 1928, and somehow everyone knew we were friends, and that was right.

We shot pictures in every category of our work—human interest, the lighthouse keeper, his wife, kids, pets, and the whole kit and caboodle with the German fliers, then more of the *Breman* and the flyers, showing the island people their fabulous ship. We shot every angle, every news idea, every sideline of our yarn, until Eddie and I ran out of film. Only one thing remained—souvenirs. We asked the flyers and people who lived there to write little messages about the landing of the *Breman*.

Now it was time to get the hell out of there in time to reach Natashauan before dark. We took off with our precious film. I don't know to this day if the Germans thought we were there to rescue them or not, but we were newsmen and concluded that they had figured us out and went along with the game, for we wanted them there on the ice while we returned with our pictures and the scoop.

Germans are smart people, and when I look back I don't think they wanted to leave their *Breman*, their wonderful craft, that had so capably carried them to the little haven on the North American continent. They had sent Duke and the Major for help to save the plane, but what kind of help only God knows, for no one could fly that plane off the island. It would have taken too many people and much equipment to repair her, then get it down on the ice for a takeoff—equipment that was next to impossible to get to the island. But those hard-headed krauts stayed with their ship like good captains, and with that thought we were off a little reluctantly because by this time we had all become good friends. But the newsreel training took over. 'Get the pictures; to hell with yourselves. Don't get involved. Get the goddamned pictures, and get them back!' And with that thought, as we flew home, we dumped every drop of gas left in each cache to kill any slight chance of competition.

We picked up the reporters at Seven Islands, and there was no need for them to imagine anymore. We had our pictures, so we lived up to our promise and gave them vivid ones to write about, every detail. That night while we slept, they stayed up and wired every iota of what we had told them, as if they had been on the mission. This kept the news hot in the outside world. The dramatization they gave was wonderful. However, had they been along, their weight and ours would have finished the job in the waters off Natashauan.

We were a jubilant crew as we flew south from Seven Islands. One long, safe and sound, hop to Lake Saint Agnes, with not a drop of gas behind us. It was mine, so why not dump it?

We ran into trouble. That frigging fog, all around us! No use flying back for gas. Romeo searched for a clearing, then finally banked. He saw a clear opening, a pasture in the snow beside a farmhouse with smoke curling from a chimney. Life! "Pull up your feet!" Vachon yelled. "We're going to crash." And in panic, up came our legs. We hit, then came the screeching of the skis, and silence. He cut the old Pratt & Whitney, and climbed out to check the damage. He had landed okay, but had struck what Vachon feared was a stone hedge. But it turned out to be a wooden one, and we had sheared off a stump that had been part of the structure.

We stood as the darkness moved in, night on our heels. Where were we? Finally a few people appeared. They had never seen an airplane on the ground before, and we had never met people like them; simple in one word, plain in another. They were neither friendly nor helpful, but interested in giving us a respectful welcome, as though we were celebrities. Of course, we did not fully realize what radio had been telling these folks. Where were we?

A beautiful, young school teacher answered for the little French provincial parish, "Sacre couer de Sangueney," and you can still find it on the map today. I am certain no one in our party had ever seen a stranger group on the American continent. I loved that little school teacher from the moment I saw her, and couldn't take my eyes off her.

We were shown to the parish leader's home, where we all gathered in the kitchen-living room, apparently a meeting place for the whole village because all came to view these people from another planet. Interpreters were about, and the parish priest spoke English; otherwise we would have felt we had landed in France. They spoke in a strange tongue that even Vachon and George had trouble with, but they became very hospitable, and we were now greeted by every soul.

We washed up, were fed, then informed that there would be a dance in our honor. I nudged Romeo. "How the hell does one get a drink around here? I need one."

"I do too." He went over to the boss man and pretty soon after I had given Vachon a few bucks, someone left the room stealthily as the music started. A violin blended with an accordion, flute, and a harmonica in a haunting sound, but with a very good dance beat. I looked across at the school teacher and felt that old yearn to dance. I asked Vachon if it was the proper thing to do. He, in turn, asked the head man, and someone left the party again. Then the dance started. By this time we had some fine Canadian whiskey to go with our host's Horse

Blanch ale, and everything began to look almost natural to us. Finally, in answer to my request to dance, a messenger returned to talk to the head man, who nodded to Romeo, and I got my wish. We danced and danced, and later went for a walk in the moonlight and found a comfortable hay-filled barn. *Ooh la la! C'est magnifique, c'est si bon, and vive la France!*

They didn't talk much, very serious people, but . . .

We had trouble sleeping that night. Vachon had checked everything on the plane, so our thoughts went back to Lake Saint Agnes, wondering what had gone on during our absence of four or five days. I had lost count. My fear was that someone had found a way to get to the flyers, but knew that was impossible with the gas situation, and felt better. But I worried anyhow.

Before dawn, Vachon and Oulett awakened us, saw to it that we had a good breakfast, then after the oil and wing routine and all the cheering and waving from the villagers, we reached once again for the clouds. It was a relatively short flight to Lake Saint Agnes and on approach we observed the scene below with unbelieving eyes. I had expected something, after receiving a wire at Seven Islands, which said: "Fervently hoping for a scoop. Good Luck. E. Cohen."

But below, on the ice, we saw the strangest of sights. There was a long dark line, like an aircraft landing strip, and at one end stood a black monoplane, prop spinning. I feared it was a competitor waiting to ruin my lead, hoped for scoop, and exclusive pictures I had. Many other ships were around the plane, mid hundreds or people scattered about the hanger and offices nearby.

Romeo Vachon circled, leveled smartly, touched our skis down to a perfect landing, and taxied up to the black aircraft. I had the door to our plane open and the magazine case with the precious film in my hand. "Mac" MacKean, our assignment editor, came running for all he was worth, as I jumped out.

"Where's the film, you son-of-a-bitch?" he shouted, hugging and banging me on the back. He grabbed the magazine, then raced to the big black monster with wheels, not skis. That explained the dark runway we saw from the air. The snow had been scraped clear, leaving a smooth strip for the heavily loaded plane. Two men hung onto the struts, and within seconds the pilot revved the engine to the maximum, while the men tried to hold back the aircraft, as it broke loose in a blast and catapulted far down the runway, trying desperately to become airborne. Finally, just when it looked as though it would crash, the pilot pulled fiercely on the stick and the plane slowly, gradually gained altitude then swung about and headed straight south to New York.

I asked one of the men what that was all about. He explained that MacKean had brought the plane from the States, the cabin was crammed full with five-gallon gas cans of aviation fuel, and had installed a waddle pump, so he could refill the plane's tanks in flight. The aim was a non-stop flight to New York with my film. I found out later that only once did they see the ground, and that was not until they were near New York's Curtiss Field. I stood there, suddenly alone on Lake Saint Agnes, feeling completely deflated. Romeo Vachon came over to me. "Come here, Swede. I want to show you something."

We walked over to our plane, and he pointed up to a section of the fuselage, where the big engine was mounted. Then I saw it. A quarter inch of sky showed between the two sections. Another few minutes and we could have lost our motor and crashed. "God!" I whispered. "Thank you, God."

The original photograph of "Swede" Fernstrom as he first steps off the Fairchild at Lake St. Agnes. Notice Paramount's Assignment Editor Mac MacKean grabbing the film magazine and racing to the awaiting Black Monoplane for the non-stop flight to the lab in New York. The film screened that night. "Scoop."

Eddie Jackson walked up to me. "How are you going to get back to New York, Swede?" I hadn't given it a thought. "Let me fly you with us to Hartford, Connecticut. There, you can make arrangements to get back to New York."

Eddie's office had supplied him with a large cabin plane, so I flew with him to Hartford, where we bid each other farewell for a job well done, and he took off in his Waco. I phoned E. Cohen collect, from the airfield.

"Charter a plane, and land at Curtiss, Long Island. We'll have some boys meet you," he instructed. And that's what I did. We landed at Curtiss, where I was surprised to see our guys shooting pictures of me and the plane. It hadn't dawned on me that during that flight to Greenly Island and back, our expedition had become such important news. The suspenseful buildup the two reporters had wired home had made our trip exciting reading.

Then I heard about all their efforts, the preparation for our arrival at Lake Saint Agnes with the film, and to hell with me and my camera. The pictures were the interest. That's all Mac wanted. Poor Mac! I guess he waddle pumped his way from Quebec to New York, and almost passed out by the time they landed at Curtiss where Al Richard, assistant editor, grabbed the magazine case of film, jumped into an Ireland amphib, flew to the Hudson River, hopped into a speedboat, then a motorcycle with a sidecar and a police escort, up the wrong way of a one-way street, West Forty-third, and directly to our office lab.

While talking to Cohen on the phone in Hartford, I had read off all the captions for the film to him, so the titles were ready by the time Al got there and within an hour theaters all over Manhattan had our pictures, our scoop.

Then came the surprise of a lifetime for Eddie and me. While we were gone, it seems the Associated Press (AP) and my boss had gotten together and agreed to cooperate so AP could have still photos made from my negatives. Something I had never heard of, as AP had never had photos of films before nor shown interest in them until this story broke. Cohen, ever alert for anything that would build up Paramount's prestige, had agreed to supply them with my stuff.

Eddie Jackson had made a fast retreat to Governors Island and his office, but there throughout a special issue of his own newspaper, were my pictures, printed hours before Eddie's arrival. He gazed in disbelief at his paper and the credit lines. "Paramount News—Associated Press Photos."

That was the birth of the great Associated Press/newsreel cooperation and my pal Eddie hasn't spoken to me since. I don't blame him. Even had I known it, which I didn't, I probably would have double-crossed him anyway, for that's how fierce the competition was among us bastards in that golden era of news gathering.

Mr. E. Cohen called me on the carpet when I submitted the expense account for that trip, but he signed it, and gave me a fifteen-dollar-a-week raise and a five-hundred-dollar bonus. The following morning, he asked where I had been the night before?

"Out doing the town."

"Well," replied Cohen, "you lost five hundred bucks, because I tried to get you to make a personal appearance at the Paramount." That one scoop became a special issue with Paramount News, and it ran in theaters all over the world, until finally my old friend, Bernt Balchen, in a Ford Tri-motor equipped with skis,

GREENLY ISLAND AS SEEN FROM
PARAMOUNT PLANE AS BREMEN DID

(Telephoto View by Paramount News-Associated Press)

Newspaper clipping of the big story. Photo, adapted from Ray's newsreel, shows Greenly Island as taken from the Fairchild. Note the credit lines at the bottom.

could get to Greenly Island and bring the German fliers to civilization and a Broadway ticker tape parade.

Paramount News received a whopping amount of money from the newsreel accounts of our successful expedition, close to a million dollars, which was a lot of money in those days. Now our newsreel was number one, and everyone was happy. This meant we had to fight even harder to stay on top.

People and Personalities

Our assignments spread out even farther. Anything of photographic value was covered, and we cooked up as many feature yarns as we could think of or dig out of magazines, newspapers, or any other source. The newsreels still had their spies, like newspapers, ever alert for an item for which they received payoff tips. I became adept at covering everything; football, baseball, polo, horse races, sailing yachts, speedboats, and ships of all kinds. The wonderful Akeleys, with their smooth panning, tilting, and close-up following of any action, became the standard workhorse of every newsreel cameraman.

We were young, wild, and able. We drank hard and lived it up, chasing any girl that came within reach or sight, ever competing, for everyone wanted to be better, tops, first. 81

Paramount News

FIRST PICTURES OF BREMEN AND GERMAN-FLYERS AT GREENELY ISLAND

Paramount News has done it again.

THE story . . . first.

Capt. Koehl and Baron von Huenefeld, marooned with their broken ship in the wilderness. The greatest news story since Lindbergh!

The flight made by the Paramount News cameraman, Ray Fernstrom, to reach Greenely Island was an air epic in itself. The ship faced the same difficulties that forced down the Bremen at the end of her voyage. Icy fog; snow-laden gales whipping across an open, desolate land.

From Murray Bay, 100 miles north of Quebec, where he had been first to arrive, Fernstrom hopped for Seven Islands, 250 miles north. He was the first to greet and photograph Commandant Fitzmaurice, Irish flyer, on his way south for repair parts. The commandant himself brought Fernstrom's film on south to Murray Bay.

Fernstrom was bound north. Bitterly cold north winds were blowing; he didn't hesitate. In five hours the Paramount News plane sighted Greenely Island — the only news cameraman to reach the Bremen.

From Tuesday to Thursday, using every one of the few good light hours, Fernstrom recorded the picture story of Capt. Koehl, Baron von Huenefeld, and their ship the Bremen. The screen tells how well Fernstrom did his job.

Back he came, fighting headwinds, fog, cold. Twice he was forced down by gales. Friday morning at dawn he arrived at Murray Bay. Straight as a homing pigeon, the Paramount plane then headed for New York. Fernstrom's negatives were rushed through the laboratory, edited, printed—and distributed . . .

The first pictures of the German flyers and the Bremen—a 500-foot special!

I feel that both the exhibitors and the public will join me in extending heartiest congratulations to Ray Fernstrom for his splendid work on this story. It is a wonderful and daring piece of work.

EMANUEL COHEN,
Editor Paramount News.

Yours to you all Ray.

"THE EYES OF THE WORLD"

Paramount News Special
First Pictures Bremen and Flyers at Greenely Island!

1. Paramount News brings to world first scenes showing Capt. Koehl and Baron von Huenefeld with their plane, where they were forced down after making first westward trans-Atlantic flight.
2. Facing same storms and icy fogs that forced Bremen down, Paramount News cameraman achieves one of the most daring exploits in newsreel history, flying more than 2,500 miles to this isolated post and back. (map shows route).
3. Paramount News Ace! Cameraman Ray Fernstrom, who made first pictures of Bremen and the flyers, receives congratulations.
4. Greenly Island! Fernstrom grinds first view of desolate spot as his plane approaches, showing lighthouse which attracted flyers' attention.
5. The Bremen! First pictures show her disabled, exactly as she landed after completing famous flight.
6. The German flyers face their first American motion picture camera! Capt. Koehl and Baron von Huenefeld.
7. As the Bremen pitched forward in landing, Capt. Koehl was hurled against instrument board. Notice bruise on forehead.
8. Capt. Koehl and Baron von Huenefeld pose with Mr. and Mrs. John Le Temple, who took weary men into their home when Bremen came down.
9. The Baron accepts a smoke from his hosts. . .
10. Greenly Island's youngsters get the thrill of their lives! The trans-ocean flyers tell them how the sturdy Bremen crossed the sea!
11. The youngsters reciprocate! They give the flyers true gifts of the Northland. . .
12. "We flew for hours and hours over country like that," flyers tell their hosts, pointing out desolate stretches of ice surrounding Greenely Island.
13. The flyers point out for Paramount News the damage to the Bremen.
14. The landing gear—hopelessly out of commission until repair parts arrive.
15. Inside the Le Temple home, . . .
16. The family and its distinguished guests at dinner.
17. The "good luck tokens" from Ireland. . . Flyers show miniatures of Shamrock, with the lucky pig symbol. These the airmen received just before taking off.
18. Commandant James Fitzmaurice, gallant Irish aviator who accompanied the German flyers as co-pilot with Capt. Koehl.
19. Commandant Fitzmaurice went to Murray Bay by relief plane, seeking repair parts for Bremen.
20. Conferring with Miss Herta Junkers, daughter of Bremen's designer, about repair plans.
21. Baron Ehrenfried von Huenefeld, who spent his all to make flight possible. The Baron, undismayed by disasters to first three attempts at westward flight, proved his faith by flying himself!
22. Captain Hermann Koehl. . . Germany's master pilot, whose unwavering skill brought Bremen safely through gales and fog to America!

Autographed edition of a Paramount News periodical congratulating Ray for his "splendid work."

Now and then a big deal would come up that needed nearly all the camera staff. One such event was a world's heavyweight champion prize fight. Whether Firpo-Dempsey or Dempsey-Carpentier, or other such great events, these were legitimate news items. But there was a major hitch to our coverage—no cameras allowed. A syndicate had bought the movie rights. Were we dismayed? Never! Our staff or cameramen, editors, cutters, all the gang, went to work figuring angles, dress, disguises, until the boxes our boss bought became filled with a motley crew. There were old women, cripples, hunchbacks, raincoated and very tall men, dashing dames, sneaking in to steal as much of the fight as possible, with box mounts on tiny trips, magazines and gear heads in the smallest pieces possible. This became a game between newsreels and the strong arm men the syndicate circulated to find us. Out of ten men, we always managed to get our pictures, and so did the other reels. One could see on the big screen pretty much the same coverage the next day.

My wife was still in Sharon awaiting our firstborn. Naturally I attended lots of parties. A sidekick of Phil Coolidge was in New York from Boston, and he invited me to a swank soiree in a gorgeous penthouse apartment belonging to a prominent couple. A grand time was had by all, and I had many drinks and dances with the beautiful hostess. Then she asked me to stay after the guests were gone. This I agreed to without the slightest reluctance, for she was gorgeous and those French seventy-fives we had been drinking had mesmerized my other abilities to judge which course the evening should take. Besides, I had nothing but an empty apartment waiting for me across the Hudson. As I laid on a long luxurious couch, the room empty, soft music playing on a record machine, she drifted into the room and over to me, wearing nothing but a flimsy wrap and perfumed from tip to toes. She bent over me and the wrap fell open revealing her pink charms as she sat down beside me. "Tell me more about your wife having a baby," she inquired.

I did and said it was our first, and I had a brother and two sisters.

"Then you come from a prolific family!"

"Sure do!"

"Will you give me a baby?"

"Well, I don't know. What's wrong with your husband? Aren't you married?"

"Yes, but he keeps using those rubber contraceptives. He doesn't want a child yet, and I'm dying for one!"

"Well, in that case, I'll help you out. And if we succeed, tell him the rubber broke." I was very helpful and a year later, a card arrived for me at Paramount News, which said, "We are having a wonderful time in Paris, my husband, the baby, and I. When we return, you must join us for dinner some evening." But I never heard from her again because I moved about too much to get word, even had I wanted to see them again. For discretion purposes and the public awareness of their stature in life, and the fact I am a perfect gentleman in these matters, my lips are sealed forever as to who they are. C'est la vie.

I've forgotten the news assignment that sent me to Boston, but after a visit with Jerry and the folks in Sharon, I drove off to meet the other guys at Paramount's Metropolitan Theater. We had a few belts, then went to see Paul Whiteman's Orchestra and the Rhythm Boys. Across the street were the girls who danced in Rio Rita, a musical, so naturally a party was planned after both shows up on Beacon Hill of all places.

During the party, we played football out in the spring snow in our BVDs, and a more alcoholic, wild game was never performed. I think the girls in their undies won because the rest of us came down with pneumonia the next day. I don't recall if Bing Crosby participated on our team or not, but I suspect so. That may account for his becoming the "groaner," for all of us groaned for quite sometime after.

We were young and crazy in those days, and the demands, orders, newsreel admonishings, warnings, and threats meant that we were trained to be go-getters. We were to get the pictures at all costs, so it was natural that every other of life's pleasant challenges be met the same way; head-on, no holds barred.

Our New York assignments reached farther outward. Mine, in the direction of Washington, DC, where we already had two men under the direction and care of a former Associated Press representative, my friend Steve Early. The two men were Bob Denton and Hugo Johnson, a pair of fine gentlemen, cameramen, and diplomats, who were increasingly in need of more coverage assistance, which was due to the greater number of stories in the DC area, and especially aerial jobs. I got the brunt of those assignments and was deeply and financially grateful.

Eventually, Mr. Cohen transferred me permanently to Washington, DC, and Steve Early became my local boss. Steve and I became very close friends because we never tried to steal each other's girlfriends during all the partying. 83

He was a very serious, dignified, southern gentleman, who looked a bit askance at this crazy Swede.

When we took assignments, Bobby Denton covered the White House, Hugo the Capitol, Senate, and House of Representatives, while Steve and I took the exciting stuff, including the air. Our first was the speed trials of Al Williams and his seaplane racer, trying to make the Schneider Cup Finals. Later we did the inauguration of Herbert Hoover in March 1929. There was a great parade as usual, but on that great day everything that could fly was to form an aerial armada in the sky, which to date nothing like it had ever before been seen by man. It was to be led by *my* giant dirigible, the *Los Angeles*, with every army and navy blimp flying around her. Squadron after squadron of army, navy, coast guard, and marine aircraft of every description were to add to the formation. Planes of varying speeds flew at different altitudes, so the slower, lighter-than-air blimps and the dirigible could fly the lowest. Each in increasing speed ranges would sweep across and above, forming a waving armada, like an umbrella, over the parade up Pennsylvania Avenue.

My camera and I were mounted in one of the fastest planes so I could shoot down with a wide-angle lens and get in as many of the crafts as possible, along with the action below. Synchronizing so much aerial activity with the city beneath was not easy, and we all wanted to rendezvous when this mass of aircraft was at its thickest, right over the presidential parade. The dirigibles and blimps first, then the slowest airplanes, and the faster groups following.

The plans worked well. We were exactly where we should be, gathering en masse over the city when, unexpectedly, a deep, fast moving, thick Chesapeake fog rolled in and met the entire massed mess just as we approached the parade. The wind that accompanied it struck the lighter-than-air ships head-on. Confusion hit the rest of us. Formations broke, each on his own, trying to keep from flying into one another, and particularly the airships.

My pilot dove, missing planes, blimps, and the giant *Los Angeles* by inches, until we were almost on the ground where we headed for Bolling Field. Later some of the blimps landed there at the navy end, Anacosta Naval Air Base, where they had landing facilities. Two were blown apart or deflated. If it was an accident or on purpose, I never found out. That was the extent of the damages, other than I got no pictures for recorded memories for you or me of that incredible day.

In July, Jerry gave birth to my oldest daughter, Barbara, in Sharon. I was given some time off, so drove to New York, saw my friend the Auburn distributor, and traded off the Speedster for a Navajo red Auburn Phaeton, four-passenger convertible. It was too red, so I added a couple of black panels across the top of both doors on each side, which also gave it a lower look. So with a new baby and car, we returned to Washington.

The birth of our new baby accompanied a new birth in the newsreel business—sound on film. The old silent days were on their way out forever. (However, I hung onto the air stuff with no sound as long as I could.) Paramount's "the eyes of the world" became "the eyes and ears of the world," which we guys dubbed immediately, "the eyes, ears, nose, and throat of the world."

During preparations for our first issue of the sound newsreel (We continued to carry the silent one, too), our boss wanted special ideas for something newsworthy to send off our new reel.

The army helped us with my idea of landing a blimp on the lawn of the Capitol plaza. A dignitary arrived in one blimp, while I shot the air stuff from another. Then he spoke at the dedication of our sound reel. The two blimps were from Langley Field and flown by Andy Anderson and P. D. Ent, both of whom later became generals. Herbert Hoover appeared on the lawn of the White House and congratulated Adolph Zukor on our sounds birth.

A US Army blimp on the lawn of the Capitol in Washington DC celebrating Paramount News' first sound. Swede is in another blimp taking this picture—it was his idea.

The months rolled by. My assignment editor arrived, and I reminded him of his promise for more expense money. This was Washington!

"You're right," he said. "You representatives are dealing with all the military and aviation news. I'll see to it you have a good expense account." Entertaining those in service who could help get news stories or ones we cooked up as exclusives without the other reels crashing in on our ideas wasn't easy and took a lot of buttering up.

I had to do a lot of entertaining in our grand suite in the new Saint Albans Tower Apartments in one of the swankiest Washington, DC areas. We had room service and quality gourmet food wheeled in. I purchased liquor from our established New York bootleg sources "right off the boat." It was excellent booze, and everyone knew it.

We had beautiful parties, and women from all over the world attended in exotic garb, kimonos, saris, etcetera. Jerry had a lot of girlfriends and the military cooperated in appreciation. Army, navy, and air corps all put on their best parade efforts, proving themselves in drills in our apartment. We were all young then, including the service officers, who shall remain anonymous, as they grew up in experience, peace and war, and became our highest ranking men in the armed forces. I am certain none of them ever forgot the Paramount News parties thrown for them so long ago.

Suddenly my greatest fears were realized. I was called back to New York to learn about shooting with sound. This would mean splitting my expense money with some square sound man and toting heavy junk, cables, batteries, and other mysterious paraphernalia in a truck. Oh Lord, what was happening to all the fun we had? But I worked hard, studied, and learned. My first sound engineer was Glen Glenn, and the truck was a monster. I taught Glenn our angles and he schooled me in their job because without cooperation no organization can build, especially in our field. I learned to pick subjects in which sound enhanced them.

Author's note: Glen Glenn went on to become the sound man of Hollywood during the next several decades. One would be hard pressed to find a movie that didn't have his name on the picture sound credits.

We received newer and lighter trucks and the sound equipment was lightened and reduced in size, but the cameras remained as large, heavy, cumbersome, and as Rube Goldbergish as ever. They were designed by engineers and mechanics who neither had to lift or use them in the newsreel world. Western Electric designed the sound end and Akeley the camera, but it appeared both had forgotten everything they ever knew. The new Akeleys had a much heavier trip and legs, which had been strengthened, all adding to the busting down of the newsreel cameraman. Along with this came cables for the camera motor, sound light, recorder and mixer. It seemed we were being entangled and wrapped in cables. But this situation began to clear up as we became a better team with more actual working experience. But one time we were too late fastening the cables.

I now had a regular sound man and a little three-quarter-ton sedan delivery truck, a Wolverine built by Reo and painted blue, red and gold, the Paramount colors, with silver touches here and there. The vehicle was a beefed-up little beauty, with overload springs and oversized tires. Every inch of the interior was crowded with equipment stacked away by newsreelmen who really knew how to design an area to hold the utmost.

My sound man was Leslie Norman, middle name Charles, who in later years became Charlie Norman and worked as sound engineer with NBC. But to me in our happy newsreel days, he was Les Norman. Les was half English and half Swede. We had a grand time together, and the expenses were doubled with him along. He was happy-go-lucky, and as let-go as any newsreelman I'd ever met. He's deceased now; probably died in a dull bed somewhere. But during our escapades, he was a true buddy.

On one of our first assignments, we awaited the arrival of another visit from Germany, the Graf zeppelin and an old acquaintance, Dr. Eckner, in his usual mystery. Our editors had anticipated every departure from Germany as a possible news story, and this was to be the first around-the-world flight for the behemoth. And we were ready. We arrived with the first newsmen at Lakewood, a fast jump to Lakehurst Air Station where some of the greatest air hangers ever built were located. They could hold several dirigibles and four or more blimps at one time.

We were at the bar having a refresher when our Western Union spies reported the imminent arrival of the Graf at Lakehurst. We put on a burst of speed, each sound truck carrying its crew plus reporters and other pals. We arrived ahead of the Graf with lots of time to spare. Everyone covered the landing, then office airplanes carried the film, which contained Eckner's guarded speech, back to New York. Meanwhile, I wondered if he knew I was the newsreelman who had tried to fly through his damned balloon in another episode.

We returned to the hotel and had a merry time waiting for a spy tip-off of Eckner's plans and action. But word came just after we went to bed when none were feeling any pain. That German, Eckner, was sneaking out of the hangar! We had gotten the tip-off in time, but awakening was another matter. Nevertheless, the trucks tore off toward Lakehurst with motley crews of news bugs hanging on all sides. We were dressed in shorts and pajamas, half clothed, freezing, and sobering up by the minute. Finally, we saw the hangar door in the distance, and sure enough it was opening slowly.

I thought fast. Norm was tense, too. We knew we couldn't get any closer and still have time to set up the camera and sound equipment unless we stopped right now. I could cover it with a long lens. I wheeled over to the side of the road, bodies flying everywhere, and grabbed my camera, tripod and magazine, then set up, threading the film and grabbing the camera cable from Norm. I locked it in and to my horror here came the zeppelin, smoothly floating out into the early New Jersey dawn. I covered her as well as anyone could, and off she sailed majestically. I gave out a relieved, deep-bellied exhale.

Then I heard a sputtering, gasping, angry, frothing Norm. "No sound!" Poor Norm; he forgot to attach the light cable, and he was responsible for sound. Who the hell wanted silent film anymore?

"What did you get?" I asked.

"No light cable—nothing!"

"Nothing exposed on the sound side of the film?" I pleaded.

"Nothing," he gasped in deadly fear.

"Wait a galdarn minute here," I muttered thoughtfully. "No exposure, no picture, no sound exposure, no sound; unexposed sound, exposed picture." I should still be able to record sound, I thought, since the recording light showing through the vibrating electronic strings is off. We have a chance! "Norm," I began, "listen closely. We may save this stuff yet."

"God, I hope so, or I'm whipped!"

"Now, here's what we are going to do," I instructed. "We shot four hundred feet of film, exactly. I'm going to cap this lens, for I've already exposed my film. Then we will wind it back in the camera to that exact distance on the footage counter and install the only sound a zeppelin makes and people hear of it taking off—motor."

"How do we do that?"

"Listen to me, stupid, and practice what you heard. Burrrr. Burrrr. Burrrr. Let me hear you, you dummy; your job is on the line on this crap!"

"Burrrr. Burrrr. Burrrr. Brummm." We both practiced until we ran out of breath. Then I told Norm to start up his sound. "Get everything ready before I tell you with a hand signal that the film is ready to roll forward again. We're going to put sound on this goddamned picture right now!" I gave him the signal and rolled the camera; only sound, of first my burring, then, as I nodded red-faced, he picked it up. We burred into the mike while he looked at me frantically, explosively red. I picked it up again, smoothly and a little more faintly now as she sailed off, until 405 feet of our burring ended.

We turned in the film to the lab, and Norm and I received a bonus from E. Cohen for the best picture and sound; the most stupendous coverage of a zeppelin he had ever witnessed. This is the first time our boss will realize if he reads this just how we actually accomplished what we did. Forgive me, Colonel. Just get the pictures and er, ah sound!

Paramount signed Maurice Chevalier to a contract. He was to arrive at Pier fifty-seven. We were told to get down there and interview him. Off we drove, then onto Pier fifty-seven to a spot where we could get close to the first-class gang plank and set up. Suddenly, a gruff voice growled, "Hey, yous!" A male mountain walked over to me, sitting behind the wheel of the truck. "Where's yous union card?" A bailing hook with a wooden handle and a sharply pointed steel curve of death hung from his huge hairy right hand.

"Back at the office," I replied.

"Go git it."

"But I've got to cover the ship docking!"

"Go git it." The hook swung menacingly.

I jumped out of the truck and caught a taxicab.

We had been warned during the start of unionization of cameramen by the International Alliance of Theatrical and Stage Employees of the United States and Canada (IATE) that anyone joining the union would be fired. But in our code, the picture came first. So off I went to get a union card at the seventy-five-dollar initiation fee. The card was made out and I was informed that the fee had jumped to five hundred dollars, that us guys at Paramount "shun'ta held out like dat." So I paid.

"Here you are," I told the owner of the bailing hook and nervously handed him the card which now looked old from being clutched in my sweaty hand. The steamer was approaching the pier. I got more nervous. "Where's my truck?" I demanded.

"Okay, fellas," he yelled, jowls quaking, as he turned. "Give 'em da truck!" A mass of bales and cases of junk were moved aside and there sat our truck, Norm hunched in the seat. Then to add injury to insult, "Next time don't forgit da union card, or da truck'll end up in da river!" I believed him.

We got the interview and the hell outa there. Welcome, Chevalier!

When the boss found out about the union card, as he did everything else, I expected to be fired. But all he said was, "Now all the boys are going to have to join the union, and I'm paying all their initiation fees." This he did, and he didn't know it but he paid mine, too. It took a lot of padding of the expense account, but I covered it.

One fine day in Menlo Park, New Jersey, I was honored to meet a real genius, Thomas Alva Edison, and his assistant, Charles Ott. I had a scheduled interview, which in light of historic events, became a re-stage of the start of our profession. Edison's first close-up with a motion picture camera which he had invented was of Ott. This event we re-staged with his old camera and Mr. Edison himself turning the crank while talking to us, as Ott posed as before. That was one of the last interviews the great man ever held. A moment to remember.

Jerry and I stood up for Norm and his bride when they were married, and the next day he and I and our baggage, without our wives, were shipped out on assignment to Cuba and the West Indies for planned sound stories aboard the *SS Mauritania* of the Cunard line heading south out of New York.

We repaired to the top deck salon, where we imbibed in refreshments and listened to good music while watching the dancing. Across from us sat a merry group of ladies and gentlemen. One of the gentlemen asked if that was our movie equipment they had seen when they boarded.

"Yeah, that's us," I answered.

"Well, boys, we are the Warner Brothers—Al, Jack, etcetera, etcetera."

The Warner Brothers had brought sound to the screen.

Norm and I were sure our legs were being pulled, so answered dubiously, "Oh, is that so? Well, we're from Paramount," I replied. "And this is Jesse Lasky and I'm Adolph Zukor." Everyone laughed. We danced with the ladies, and everyone had a good time. But they were not kidding us, and I've been privileged to do a lot of work for the brothers throughout my career.

We disembarked at our first job site, Havana, Cuba, and waved adieu to the real Warner Brothers and their party, as the *Mauritania* continued toward her West Indies tour. Then we checked in at the Siboney Hotel, locked up our gear and went directly across the calle to renew our friendship with Raoul Sanchez at his beautiful Cunard Bar, where we discussed our visit and purpose. First, we had the job of covering the memorial service at the monument of the USS *Maine* where dignitaries were to speak. But Raoul told us of a nightclub way out in the sticks, Le Verbena, that he was certain we would enjoy. So that evening, in a horse-drawn carriage we rode out there, along the lovely Mercado, down the calle.

Raoul was right; it was grand. We heard new tunes and saw a dance that simply had to be on film. The manager arranged with Raoul's help a daytime set-up so we could photograph the dance and record the sound in that native tropical background.

Later back in New York at our office building, Rudy Vallee and his orchestra were rehearsing in our new upstairs sound studio when our film arrived. They were invited to listen and watch our new stuff. The dance we had photographed was the rumba, true native style. The tune became known after Rudy Vallee introduced it in New York at the Paramount Theater as the *Peanut Vendor*, and it became a smash hit for Rudy.

We made a botched try at interviewing Rudyard Kipling in Trinidad, then were ordered home to Tennessee to do an army recruiting film of the great World War hero Sergeant Alvin York near Pall Mall. The army would cooperate with us. This was to be a typical human interest feature of which we had filmed thousands.

We made our pictures of the famous sergeant in the hill country at a turkey shoot, in which the shooters used long rifles. The guns were accurate and while shooting these scenes, I realized how wonderful our civilian soldiers are at war. Their hometown training had taught them more in independent action than any stylized army teachings could ever accomplish.

We were staying at the Mark Twain Hotel when we ran out of moon. So our escort, the Major, and I went to a gentlemen's mountain shack to do a little bartering. We had been directed there by a gent in the know for some "good likker." But as we approached his diggings, we were met with the serious end of a double-barreled shotgun.

"You revenoors git outa har, now!"

What the hell did he mean? Then it struck me. That jerk of a major was wearing his army boots, khaki shirt and pants, and looked just like a revenue agent. We returned to the store in Pall Mall, left the major behind, and got a local gent to obtain the thirst-quenching corn for celebrational fun. We had completed our work, and now it was time to play.

Newsreels were rapidly losing their grip on the people's imaginations. The crash of the stock market had taken the starch out of so many things, and the arthritis in my back was killing me. Those goddamned heavy sound cameras (or was it the moonshine) had taken its toll. Norm accepted a great position out West as a sound engineer at NBC Radio in Hollywood, California, and E. Cohen told me to see the Paramount doctor about my bent spine. The doctor strongly suggested I move to a warm climate, so the boss gave me three months' advance salary and said, "Go and get your health back, then come back to Paramount News."

I sold my car, cashed in everything I owned, gathered up my traveler's checks, bought three tickets aboard the steamer the *President Harrison*, took Jerry and baby Barbara aboard the huge ship, and we sailed away south through the Panama Canal for sunny California. I knew in my heart I would never go back. So long Paramount News! It's been a ball and my thrills behind the newsreels!

⇒•⇐

Finally, Color

Swede had his camera, equipment, and trusty old relic of a typewriter, and he began to write to the Swedish-American line, The Swedish State Railways, et al, as he had planned a series of color travelogues after discovering the existence of Multicolor and was itching to create. He had met with the head of Multicolor's camera department, Emil Oster, but couldn't get the financing needed. So he looked up John Boyle, with whom he had first worked in Hollywood at Paramount Studios years earlier. John was very interested in what Ray was planning.

Ray had already spoken with his contacts at Metro-Goldwyn-Mayer about doing six one-reel travelogues of Sweden, Norway, Denmark, Finland, Holland and Belgium, all in glorious color. They had nothing on file except black and white, so they were interested. They made a gentlemen's agreement for a contract should Ray manage to bring back material acceptable for the six eleven-minute shows. Very simple, since Swede's contacts in Europe immediately opened the doors to the continent and beyond, with free first-class transportation by ship and railway; everything he had hoped for and more. He knew how much they wanted American tourists there and publicity here. Every detail was settled, except money. It was so tight.

One day at Multicolor, John proposed that they team up, with John supplying the money on an agreed basis. He bought a new bi-pack Mitchell camera with a set of double magazines, and one red-orange and one blue-green negative. Yellow or lavender were not available in those days, but they could stretch the stimulation by staying away from the colors they were obviously unable to record. No one had yet brought out a practical full spectral reproducing system.

A deal was drawn and Ray felt personally committed to his Scandinavian friends; thus he had to sign, even if it did take the control of the operation away from him. He was now a five-percenter. But he was able to leave enough money for his family to exist while he was away in Europe that spring and summer.

The president of the line, Hilmer Lundbeck, threw a plush party on board the Swedish flagship *Kungsholm* in New York Harbor. Everyone was in formal dress, with the usual speeches from the Captain, John Boyle and others. After *skäling* one another with a few blasts of 150-proof akvavit, John announced, "Instead of six one-reelers on six foreign countries, we are going to make a feature-length documentary on Sweden." This delighted the predominantly Swedish audience.

Ray wondered what they would do about showing it. Later John told Ray, "We'll roadshow it!" What did they know about roadshowing? John was a Hollywood studio cinematographer and Ray and ex-newsreeler. He had no choice but to go along. It was John's money.

While at the party, the chief engineer and Swede had been discussing color photography when Ray innocently asked why the lovely yacht-like Swedish motorships were painted black instead of white or light blue. When the president of the line asked what the two of them were discussing so intently, the engineer explained, and to Ray's amazement, the president announced, "Ray's right; we'll paint them all white! It will be cheaper to maintain and much prettier." Swede was pleased because he had planned to photograph the sister ship at sea one day after reaching Sweden. In only nine days, Sweden's entire fleet was painted white, and white is to this day is associated with luxury ocean liners.

John's first inspiration, as part of the Swedish documentary was a trip across the Atlantic, and while they prepared to sail, Ray wrote a script. They shot montage flashes of the great liner leaving New York, careful not to get the as yet unpainted black sides in the picture, so the scenes they would shoot in Gothenburg of the white liner would blend.

The big problem was John with his Hollywood studio training. He ran three hundred feet of film on the first scene. The magazines only held four hundred! Ray threw the script overboard. Somehow they would have to bring the thrifty use of film in newsreels together with the

Hollywood give-a-shit attitude of shooting. They would work that out later at sea.

Ray was thrilled to at last be working with color. His imagination knew no bounds. The two men worked out all the details, covering every aspect of the trip within a reasonable budget for the pioneer feature full-length color documentary with as much action, humor, and human interest as possible. They hoped desperately that it would be a success.

By the time they completed the long shots of the other ship off the Swedish coast as she plowed white and lovely through the green sea against a blue sky filled with billowy clouds, both felt secure the film had begun well.

However, it was one thing to make a one-reeler interesting, but to hold an audience through an hour or more took a bit of doing. They had to create novelty, entertainment, and the unexpected.

During their spare time aboard the ship, they studied Swedish history, both within her cities and all twenty-four of her provinces. They gleaned help from everyone aboard who related stories about life in the areas in which they lived. This was of immense help.

They readied to meet the challenges ashore and learned that the cooperation of the Swedish State Railways was as complete as that aboard ship. When Swedes cooperate, they go all out. Ray and John wanted to make a complete little railway yarn on the express run from Gothenburg to Stockholm, and not just any old train would do. It had to be assembled in a grand manner—a special car to supply the electricity for the huge array of photo floods and a dining car for the longer Lapland runs, plus a sleeping car and day Pullman. They needed scenes of the train dashing beautifully through interesting settings. This was quite a project for any railroad, but the Swedes brought it off with their usual efficiency. The passengers on board were cast like a Hollywood production, even to a Swedish beauty going to bed on board. The dining sequence was spectacular with the tremendous picture windows and scenic countryside for the background.

After the rail job was completed, they returned to Gothenburg for a cross-country trip by steamer. These miniature white steamers drop through locks down to Lake Vattern. At some points, they can be seen chugging through a farm past grazing cattle, with no water in sight. It was below the land like a mirage.

Ray and John traveled through the tiny Gota Canal with its locks, then journeyed through the countryside greeting lakes, and finally to the Stockholm Sound and the gleaming capital. They covered Stockholm in a travelogue manner, but for excitement the two cameramen went to Dalecarlia, where the good people dragged out their ancient Viking long-boats which no longer had sails, but the many oars were intact. Proudly, they removed the boats from the museum, then caulked and varnished until they looked like new. Then the natives staged a scene in their national

Dalarna costumes and crossed Lake Sylvan to the little white stone church at Leksand. A tradition was started. To this day, every Sunday the Swedes reenact the scene with the longboats for tourists to enjoy.

Next were scenes taken on the Island of Gotland with its walled Hanseatic League city of roses and ruins, Visby. There were many crumbling cathedrals and decaying protective walls from earlier centuries. There they did a stunt through the magic of the color camera, which took the viewer back to the early tenth century and showed how the city looked and was occupied at that time.

They went to the museum. Clothes were reproduced; armor, spears, and swords were made to look like new again. The film appeared as a series of moving paintings. Ray used the most beautiful girls in town, who wore high peaked hats with trailing gossamer veils and traditional costumes, and waved from windows as people strolled by. At the toll gates, soldiers stood in full armor, farmers pushed carts, and nuns meandered about the cathedral grounds, while one kneeled in a particularly beautiful ruin with smoked sunlight streaming over her, adding to the magic.

Ray was happy to have covered Stockholm so thoroughly, because in the back of his mind his contacts at MGM loomed, expecting six short reels of different countries, and Swede had convinced John to do a quick series of highlights on the other Scandinavian countries for a tie-in to Sweden.

Springtime moved swiftly into summer, while they did a fine film on Denmark, Hans Christian Andersen's storybook land of dairy products, lovely girls, and the castle Elsonore of Shakespeare's *Hamlet*.

Next came Finland, and again they did well, especially the novelty sequence on Lake Ladoga on the little island of Valamo. It was completely inhabited by monks of the Russian Orthodox Church who went about their chores dressed in dark brown, high-topped hats, and flowing beards. They made shoes, baked bread in huge ovens, worked in the fields, and one even raced by chasing after a runaway horse and cart, his skirts hiked high.

They filmed the many colorful cathedral towers that rose above with chiming bells calling the monks to worship. Through an arch, they shot crosses in a graveyard and all in glorious color. Ray felt like a Rembrandt with a camera instead of a brush, as he painted picture after enthralling picture.

Summer was waning; all the film was gone, and so was nearly all of John's money. As usual, they had spent more than expected. They sailed home hopeful, but with only three countries in the can. Swede had misgivings.

When they arrived in Hollywood, John agreed to a finished one-reeler on *Stockholm, Queen of the Baltic.* They rough-cut a one-reeler of Denmark and another of Finland. Then they went to MGM.

First Ray asked them to screen the Stockholm film. When the end appeared and lights came on, the spokesmen for MGM, Irving Thalberg, said, "Gentlemen, that is very high class entertainment." Swede held his breath. Then Thalberg asked, "Do you have anything from other countries we can see?" John had them run the other two reels. On came the lights.

"Excellent," Thalberg exclaimed. "What other countries did you cover?"

"Those were the only three," Ray explained.

"Well, we can visualize the problems of foreign shooting with a short summer. If you will make a one-reeler about Canada, one on Mexico, and a final of Hawaii, we would be happy to give you a contract."

John's answer was a flat abrupt "No! I'm going to roadshow the feature. No contract."

With the help of the wife of another cinematographer who was secretary to Sid Grauman, Sid agreed to run the Stockholm reel instead of a newsreel, and Ray enjoyed his first Hollywood premier in living color at Grauman's Chinese Theater. John did roadshow the feature but was only able to recapture his initial investment and Ray got nothing from the nonexistent five percent share. "So much for roadshow crap!" he was heard to say.

Again, Swede was out scratching for work. He did some piece work for Universal, which covered a flood that nearly swept the Warner Brothers Studio into the Los Angeles River, along with a lot of homes.

Then the Olympic Games of 1932 came to Los Angeles, and that kept him busy for a while. Finally, one of the highlights of Ray's career occurred. He met his best friend, Hartley Harrison, a gentle, honorable man, and Hartley's pal, Art Reeves. The two men had obviously seen some of Ray's work, and they invested their money and friendship in him.

Hartley was one of those quiet, soft-spoken, thinking, genius-type of individuals who was always coming up with some new idea to improve and advance the world. He owned Harrison and Harrison Optics in Hollywood and was listed in *Who's Who*. Over the years, he would supply Ray with the latest in new lenses and special products he had invented for Ray to test and only for Ray's use. *Author's note: Hartley told Swede NASA used Harrison lenses for the first moon landings.*

One day, John Boyle called to say he couldn't take a job and had recommended Ray. It involved going to Europe again with the first three-color Technicolor camera. Full spectral color had arrived at last. Ray jumped at the opportunity, reported to the big Technicolor lab, and was introduced to George Cave.

Swede needed the work, for by then his oldest son Russell (coauthor of this book) had arrived, and was born at the Lagerloef Estate in Weehawken, New Jersey while Hans, Jerry's father, had sailed to Sweden aboard the *Drottningholm* for his annual visit. Ray had stood by while Jerry gripped his arm. When the baby first glimpsed the light of day, the doctor exclaimed, "What a head; what a pair of shoulders!" Many years later, Russ would become more of a brother to Ray than a son.

Mr. Cave explained the details of the job. Swede would have a color technician with him all the time—John Hamilton, who had been taught strictly; a scientist type, with the Technicolor rule book in one hand and a slide rule and report chart in the other. They would have a week of testing, along with Swede's friend, the dean of Technicolor consultants, Ray Rennahan. The two could shoot a thousand screen feet of film, which is actually three thousand total. The three-strip camera had a red, blue, and green record, which, with their imbition and stenciling process, gave natural colors by stenciling on cyan, magenta and yellow.

Swede met the master, Rennahan, and the two started tests. After a few flowers and long shots of UCLA, Swede suggested they make a one-reeler since there was nearly a thousand screen feet in the camera.

"What do you have in mind?" Rennahan asked.

"Let's do *meditation*. Get a gal to walk through those beautiful areas in the Hollywood Cemetery, the Reflection Pool, and the Clark Mausoleum. Then we can play soft music to accompany the showing." Swede peered around and spotted a pretty girl with a nice posture. They asked her if she would like to make a screen test in the new Technicolor. She consented excitedly. The two Rays rented a Grecian toga, sandals, and a blonde wig with a Grecian cord entwined to cover her dark hair. Then they all went to the cemetery.

John Hamilton had a strange gadget; a fancy exposure meter, something brand new in cinematography, the very first. Rennaham and Swede studied the massive camera while John took a reading with the meter. First straight at the camera, then one to the left and right, as he scribbled notes on his report card. Then he made a lens setting from the three readings.

Meanwhile, Swede looked through the camera viewing tube, eyeing the image he saw in the prism inside. He topped down the lens visually and slowly, as he had in his many years of experience with the old Wilart and later the DeBrie cameras, then opened and stopped down the lens until the image was just visible. Perfect, and he figured he could judge the correct exposure by eye. This simple method, he was sure, could be applied to the color camera. But when he studied the new attached lens, he noticed something else was different. The Technicolor calibrations were one, two, three, through to ten, instead of the old familiar F 2.3, 5.6, 11.0, etcetera. Excited, Swede called Rennahan over. "See what I have for a stop on the lens now."

"You have it at six," was the response.

Swede explained what he had been trying to do. Rennahan went to work studying, too, and both arrived at six. Then Big John came over with his triple reading crap to set the lens—at six. Swede whistled the tune, *Happy Days are Here Again*, then said, "It's a snap!"

Rennahan and Swede experimented again and found it possible to hit the same readings or within a safe margin. Swede explained the reasoning to John that there would be times in Europe when they might have 95 to forget the book and shoot fast. And with only one exposure meter, anything could happen. "It's called insurance, John." Swede told him. But John was bewildered. The technical *Bible* had been his entire job. It was his boss, his life for technical genius.

Ja, ja, Swede said to himself smiling, as they began their artistic production.

Rennahan and Swede practiced their extinction method while John pursued the ordered course. They enjoyed composing real art in scenes which looked like ancient Greece with columns and lily ponds, while the girl meditated as she moved slowly, quietly in front of the lens.

After Technicolor's processing, they ran the test with an added musical background for Dr. and Mrs. Kalmas. Mrs. Kalmas gasped, "It's so beautiful!" The R&R boys had made their point!

Swede and John left for New York to meet the man who had hired them and their massive equipment, James A. Fitzpatrick, and his famous *Travel Talks.* During lunch, Fitzpatrick explained that his work in completing the last cutting of his latest monochrome would keep him in New York. His wife would accompany them and handle the money. She also knew all his story ideas. Thereafter, they sailed on the French liner *Champlain* to England. *Author's note: The ship would later be sunk by a German mine off France at the beginning of World War II.*

En route, John taught Ray a few of the difficult jobs required on the huge color camera which was heavy enough, but the wet battery required weighed two hundred pounds and had to be carried with two sedan chair sticks like Cleopatra, with Swede on one end and John on the other.

Their first assignment was in Ireland where Mrs. Fitzpatrick said, "I don't know what we are going to do with Ireland."

"Let's take the ideas from the Irish songs that are so popular in America," Swede suggested. And they did, then hopped, skipped and sailed over to France, en route to Holland in the Netherlands. Swede felt this was exactly like the series he had just finished with John Boyle, but this time with full spectral color. He made up his mind to surpass anything he had done before. People would view the most beautiful color photography and composition ever seen to that date.

Ray had been looking forward with keen anticipation to visiting every art museum in Amsterdam, Den Haguye, Utrecht, and any others in which he could find works by the old Dutch Master artists. As in most museums, monochrome and color postcard reproductions of the paintings could be bought, and Ray purchased copies of everything they had, primarily Vermeer and Rembrandt. He studied their style carefully, hoping to emulate techniques, compositions, and lighting effects in the same settings, using live people in modern dress. In Volendam and Amsterdam, he did his best Rembrandt copies in "motion painting."

When they arrived, it was raining a little in the picturesque seaside village. But they figured that the clouds would roll by and the tiled roofs and cobblestones would shine in the sun, so they set up in a closed lorry with the tarpaulin end dropped to protect the camera. Then the sun came out, and all that was needed was to set the exposure while John raised the tarp. But somehow, the one and only exposure meter dropped from the truck to the cobblestones and broke.

"Can't shoot!" stated the frustrated and shaken John.

"What in hell do you mean we can't shoot?" Swede yelled.

"Says so in the book."

"Forget the goddamned book. I'll set her by eye. We'll never get this scene again." And he shot, much to John's bereavement. His *Bible* had been violated, and he would certainly be castrated by Technicolor for breaking their strict code.

Rules, shit. Fuck Technicolor. Get the gawdamned picture! thought Swede as he remembered Paramount News' motto: Get the picture, for tomorrow may never come. "Don't worry, John. I've been fired before. I'll take full blame. Let's go!" John stood looking at the broken meter in his hand as if the world had just ended.

What a sensitive, mental man, Ray thought. Not a bit like me, the tough, ornery, unfeeling jerk cameraman, Ray Fernstrom.

John got into the swing of things and was a great worker, but continuously nervous about the broken meter. The book said, "yap, yap, yap."

"Don't worry, John; keep at it," Ray encouraged as the assistant worked over the meter. Finally, the thing began to function again. They made tests and found Ray's guesses to be less than a quarter of a stop overexposed, which in photography is as close as anyone can judge with the naked eye, and well within acceptable limits.

They were about finished shooting in Volendam. Swede placed some Dutch sailors against the sails of their pudgy boats, their tobacco pipes smoking, with the cross lighting Rembrandt preferred. A light color in the center called attention to a little Dutch girl, the daughter of one of the fishermen. Ray was proud of the effect and felt even the Master himself would have liked it.

They photographed large tulip flowers, pouring strong light through each petal, until the flowers would later seem to pop out on the screen. They found a poppy field with a Dutch windmill in the background for a slow panoramic scene, and realized they needed Dutch costumes for the people, and the vanes spinning on the mill. A small motor took care of the latter, which spun lazily.

Spring turned to summer, and they were off to do another reel about Zeeland, a province much like Holland. Then the mountains of Switzerland beckoned.

It was now 1934. One could already smell the approaching war in the air. But as always, Switzerland was peaceful. They photographed Zurich, then drove the country roads.

At the hotel in Interlaken while enjoying a view of the Jungfrau Alp, Ray met a young damsel from New South Wales, Australia, opening up a sequence of events. She, too, was going to Jungfrau the following day with her aunt.

Ray enjoyed her company on the little train as it chugged up toward the mountaintop. The view of the valley was fantastic, falling away and spilling toward the tiny townlets set in postcard views of green and blue violets and little white churches. The train climbed slowly upward toward a hole in the mountainside and into a winding tunnel that ended at a little station.

Ray and the girl walked up to the hotel at the very top, built in half rock, hanging out over the slope like a balcony above the Jungfrau glacier. Their breaths came hard, as the altitude was thirteen thousand feet. Ray set up his camera and took the shots of the glacier in daylight, leaving it for a dissolve as the colors of sunset flooded the ice wastes below. The first day was over.

"Wrap it up, John," Ray said. He stowed the gear while John went about busily making tests and referring to the book.

Mrs. Fitzpatrick was feeling the altitude and went to bed early. Ray had not seen the Ice Palace yet, so with a bottle of Scotch, he enticed the little Aussie lass to climb the icy steps of the palace, which were softly lit in blue and led to the very top of the glacier. There, standing on top of the world in the soft moonlight between slugs of Scotch, they rested on the soft snow and surveyed the majesty of God's work.

Ray pondered the right approach. "Just think," he opened, "here you are from Australia, while I'm from Hollywood; both of us on the highest Swiss Alp."

"Yes," she purred, "isn't it romantic? He kissed her and she was warm, cuddly, soft, yielding. The night was balmy, the snow soft. Then history was made, and so was she. Ray never had a thought about Jerry patiently waiting for his return while caring for their two children.

In their search for the best composition for each scene, they often had to carry the heavy battery, camera, and the rest of the gear away from the mountain roads. At one such time, as they were about set up and ready to shoot a scene of rushing water from a mountain stream in the foreground, midst snow capped Alps, flowers, beauty, action and color, John suddenly announced, "It's time to clean the prism!"

"Not here, John. Not now. Wait until later, back at the hotel," Swede suggested.

"No, it says at four hundred feet of film, check and clean the prism. It's in the book!"

"Aw nuts, go ahead and clean it. You and your goddamned book!"

John opened the three doors on the camera, unbolted the prism mount, then held it up to look at the glass. He sloshed a few droplets of cleaning solvent on the top, then wiped and sighted it expertly, carefully. Suddenly a speeding Porsche came tearing down the dusty mountain road near them. A second later, there in the settling dust stood a gray-brown statue of John, holding his revered, dust-covered prism, dirt swirling in and out of the camera. He was frozen in position as Swede snarled, "What does it say in your fucking book about that, John?"

The assistant was up half the night cleaning and putting the camera back together. Later Ray was sure he heard John reciting the Rosary beads before he fell asleep.

Switzerland completed the journey to Europe. Technicolor had become the cathedral of opportunity for Swede, and he suffered great

Sometimes even Swede had it tough. The strenuous years as an "Ace" Newsreelman clearly show on his face.

anxiety as to others' reaction to his beautiful composition. He knew deep down that he wasn't their "book" type, but who could deny the creativity?

Back at the head office, all the top executives were present when the reels were shown. Ray sat next to the general manager, J. Arthur Ball. "Don't you like the composition and lighting?" Ray asked.

"No! It wasn't done according to the book!"

The damned book! He had copied Rembrandt. Swede was fired on the spot. But there was little doubt that he could have written a dozen books of better ilk on the subject, for to many in the industry and among his peers he was considered the finest cinematographer of them all.

Ray was invited to the monthly meeting of the American Society of Cinematographers and allowed to screen the four pictures. Now he would be judged by cameramen, the best in the world. He had named the features *Holland in Tulip Time, Zeeland, Unknown Paradise, Ireland, Emerald Isle,* and *Switzerland the Beautiful.*

When the screening was over there was a hush in the room, then slowly the audience rose to a standing ovation. He was immediately invited to become a member by John Boyle and Elmer Dyer, and unanimously accepted by all members. At last! One ambition was realized, another lost. Slightly disheartened but never broken, Ray, the intrepid cameraman, headed home to his wife and a time of deep thought.

California Highways

During Ray's absence, Jerry had become fast friends with Frank and Vita Kowalski while living at the old Colonial Court in Hollywood. Those were lean years and they shared every nickel they managed to bring in for food, rent, and clothes. This early friendship was to last a lifetime. Later the Kowalskis moved, but remained only a phone call away.

James A. Fitzpatrick's *Travel Talks* were shown throughout the world to viewers that included Ray's father-in-law, and for once he was impressed. Eventually, Ray and Jerry used the break in the ice to borrow two thousand dollars which Ray needed for a new project offered him through his good friend Hartley Harrison.

Hartley had designed and patented a new method in optics for the building of the Dunning color camera. Ray was picked by Hartley to do the testing. Dunning had developed an entirely new color process, which when fully developed would become active competition to Technicolor. The camera would carry three films, one facing the lens, while the other two faced optics that Hartley had designed.

After the camera and printing process was developed, Dunning was able to contract for a full-length film on the state of California for the Division of Highways. The state needed this for a referendum which would be submitted to the voters and guarantee that all gasoline tax funds would be used only for California's needed highways and not siphoned off by politicians for other constituents' purposes.

Ray received the assignment, along with Snuffy Cowper, to write and shoot the picture. California Highways was the theme. He studied California's history pertaining to movement, the methods used, and paths taken. Then he took the money borrowed from Hans and purchased a little Ford sedan delivery truck, which was a panel job with overload springs and heavy-duty brakes, as he was always a nut for good stopping power. He had the top of the truck modified with an opening hatch for mounting the camera with airplane mounts for high shots and moving ones as they sped along.

Ray and his camera truck shooting California Highways.

The idea was to show the progress California had made from the very beginning of a path and Father Juipero Sierra's feet, to dusty roads, horses' hooves, wagon wheels, then rubber and rubber with air in it.

Ray planned to film everything in the steps of progress, beginning in a dusty little town on the Mexican border and ending with the building of the great bridges at San Francisco, with the Oakland Bay Bridge and the impressive one-span, Golden Gate Bridge.

The only information they had received from the state were road locations. So they found a monk and a burro to illustrate the good Father's trek from the border to the northern reaches of California. This 101 turned out not to be a problem, and the project began on a pleasant note.

The filming took over a year before completion, covered approximately fourteen thousand miles of the state's roads and highways, and explored predictions of the freeways to come.

Sequences obtained included traveling to all parts of the state, with some of the middle scenes shot first and many others out of sequence. But all would be cut and edited in proper order.

They met an old friend of Snuffy's in San Bernadino who had many motor cars in perfect running order, so they did the original auto sequences with the first roads traveled in cars without horses pulling them. The movie depicted bumps, holes, dust, and the putt-putt of the little engine of an old 1838 locomobile driven by the old gent in duster, goggles, and motor cap. The auto was cute in that it didn't look much larger than a buggy. They showed dusty roads, the first paving, and highways, then progressed to the present and a final look to the future.

On the way North, they picked up Jerry for the balance of the shooting. The Kowalskis kept the children while she was away.

They were shooting in the famous Mother Lode gold country outside of Sonora with a stage coach dashing across the ruts of a meadowland, when they spotted several small planes landing a little way up the road. They went to investigate.

The visit resulted in an invitation to join the pilots at a breakfast of the Los Angeles Aviation Club. Jerry Fairbanks, producer of Paramount's short feature films *Unusual Occupations* and *Popular Science*, was among the flyers. He admired Ray's hatch arrangement and camera mount on the truck and invited Ray to check with him when Ray completed this assignment. He liked what he saw and said he had a good job for Ray.

They continued northward and covered all the spots needed, including the Ferry Seed Farm. Jerry, Ray's wife, was ecstatic with the beauty. Wherever they looked, there were acres and acres of flowers, row upon row, in full bloom. A perfect subject for the blossoming Dunning process of color.

During the hours and hours spent on the road, Ray kept Jerry and Snuffy spellbound as he recalled many astounding experiences from his days as a newsreelman. One particular tale left Snuffy with mouth agape, while Jerry took everything in stride. The story involved Swede and Lindbergh. The two Swedes had actually flown together. At the time, Ray was stationed in Washington, DC, while Lindbergh was taking congressmen aloft in a transport in order to make them more air-minded. Ray finally met Lindy, his personal hero, who invited him to fly with him in the cockpit, which he did. Ray had carried his hand-held Eyemo camera for shots, for Lindbergh would always be a picture and a story that would never be fully told. Ray's flight was the first Lindy had experienced with

a cameraman in the cockpit. Ray was ecstatic.

Swede recounted old stories of Charles Lindbergh, pictured here with camera buddy Willard Vender Veer.

The travelers went on to Sacramento, the beautiful capital of California, then to San Francisco, where they received privileges and help equal to everything Ray had experienced in his travels around the world. He would never forget the delightful Officer O'Rourke, of the Highway Patrol, who rode a motorcycle and escorted them.

"O'Rourke!" he said to him, laughing. "You pronounce the name like a fart in a bathtub."

After the first day's shooting in the City by the Bay, O'Rourke asked, "Would yez like a beer?"

"Would we?"

"Follow me," he yelled, and away they drove to the taproom at the Lucky Lager Brewery.

During their work on the expansive Golden Gate Park, they were joined by two little old San Francisco ladies, who tagged along as Ray and his entourage went about their chores. When they had finished the day's efforts, the ladies asked if they could accompany them on the following day's filming.

"Certainly," Swede replied, amused, "if you bring the martinis." They all laughed, but that was to be one on Ray, for sure enough they had martinis almost all day from two huge thermos jugs. There was ice, cold glasses, and all, packed neatly in two baskets carried by the ladies.

The film was processed by Dunning and shown to the powers that be in Sacramento, to another standing applause; then on the screens to the California populace. The vote was passed unanimously in favor of highways. Swede and the film received high recommendations from the state officials.

It was a job well done, and they headed back to Hollywood where Ray would make his first visit to Jerry Fairbanks at the familiar old Paramount Studios. On the trip back, Jerry, Ray's wife, told him that it had been one of the most thrilling times of her life and that she had had great fun accompanying him. It was to remain one or the happiest times of her young life.

Photo of Swede and Jerry filming "California Highways." Also shown are Ray's soundman and his wife, as well as some California Highway Patrolmen.

Unusual Occupations and Popular Science

Jerry Fairbanks and his partner, Bob Carlisle, had toured the country for their two Paramount Picture reels in a big two-and-a-half-ton truck. Now the sudden requirements at the studio demanded all their attention. They offered Swede a chance to roll around the country in his fast little camera car, with one stipulation: Ray would have to supply his own camera equipment and lights. Again, he turned to his good friend Hartley Harrison. Hartley, with his brother, Ted, bought a Mitchell bi-pack color camera, lights, cables, bulbs, and everything a one-man movie studio could possibly need.

Not only did Hartley supply Swede with the camera setup, but also his special world-famous Harrison filters; the diffusions, neutrals, fogs, the entire line, including Hartley's new color temperature exposure meter he had invented. This really began the use of color meters, as long as they agreed with the cameraman's visual judgment.

At Paramount, the camera car was embellished with color signs indicating Paramount Pictures Camera Car Number Two. Swede was provided with all kinds of charge cards and the typewriter he would use to the end. All working procedures and contacts were explained. Jerry and Bob supplied clippings from magazines, newspapers, and correspondence on subjects with a science lead or occupational interest of some novelty. Swede was to proceed to the location, introduce himself, scout the story for possibilities, write a script, and issue a shooting schedule. He'd airmail it in, then receive a wire back to go ahead, often with added suggestions. He would shoot according to his copy, and airmail back each reel. He was also given a card.

"What is this?" he inquired.

"Oh, there's a guy down in Dallas, Texas who keeps a file on everything interesting. We have a deal with him. If he has any occupation or science leads we can use, we pay him. Look him up when you get there."

Ray loaded everything neatly into the little Spanky, as his kids called the truck, and he was ready to hit the road again. He needed the job badly, for now he had three children to support. His second son, Eric, had been born at Hollywood Hospital in March 1935. Gone for a time were his dreams of becoming a Hollywood cinematographer. Gone by necessity, for this could be a steady job, and such were rare in Hollywood.

Thus began four years of covering all the then forty-eight states. It was to become an education and an adventure. When he needed help, he hired what he could wherever he happened to be, but for the greater part of his wanderings he drove alone and fast. He carried the best auto club maps as well as an alarm clock, because when he became sleepy, he'd pull off the road, set the alarm, and have a catnap. The little van became Ray's rolling home, office, camera car, and friend.

His first assignment was to film a family on the Texas border that raised armadillos and made baskets, lamps, and novelties from the little pigs' armor. The next job was deeper in the heart of Texas. It involved a lady who made all kinds of dresses, hats, blankets, and gadgets out of Bull Durham tobacco sacks, which were tiny, varicolored and novel. Then there was the old man who cut up hubcaps and made colorful fishing lures and spinners out of them.

On to Dallas to look up the old man with the filing cabinets, who turned out to be a very sharp young man with a charming wife, and both grand hosts for the galloping rover. Harry McMahan was a writer, news-paperman, handicapper, author, speaker, and an expert on anything that held his interest. His wife Judy was equally talented and an interesting person. They made Ray wonderful dinners preceded by pink mint juleps and insisted that he stay at their home while in Dallas. Ray covered as many stories as possible from their files.

Swede on the road in Dallas, Texas.

Of all the many Texas stories Ray made, none was more difficult to set and make as the one feature Fairbanks had craved for a very long time. It was a modern Texas Ranger story with a science lead, which found Swede in the Texas capital of Austin, where the headquarters of the modern Texas Rangers was located along with the Texas Highway Patrol. If Ray expected Texas hospitality there, he soon found out his mis-take. He was unable to get his foot in the door to see Colonel Carmichael, who was in charge. Fairbanks had not been successful with his visit either, so Ray decided to begin a vigil. He sat outside the

Colonel's office every day for days on end. "Good morning, Colonel" and "Good evening, Colonel."

But there was no response until one eventful morning when Colonel Carmichael invited Swede into his office. "I like your damned tenacity," he blurted. "But just because Paramount wants to make a movie doesn't mean we want to!"

"I understand that, Colonel. I'm just trying to do my job."

"Tell me just what it is you have in mind."

"Colonel, I don't really know. You will have to tell me. All I can do is explain what kind of movie we want. Under your command, we want to show the American public how the Texas Rangers of today use modern science to help in their work." Ray held his breath as the Colonel pondered the idea.

"You mean to tell me you want to do this all by yourself?" the Colonel queried.

"Well, sir, I've been doing things like this all alone, but I feel that this one is too important and I may need your help."

"Oh, there's no problem with that. If I decide to go ahead," he volunteered as Ray's hopes rose, "who is going to write the story of the Texas Rangers?" The Colonel was warming up to the idea.

"Only you or someone who really knows all about modern Ranger operations can do it." Ray's glib tongue was at its best.

"Mmm. Let me see. Captain Aldrich is your man." The bait had been taken. Aldrich soon joined them, and Ray was introduced to the storybook Texan who could recite yarns of true stories of the Texas Rangers endlessly.

"You two gentlemen get together and let me know what you come up with," Carmichael ordered.

Aldrich invited Ray to his home which turned out to be a veritable museum of Texas lore, and there he listened to the Rangers' history with utter fascination, beginning with the first Rangers up to modern day.

Days of listening passed before a script was begun. Swede's enthusiasm grew as he hung onto every fantastic tale the Captain related. This was too good a film for just ten minutes, so he wired Fairbanks for permission to make a feature half-hour documentary and was given the go-ahead. This would surely get the Colonel's approval.

Carmichael read the script with a smile on his face, then turned to the cameraman. "Select all the men you need and shoot all the headquarters stuff first; the lab and ballistics, and ending with the fingerprint department, which is second only to the Federal Bureau of Investigation's."

This gave Ray the opportunity to meet more of the personnel, including Deputy Commander, Colonel Garrison. During the filming, Swede was invited to Colonel Garrison's wedding and reception, and he felt well accepted but careful of his Texas manners. It seemed that once one was accepted in Texas, nothing was beyond reach.

"What's holding up the film?" Fairbanks asked in a wire. Ray fired back the coverage of headquarters, and explained the script. "Go for it!" came the response.

The Colonel called them into his office. "Guess I'll go along with you boys. I can't see anyone else doing the job with our Rangers." Ray couldn't have asked for more.

They headed for Captain Bill McMurray's ranch in Hebronville and stopped for breakfast in the little town of Alice. It had been a long trip, and they were starved. What a bunch of lawmen, Ray thought. Mean, weather-beaten, strong, forceful men, given to only a few words. But they had a sense of humor. A deadly sense, and were not to be kidded around with, as Swede found out.

While they were eating a steak, eggs, and potatoes Texas breakfast, the town constable came rambling in. When he saw all the badges and guns, he asked every one of the younger Rangers to show him their commission cards, and each obliged.

Ray was decked out in a black cowboy hat, Levis, shiny black boots with silver spurs, silver belt buckle, but no gun or badge; a real Hollywood cowboy. Bill Oldham sat at the far end of the counter. Swede had been introduced and had shaken hands with him earlier. His hand still hurt. He didn't know if Oldham was throwing a steer or just being Texas friendly. "Now that's a handshake!" he had commented.

The constable finally asked Oldham for his card. Bill turned slowly, looked him up and down, and still chewing a hunk of steak, pulled a sweaty, worn card from his saddle-scrambled wallet. The constable nodded. Then as quick as lightning, Oldham rammed a stiff finger in the constable's gut and drawled, "Where's yours?" The poor constable didn't have it on him. Bill grabbed his arm, dragged him over to his own jail, and locked him up. He returned and gave the key to the gent behind the counter. "Here, let him out after we've finished eating in peace." Thus Ray had his first experience with a Ranger, the most feared lawman that ever lived.

They met other Rangers in Hebronville. *Author's note: Today, Rangers travel in pairs, but in those days the Rangers moved about alone, each dragging his mount in a single-horse trailer.* Ray, Captain McMurray, and the caravan set out for the McMurray Ranch, located way out on the range, midst a few scattered trees, a water tower, and a corral.

The group settled into the bunkhouse, and later ate around a campfire, while the Colonel explained in more detail just what the hell all this fuss was about.

Before long, Swede became known as Ol' Hollywood to the gang, and the fun started. The Colonel suggested that Ray throw his hat in the air, which he did. It came down riddled with bullet holes from everyone's guns. Then Joe Bridge came sauntering over. "Hey, Hollywood. Here's a gun given to me by a Mexican general. Even you can handle it. Draw a bead on those cans over yonder." Swede did, and a steady bam, bam,

Only picture I have of Swede "Ol Hollywood" with a Texas Ranger. The only other one of Swede on horse in full Ranger git-up was lost by the Smithsonian Institute in Washington. Circa 1936-37.

bam followed, while the gun rose higher and higher up and over his head. It was scary as hell, for it was an automatic which acted like a machine gun with powerful recoil, to Ray's surprise and the entertainment of all.

They traveled across the rugged terrain until they came to a perfect setting, and made ready to do the first pictures. By then, it was lunch time. They had brought a couple of Mexican cooks and a chuck wagon with them. One Ranger rode out to the grazing cattle, cut out a calf, killed it, and they cooked it on the spot, devouring it with beans and hot coffee. Ray was so hungry he ate like a Ranger. Later they staged a cattle rustling sequence, with Rangers playing bad and good guys. Ray filmed the back end of a trailer with cattle being shoved in, as two Rangers came galloping on the scene, firing their rifles at the rustlers. Earlier, the Colonel had suggested blanks for the guns. "No sir, Colonel. If Ol' Hollywood don't trust our shootin', ain't a goin' to dirty up our guns with no blanks!" The bullets hit the sand at Ray's feet and around the camera as he worked. His hand was not too steady.

From Hebronville, they drove south to the Mexican border town of Rio Grande and stopped at a tiny cantina for a couple of *cervesas* (Mexican beer). Then on to new locations which would show Border

Rangers at work. Ray had heard stories about them that had made his hair stand on end.

One ranger, Alf Allee, had captured a bandit and put him in the seat beside him as he drove the culprit to jail. The outlaw grabbed at Alf's gun, and with one hand on the wheel, Alf killed him dead on the spot.

While the journey progressed along the border, the Rangers kept up their Ol' Hollywood gags on Ray. After he had been subjected to every joke they could think of and his lessons on shooting and "iron handlin'," one Ranger suggested, "Say, Colonel, everyone's a Ranger in this picture, 'cept Ol' Hollywood."

"Yeah," another added, "and he's gittin' ta be a pretty fair shot, too, Colonel."

It must have been planned ahead, because the Colonel issued a badge to the Swede. It gleamed in his hand, number twenty-nine, Department of Safety, Texas Ranger, State of Texas. Ray stood astounded as the Colonel gave him a commission card with Ray's name on it and two authentic Ranger six-shooters, which made him an official Texas Ranger. Along with this came an assignment to fire two rounds of ammunition in every state in the union to let them know a Texas Ranger was there. Texas was a strange and fascinating place.

They drove on, cutting wire and neatly repairing it after passing through, across ranges and streams where the camera car often bogged down. The good Rangers would lasso the vehicle like an old cow stuck in the mud and pull it out.

As they approached another little town on the Mexican border, the group decided to see if Ol' Hollywood could live up to the title of Texas Ranger.

It was early in the evening when they camped around a fire. Lights glowed through the windows of an old shack, while soft Mexican music drifted through the air. Again, Ray was told that he must prove himself before they would accept him as a true Texas Ranger. He swallowed hard, thinking, what now?

"That's a cantina over thar with plenty of Mexicans from across the border visiting amigos."

It was well known in those parts that while one Ranger would throw the fear of God into a border town, two could create havoc. And such a large group as this caravan had would scare the holy hell out of the small pueblo as if war had been declared. The Mexicans feared and hated the Rangers along the border and would just as soon stick a knife in one if they dared. Everyone had disappeared; Mexicans and Texans alike.

"Hollywood, all you have to do is go into that cantina and order a *cerveza*. Drink it and walk out."

Easy? Ha! Swede knew he was really being tested, and a knot rose in his stomach. But how else could he get the film in the can if he didn't gain their respect? So off he hobbled, wearing those damned cowboy boots, corns aching, as he doffed his bullet-riddled hat, smelling like a pig, two guns hanging heavily from his hips.

He went to the swinging doors of the cantina not knowing if he would come out alive. Slowly, he advanced toward the bar as a hush settled over the drunken bunch. He heard a hissing, "Reenger," and the skin crawled up the back of his neck as he expected a knife to be thrown any second.

"*Uno cerveza*," Ray ordered in a gruff voice. When he was served, he gulped it down, then turned slowly and headed for the exit. Just outside

HOMER GARRISON, JR.
Director
JOE S. FLETCHER
Assistant Director

TEXAS DEPARTMENT OF PUBLIC SAFETY
5805 N. LAMAR BLVD.
BOX 4087, NORTH AUSTIN STATION
AUSTIN

Commission
C. T. McLAUGHLIN
Chairman
TOM HICKMAN
W. E. DYCHE, JR.
Commissioners

January 20, 1960

Mr. Ray Fernstrom
Camera Department
Warner Brothers Pictures, Inc.
West Coast Studios
Burbank, California

Dear Ray:

This will acknowledge receipt of your good letter of January 15 in reference to your previous service as a member of the Texas Rangers. I can well understand why some of your compadres do not believe that a Hollywood cameraman would ever qualify for this rugged duty. You will recall that at the time you were here filming a picture of the Rangers, Colonel Carmichael was the Director and I was his Assistant. I do recall that he gave you a Ranger badge, a Ranger gun and told you that during the filming of the picture, you would be a Texas Ranger. There was no record ever made of this commissioning. I do remember, however, that on your trips out of Austin, you were traveling with the Rangers garbed in Ranger regalia with a Ranger star on your breast and a Ranger gun on your hip.

It is always good to hear from you and I hope that if you are ever over this way, you will drop by.

With best wishes, I am

Sincerely yours,

Homer Garrison, Jr.
Director

HGJr:dne

Letter from Colonel Homer Garrison acknowledging Swede as an honorary member of the Texas Rangers.

111

the swinging doors stood four of the meanest looking Rangers Ray had ever seen, watching his every move. They looked like saints.

The final scenes found them in El Paso, where Ray met the true Lone Ranger who covered the entire Big Bend country by plane. At that time, the coast guard supplied the Rangers with aircraft, but that wouldn't do for his film. He rented one and had the sides painted with the Ranger badge.

The aerial sequence opened with Big Bill Thompson loading his gear into the plane, then showed the taxi and takeoff. Flight shots were made by Swede from a second camera plane, which showed Thompson directing the ground Rangers and talking to headquarters while he searched for signs of rustlers. *Science and the Texas Rangers* was in the can.

The job was finished and cameraman and crew headed for home. It had been quite an experience. Ray carefully packed his badge, guns, and tons of memories into his suitcase, and after fond farewells to the tough bunch he was off to his next adventure and a mysterious beauty.

CHAPTER FIVE
Memories of Monetta

For every person, there is a once in a lifetime experience; for Raymond G. I. Fernstrom there were many.

The cameraman leaned heavily on his thoughts as he traveled the lonely, dark Texas highway. It had begun with the ringing of the telephone. He and Taylor "Cowboy" Byars, a local cameraman, were sharing a room. Ray grabbed the phone. "Hello."

"Hello, is Taylor Byars there?" the voice said sweetly "He sure is, honey; come on up. We're in room 302."

Ray opened the door and gazed at the lovely olive-skinned young beauty and asked flippantly, "Where's your mother?"

Before she could answer, Byars shouted from the back of the room, "Hey, come on in, and welcome." He pulled up a chair and seated the girl. "This here little sweetheart is an old friend of mine," he explained to Ray. "Her name is Monetta."

Ray's trained eye examined the marvelous lines of the young face. There was exquisite beauty in the cheekbones suggesting Indian heritage, and a mouth that would compare to Cleopatra's. "How old are you, Monetta?" he asked.

"I'm almost fifteen."

Ray studied her closely. God! What a face, he thought. "Would you like to go to Hollywood and be in pictures?"

"I've already been to Hollywood. Twice. Once on the *Gateway to Hollywood* radio show, where I came in second, and a screen test. After the viewing, they sent me home and told me to grow up."

"How old would you like to look?" Ray inquired.

"I wish I could look about eighteen."

"Do you want to be in movies, Monetta?"

"Oh yes, more than anything in the world. I dream of it every moment."

"Okay." Ray turned to Taylor. "We'll do an occupation theme with her, using all my techniques and Harrison's lenses. I'll make her look grown-up. Let's help the beautiful lady become a star." They set up a story on finger painting, a class Monetta was attending. Ray posed her with the correct lighting, slanting his camera to show a mature image free of baby fat. It worked. Her face recorded on film like a Madonna.

Swede discovering Monetta in Dallas, Texas, during the filming for Paramount's Unusual Occupations.

"Monetta," Swede asked gently, treating her like the child she was, "what is your last name?"

"My name is Monetta Darnell."

Swede ran his fingers through his hair, thinking. He gave the name a lot of thought. Darnell sounded good, but Monetta? That would never do in Hollywood. He scoured his mind. Mona? Monique? Laura? They all stunk. Let's see, how about a Swedish name? Jenny Lind? Nope. Linda? "How does Linda sound?"

"Yes, that sounds nice." And from that moment on, she became Linda Darnell.

Publicity photo of Monetta, now Linda Darnell in her first motion picture "Hotel for Women." These pictures were sold world wide in 5 & 10 cent stores to sell picture frames during the heydays of Hollywood. Note Linda is misspelled.

Author's note: Ivan Kahn, a Twentieth Century Fox talent scout first spotted and screen-tested Monetta Darnell from the Gateway to Hollywood radio program. When Darryl Zanuck and his wife saw Ray's Linda Darnell occupation short, Zanuck had a print sent from Paramount to Twentieth Century Fox and inquired, "Who's that girl?"

Kahn took a look, then exclaimed, "Why, that's the little girl from Dallas we sent home to grow up."

"Who sent her home? She looks grown up enough to me!"

"Why, you did, Mr. Zanuck."

"Well, get her out here and sign her up," Zanuck ordered. And Linda went on to stardom. She would eventually marry a cinematographer, Perverell Marley, A.S.C.

Ray had several other stories to make before he left Dallas, and each day Linda helped him with lights and cables, and made herself useful. She wanted to learn everything she could about movie making.

Linda lived an easy life, as evidenced by the fact that one day when Ray went to visit, her pet rooster wandered past them through the living room. Her father greeted Ray with Texas hospitality and often apologized for his absence when he had to go on his daily mail route, which encompassed miles.

Swede and Linda remained close friends for life and saw each other on the movie lots and at numerous Hollywood bashes. Linda never let success go to her head and remained the sweet Monetta that Ray had first met. Now and again, Ray pondered the question, What if I hadn't helped her? Would she have married and stayed with her family in Texas? No! She wanted stardom more than anything.

Author's note: Linda Darnell met a tragic death at an early age. Headlines blared the awful news: "Famous Actress Burned to Death in Fire." She had tried to rescue the children of a friend she was visiting. This deeply affected Ray, so much so that he was never quite the same person. The Cloud had struck very close to Swede. His beautiful Monetta was gone.

Here's How and How Not

Time flew. Ray went to Mississippi to film *Science and the Penitentiary.* The science subjects went on endlessly. He shot boxing scenes, cotton harvests, timber workers and road builders. Anything to earn a buck. He felt like the proverbial rolling stone. The more he'd seen, the more he'd done, the less he had. All he really seemed to gather for his work were memories and miles and miles of roads and color film.

One day Jerry Fairbanks called and wanted Swede to shoot several subjects on the East Coast. Ray drove almost nonstop to New York and was surprised to find his wife and children waiting for him in the same little apartment he and Jerry had shared during his reel days. He was happy to see them but felt a choke of dependence hanging on his neck.

Ray's favorite photograph of his wife Jerry. She's shown with daughter Barbara, my sister, and yours truly Russ.

Ray stayed in the apartment and was startled to realize that he hardly knew his wife any longer, let alone his children. His reflections of past, present, and future life he considered wonderful. He had loved his career and work from the first day. He felt himself born lucky, blessed with hands that were free, a light heart, sharp eyes, and with a physical vigor that knew no disease, no pain, no bothersome conscience; just free, wild, and eager. He had escaped the traps, missed the potholes, leaped high, and lived big happy memories, forgetting the bad, remembering the good. Yes, he thought, I am really living. And he was determined to keep it that way. No shackles on him!

Ray had hardly settled into the apartment when he was given two assignments. One, Macy's great Thanksgiving Day Parade up Broadway, the another an occupational tale, *Doodling and Doodle College*. It involved two sophisticated ladies who analyzed celebrities' doodles on paper. This he shot at the Sherry Netherlands Beauty Parlor and at a table in the El Morocco. Then they went up to Lanny Ross' apartment, higher to Jessica Dragonette's penthouse, and on to old Ben Bernie's suite. The finale of the doodle story were the analysts themselves, who explained the meaning of doodles. Then Fairbanks edited it in Hollywood. Ray knew one thing, though. Fairbanks didn't have as much fun as he did on that little subject of *Unusual Occupations*. Oh my; did those two ladies analyze his doodle!

Swede received a wire from Hollywood to make an end of story on Edgar Bergen and Charley McCarthy's new friend, Mortimer Snerd. A lady in New York had just completed Mortimer's head, and Ray was to film the reenactment of her designing and making him, or it, which was done in a routine manner.

Another wire arrived from Fairbanks in Hollywood: "Head to New London, Connecticut. US Coast Guard academy training base at Groton, CN. Assignment waits."

So off Ray went after hiring an assistant from his old locale in New York. He was an Englishman and was trained. Good, Ray thought, I don't have to train the bastard. Later he found out his new assistant had a flaw in his character. He was superstitious and could be scared. This could be really bad for him with a fearless rascal the likes of Swede.

———————◆◆◆———————

The following is taken directly from Ray's memoirs, as only he could tell it:

Have you ever been below the sea? That, my dear friends, is the next space age to truly become discovered. It may not be as far to the bottom of all the vast seas as in space exploration, but of it we know even less.

Science and the underwater world of our navy, I guess, is the best way to tell the film story I made. Training way down deep. Compression, decompression chamber, but my story is of me and that gol-ding-dang submarine . . .

We had done a good job shooting ashore. Now the officers and men in training were to handle a submarine for the first time. I had breakfast with the skipper.

Cook was his name, I believe; Lieutenant Commander Cook. We understood each other pretty well from the opening guns. He was a submariner; I was pictures. Subs first. That was okay with me. He told me about the history of the submarine we would sail on and asked me if I was superstitious. Me? Hell no I'm too stupid to be chicken. Fear? No. I'll do anything for pictures. That's how infectious the photo bug is. Especially the movie kind. And I had gone from acute to chronically afflicted with it. What the hell. Death is just another picture to a picture nut . . .

So off we slid out of Groton. Crew of officers, officer trainees, crew trainees and us picture guys. I remember thinking we had enough crew to sink a battleship. She slid smoothly to the sea and I lit up all my photo floods from their batteries. Shooting first, every training dive, gauges, men at stations, valves being operated, the whole topside, submerge, crash dive, bottom leveling, the works. Then suddenly I found I was short one New York assistant.

So I took a coffee break. I found the bastard ensconced on a bunk—the skipper's at that, sipping tea.

"Having a good cruise, old bean? Are you comfortable?" I sarcastically inquired in a newsreel voice that cut like a stiletto.

"Oh yes, quite, old chap," he yawned.

"Well, that's great," I added in a cold, quiet manner, sweat pouring from work he should have helped with. "Are you superstitious?" I asked with a faint smile crossing my lips.

He cocked an intense, "Why?"

"Oh, nothing, but this training dive is our thirteenth and the crewmen are very edgy."

"Wow, I didn't know that," as he sat bolt upright. So I knew I had my fish on the hook. "By the way, do you know the history of this sub and what it used to be called?"

"No, what?" he asked, rather getting more nervous, which this old bastard encouraged.

"Why pal, this is the old S-51 that sank off Provincetown years ago and drowned a bunch of guys."

"No kidding. Let me out of here!" he yelled in panic.

"Aw, you can't go anywhere. We are down two hundred feet in the Atlantic."

"What are we going to do?" Now he was a little more than roused.

"Why," I went on, "we're going to make movies."

"Not me, I'm going to stay right here in this bunk!"

"Oh, by the way, that's the bunk the ex-skipper's body was found on when the S-51 was pulled out of the deep." That did it. He shot out of that bunk like a rocket.

I was told our dives could now be executed. All training was over. All exercise fish (torpedoes) had been fired and it was our turn for pictures.

So on the surface we set up my camera above the conning tower deck, so I could stand on the rail and shoot. The camera was chained down tight with turn buckles and I was ready. First a wide angle lens.

My shots of the sub under me, diving to a point where it looked like the camera was about to go under. The skipper, Cook, had it figured to an inch. Boy, was he good. So the hatch was battened down and we began to move faster. I was alone on top and outside the sub; my superstitious assistant below deck.

Now it was full speed ahead and I was ready for a crash dive. I kicked the hatch rail hard. They got the sound signal to dive and I started the camera. Beautiful shot. Good dive. Up came the sub, hatch opened, Cook's voice, "How's at?"

"Not fast enough, Captain. Not fast enough!"

So the double-crosser that I am, switched to a 40 mm lens. This time it was even better; faster and a little deeper. But still not deep or effective enough for me. Again the Commander's voice, "Okay, can we go in now?"

"Gee, Commander, please try just one more; deeper and more of a serious crash dive!"

Slam-bang went the hatch. He was getting angry, which always helps pictures. So I put on a two-inch lens. Now I was giving my cutter, Bob, back at the lab really something to play with in speed cutting action. It was great. But here came the skippers voice again, "We've had enough of this. Now I want to go in. That was a perfect dive!"

"Yes sir, it was," I pleaded, "but not deep enough. Please try a little deeper and I'll get the pictures I want."

I put on my three-inch lens, which made a tighter picture around the diving fins and the first third of the sub.

He blasted the water from his tanks like an angry whale. She dove, and I mean dove. As straight down as the sub could handle.

"Drown the son-of-a-bitch. Drown him. Goddamn it!"

And, boy, were those some pictures! All I saw was tail fins and Atlantic. Down she went as my camera ground away. Beautiful, great shots. Great thrilling shots, I grinned. "Jesus H. Christ, stop diving!"

Up came the water over the conning tower. Up to and engulfing my lens. And still she went down. I had a safety cable around me and a life jacket to keep me from tangling with the props if we happened to go too deep. But this really had me worried. That damned sub inched lower and lower until my balls were swimming and then my wallet. But then, thank God, up the fucking fish came and I succeeded in smiling at the grinning, red-faced Skipper as he came aloft.

"Greatest shots I've seen in years!" I said, dripping sea water, blood and cold sweat.

Then I threw a party in New London for Cookie and his bunch of dolphins. All I needed now before heading back to New York was a few scenes of subs leaving and returning. Commander Cook wished me fond adieu with a hangover. We were friends again. So off to the New York office with the greatest shots of a submarine I've ever seen. As I look back, many great films have been made since of crash dives, but that was the first and in this cameraman's book, the very best.

<hr>

Finally, Ray decided to take a little time off to be with Jerry and the kids, to whom he had become a myth or legend. He had heard them call him "the Phantom." Shortly after this, their fourth child checked in—a daughter, Selma Rae.

His batteries recharged, Ray was on the road again headed west through Dallas and a stop-off at the McMahans in their new and bigger home. While there, Mac planted a seed that Ray couldn't shake from his head. The idea grew. Mac had said, "Ray, why don't we go into making our own short films?"

"Not me," Ray replied quickly, remembering John Boyle's roadshow fiasco. "Who's going to release them?"

"Oh, we'll get them released," Mac retorted confidently.

"Not a chance, Mac. I've learned that lesson before, although there's no one I would rather go into business with than you."

They had left the idea hanging. But in the back of Ray's mind, he thought, Mac and Judy must be loaded with loot. If he ever decided to make his own pictures, he'd know where to get the money.

Back in New York a short time later, Ray was having cocktails with Lou Diamond, his old friend from the newsreel days. Lou, the money man, was now head of production and distribution for Paramount Pictures short-subject films. "Swede," he said, looking into his martini and turning the glass thoughtfully, "you're the best in the business. Why don't you make your own short films?"

"What the hell would I do with them, Lou?"

"Well, you just told me that you sometimes travel a thousand miles between leads on the two Fairbanks series. Why not make a series, and stay away from Fairbanks' and Grantland Rice's sports light techniques? Do something longer and different."

"Again, Lou, who would release them?"

"Ray, I am offering you a chance. I'll release them. I can use another color series, more diversified in character and subject matter than those we already have. Knowing you, your experience and ability, I'm sure you can do really good ones," he added seriously.

Ray studied him, thinking of what Mac had said. Here was a chance to make his own, and with a Paramount release guarantee. They couldn't miss. "What the hell can I call such a series?"

"Swede, what I taught you in the old days never changes. It's that certain element in entertainment and film making that always sells; novelty, surprise, and the unexpected. Call it anything you want. Just—here' s how to do it!"

"*Here's How*! Lou, that's it, a shotgun title."

"*Here's How*. You're right, I like it. Now go to the phone and call Fairbanks. Tell him you quit."

Fairbanks roared, "What? Again?" Swede had quit and been fired several times before, but they had always resumed their relationship.

"Yes, Jerry. I am; going to take a shot at making my own."

"Well, paint over all those Paramount signs on your truck." 121

"Okay, Jerry, and thanks for everything. See you later." Ray returned to the table.

"What did he say?" asked Lou, curious.

"Good luck, and paint out the Paramount signs."

"We'll do it with water colors until you get your own *Here's How* sign on it," and they shook hands. A handshake from Lou was as good as any contract.

Swede took a fast trip to Dallas and neglected to paint over the Paramount signs, as he figured he would need the clout to get Mac to put up the money. Elated, he explained his good fortune to Mac and Judy. "Thank God you've got the money to make our first reel, Mac!" Ray went on.

"Who me?" Ray's heart went into his sneakers. "No, Ray, all our money went into this house."

"Holy shit!" What a situation he was in now; no money, no job.

"But don't worry, Ray, we know a lot of people here. We can get it from one of them. Yes, come to think of it, there's a young man, Marvin Singleton, who might be interested."

"Mac, would you talk to him and explain our plan?" Swede's hopes brightened a bit, but he couldn't forget that he had quit a job he loved, and a steady one at that. They made an appointment with Mr. Singleton for the next day, then washed the truck, and prepared to give the big pitch, with camera all set up on the roof of the vehicle, which would be parked outside Singleton's office, so he could easily read the Paramount logos, and know that the cameraman had the equipment and experience for the project. They went up to his second floor office.

Mac and Ray outlined that initially there would be two one-reel demonstration pictures of *Here's How*, with four or five subjects on each reel, consisting of ten or twelve minutes each. A new and different voice would narrate each diversified subject. Locations would be varied and would encompass the whole country.

Singleton was enthralled but asked, "Just how much of a gamble is this?"

Ray swallowed hard. "One hundred percent my ability, my equipment, my time and travel, Mac's files, writing, and musical knowledge, and your money!"

"Mr. Bucks" looked out the window at Ray's camera truck gleaming in the Texas sun, turned to them, and asked pleasantly, "To whom do I make out the check?" The check? They didn't want any check. They just wanted him to pay the bills as they came in. Sweet relief, a rich backer! "How much is all this going to cost?" Singleton pursued.

Mac thought they could make two sample reels for five thousand each, and of such high quality they would please Paramount. They wound up the meeting by going to Mac's lawyer where the papers were drawn up involving a three-way deal and forming United States Motion

Pictures. Mac was to report bills and Marvin would send Mac checks, while Ray went on the road to shoot and ship the film.

The only known picture of Swede and his partner Mac McMahan on their ill-fated series "Here's How." Swede is on the left and Mac is on the right. The man in the center is unidentified.

Much work followed in which Mac, Judy, and Ray selected fifteen subjects from Mac's files that were as diversified as possible and as unexpected as snow in July. Surprise and novelty were their watchwords. It made good sense for them to find a Dallas location for the warm-up, and they located a goodie in the training school for Braniff Airlines at Love Field, with pretty airline hostesses.

While they waited for their first shipment of film, Mac and Ray went out to write the story and cast the picture. They easily completed arrangements, as Braniff was extremely interested in the publicity and helped in every way. Cowboy Byars assisted in casting by supplying the most beautiful girls around, and Dallas had them!

The first scene opened with a close-up of a lovely teacher. Then the classroom with girls taking aptitude tests. This gave Swede a chance to introduce each girl through each step of the training, showing uniforms and finally air pictures, which were long shots with another Braniff ship. The finish included a sunset flight over puffy white clouds, trimmed in red and gold.

Ray's mind drifted back to all the times he had flown with a camera from 1925, over the Polar ice cap with Bernt Balchen to that time over Hollywood with Vance Breese and his bomber. They had been shooting 123

Storm Over the Andes, when a cylinder head flew off and they barely made it to the Metropolitan Airport (now Van Nuys). Both had escaped the crash by a thread. Two wild guys. When their legs stopped shaking, they got sloshed!

Mac and Judy left their home in Dallas in the care of her mother and flew to Hollywood with the first subject on film. They opened a little office at the Cinecolor lab and were off on their independent venture, while Ray headed East and did a rags-to-riches story on the playing marble king, Berry Pink. Not only did it turn out to be a fascinating subject, but Ray found the making of real glass marbles as interesting as the pictures he was making.

The next event was interesting and enjoyable. Swede was to put on film the making of our flag, *The Betsy Ross Story.* He began at Fort McHenry, where our *National Anthem* was written, then traveled to Philadelphia and was given permission to shoot in the room in the Ross home, with an authentically dressed Miss Hospitality playing the part of Betsy Ross while sitting in the original rocking chair. It was inspiring, and Betsy, rather Miss Hospitality, was very hospitable to the cameraman later that evening. I just love this country to death, Ray thought!

It was on to West Point for more filming and the final shots of the Betsy Ross flag story. A West Point dress parade had to be promoted with their public relations officer. He was a fine gentleman major. Explaining to him the flag story and that he was to shoot it in color, Ray was asked to wait while the Major obtained the needed permission from the Commandant. God watches, Ray thought. And the permission was granted.

———————

Only Ray can explain in his own words the next event. So from his memoirs, he tells of his faith:

"But, you said you want sunshine. It never shines on a dress parade!"

"Major, my faith not only moves mountains, it moves clouds away from the sky, letting us work under the evening sun. Have no fear. That's as The Man wrote. The magic of believing, asking, praying and knowing that it is already so. Even though you doubters don't see it. It's there, if you believe. But, only with unquestioning faith, my friend."

To philosophize a little further just a word or two, if I may, so you'll know me a little better. I do not believe we should say *luck*. I come out with the word *faith*. God watches and I thank Him for my blessings before I receive them. I know for certain within the deepest reaches of myself that He answers me in the most positive manner. And all that has, is, or will happen in my life is His will just for me. So I'm happy at the tests, challenges, and the joys of all that I do.

The parade started. Clouds of black hid the sun. The cadets crossed from the other side of the parade grounds and turned to cross the north side. "Still think you'll have sun for your color pictures?" said the Major, coming over to where I stood with my camera.

"Positively. I only want to shoot when the cadets come company front, from the flag. There," pointing. The Major shook his head in doubt. The ranks turned. When I had the entire group, I snapped my camera on after setting the exposure for full sun. And out it came. Just as bright as I had calculated. I shot the entire parade passing with a variety of lenses. I asked the Major to do it one more time, only this time with the color guard only. Around they came, precision marching in full sunlight. With a special close-up lens I shot the entire group as they passed before us. What a magnificent color display, I thought. I shut the camera off and the sun disappeared.

I smiled with grateful thoughts toward Heaven and at the Major, who was standing there shaking his head. "I'll never forget you and your faith, my friend. Simply unbelievable!" End of flag story.

※

Over the bridge to New Jersey and through the woods nestled a tavern I knew well. There was a little hotel down the road where I had stayed many times before. Naturally I wasn't going to my room until I had a nightcap. So, to the tavern past the woods. I parked Spanky, my camera car, and looked forward to another visit with one of my favorite cross-country owner/bartenders.

Yes, it was late, nearly time to close up. Lucky me, as usual, the bar was still open. I always seem to get everywhere in the nick of time. After a few tidbits of conversation and bracing belts we turned as two of his regular customers entered the bar for a last one before heading home.

I sat facing them at one end of the bar, they at the other, as our friend introduced us. After a few more belts the owner said, "Hey Ray, why don't you show my friends all that stuff they gave you down in Texas. All that cowboy Ranger gear."

Boy, what a dumb, stupid thing to ask that early in the morning, me tired and boxed on booze. But it shows you how alcohol louses up your reasoning ability and reserve. So, like a jackass, out I went, put on the bullet-riddled hat, hung on the two guns and all the other Ranger legendary and true lore that returned to my boozy brain. A Ranger never draws his gun unless to shoot! A Ranger always accepts a dare! So, with these thoughts in mind, I returned.

I held up each gun at a distance for examination. Both were fully loaded with Texas reloads as only a Ranger can reload; heavy charge, softly rounded lead heads cased in the shell. As one Ranger told me, "These are the best bullets ever, Hollywood. They go in small and make a big hole going out!"

The owner's guests admired my *real* Texas Ranger badge, at a distance. For with two loaded guns, I never got very close to anyone. More Ranger training.

I sat down to finish my drink and leave when one of the gentlemen said, "How many box tops did it take for the badge?"

The other, "I'll bet those toy guns don't even have caps in them!"

All of this took a minute of pausing, looking, thinking, for they weren't strictly sober either. They were about as fogged as I was, the ass holes. In their eagerness to goad me, they had moved apart, leaving a stool space between them. This was a big mistake, for at that moment, one said loud and clear, "I dare you to fire one."

I guess it was the booze, or was it that sarcastic sneer on the bastard's face that did it? Out flew the iron as I'd been thoroughly taught—right between them into the mirror of a cigarette machine directly behind them. They instantly spread farther apart as I put four more slugs, one in each corner of the mirror, which was so satisfying. I spotted a star in the middle of the linoleum floor and plugged the last round directly in its center and put away the cannon. But our good friends were long gone by then.

All the owner said was, "You'll have to pay the damages on the machine," to which a sobered up me replied, "You bet, Joe. I'll be in tomorrow. I'll be at the hotel 'til then."

And I was. Asleep and snoring, when . . .

With a flash I woke up. Thick headed, gazing into a flashlight and two drawn Smith & Wesson magnum pistols, held by two New Jersey State Troopers.

"What's the trouble?" I asked bleary-eyed, not fully aware of myself or surroundings. "It's him all right," one trooper said after going to the dresser, where piled high were my guns, badge and wallet.

"Him who?" I inquired, getting awake and head sick real fast.

"Bank robber," the second officer answered. "We put two and two together. A bank robbery early this morning and a tavern shoot-up a short time after."

"Bank robbery? Did you see my camera truck downstairs?"

"Yes, we did. Thought it quite a wrinkle. A new one on us."

"Look, I'm a movie cameraman and also a full-fledged Texas Ranger to boot. Look at my badge and card!"

"That's right, Jim," the other officer said. "Here's a real card and badge."

"I can't figure this out," said the other one. "How come the camera truck if you're a policeman?"

"Oh, they made me a Ranger when I made a movie of them down there in Texas."

"Have you any movie credentials?"

"Sure do, if you'll hand me my wallet. You'll see my cameraman's union card, my A.S.C. card, my California drivers license, my credit cards and my Southern California Auto Club card. Will that do?"

"Get up, get dressed and come along with us."

"But why? All I did was have a little target practice and I agreed to pay for any damages."

Then the other officer said, "We'll just take these guns and things."

I immediately flew into a crabby sarcasm. "Since when did the State of New Jersey confiscate property of the State of Texas? Look at what it says on the pistol. Texas Highway Patrol."

"By God, he's right. It sure says that."

Then the other one calmed down and turned to me. "Fellow, let me tell you why we're taking you in. We know now that you are no bank robber; only a policeman on his off-time having a little target practice and fun. But, what you don't know is that those big ol' Texas bullets of yours tore through that cigarette machine, the wall and out into a brand new LaSalle coupe, blasting out the windshield and rear window, and that the bartender's wife usually sits in that car waiting for her husband to close up. So warrants have been sworn out with multiple charges against you."

Brother, I knew I was a cooked duck as I entered the Mount Holly County Jail. My camera car impounded, guns gone . . .

After being fingerprinted, booked and all that routine, I inquired if I could make a phone call.

"Of course," was the answer.

I immediately called Texas Ranger Headquarters in Austin, collect. I asked to speak to the Colonel, whom I finally succeeded in dragging out of bed. But, it wasn't Colonel Carmichael. I was informed that he had died a few days before of heart failure. I was talking to Colonel Garrison who was now the commander. All the satisfaction I got from him was, "Let me speak to the arresting officer!" And to him he merely said, "Please send me his commission card, badge, the Highway Patrol holster and Colt. The other gun is his. He can keep it!" Big deal. No help. Just off with my badge.

I asked if I could make one more phone call in hopes that I could get some action to help me out. And could I also wire Hollywood for money and any assistance they could give? Both requests were granted. They had that look on their faces of what the hell kind of worm have we got on the hook now.

I called the White House in Washington, DC, collect, to Steve Early, now Press Secretary to President Franklin D. Roosevelt. Remember, Steve was my former boss at Paramount News in Washington.

"What in hell's the matter, Swede," came his sleepy Southern drawl, "a callin' me this early hour?"

"Steve, get me the hell out of this stinking jail. Mount Holly Jail, New Jersey. I'm in deep shit. Bad trouble. I'm shooting for Paramount with camera and guns and got thrown in the pokey."

"Swede, you can't embarrass the White House. What the hell can I do?"

"Steve, you know me. I can be a real bastard and you know what I say I'll do! I will. Please get me the fuck out of this rat hole or I'll bug the shit out of you. I'll call; I'll wire you every chance they give me. I can't stand being cooped up like this. I'm a free flying Swede and you know it. Help me Steve. Help me get the hell out of here. I can't stand it. Please, Steve."

"Go back to your cell, Swede. I'll see what I can do."

"Thanks Steve, for old times' sake. God bless you. God, help me get out of this place."

A couple of days later the Attorney General of the State of New Jersey had me out of there. I was told to go across the street, plead guilty, keep my big mouth shut, pay the fine and damages. (By now Mac had wired me money and lots of bright letters to cheer me up.)

I was charged with carrying a gun without a Jersey permit ($50), damages ($125), and I was free. God that fresh air tasted good. Thank you God. Thank you Steve.

Ray took a few days' rest with his mother and father Fernstrom in Sharon while the film was shipped to Mac. Before him lay the long dash back to California where his family had returned and found a house to rent with an option to buy. He looked forward to seeing it.

The house was ideal, a good investment, and located in beautiful Pacific Palisades.

Author's note: It was in this house that our paths were to briefly cross with the blonde Hollywood star, Carole Landis. She was one of the blonde bombshells of the heydays of Hollywood, the thirties and forties.

We lived in this house with the intention of buying it. But Swede took an assignment in Canada, and decided to take the family with him. Carole moved in. Her career was at a peak when she fell hopelessly in love with actor Rex Harrison. She saw no possibility of marriage with the man and without a future with him, decided to take her own life. She left a note for her mother and loved ones saying how much she loved them all and begged their forgiveness, as this was her only way out.

She carried out the suicide on 4 July 1948, with a lethal dose of sleeping pills. Ironically, it was Rex Harrison who discovered her lifeless form crumpled on the floor of our old bathroom, in the house where we had found such joy. Another not so gentle nudge from The Cloud that frequents only Hollywood.

Mac had done his work in the lab in Hollywood like a seasoned producer. A composer of original music was hired for the musical score for the two completed reels of *Here's How.*

Mac had found that two short subjects on each reel and one larger feature made it more attractive, and he had recorded a different narrator for each subject as planned, including one with a woman's voice. They were extremely proud of the finished product as they shipped their baby off to Lou Diamond in New York and waited.

Meanwhile, they checked the costs and were surprised to find they had only spent a total of sixty-eight hundred dollars for both finished reels.

A telegram arrived: "Like your reels very much, Swede. Proposition follows by airmail. Lou Diamond"

"Let's accept," Mac remarked impulsively.

Lou's proposition arrived. He would pay four thousand dollars negative return on each reel and charge them thirty-five percent for distribution, leaving them sixty-five percent. Lou wanted at least six reels the first year. They had a profit of twelve hundred dollars offered even before the films started earning.

Mac and Ray were ready to wire Lou their acceptance when Mac's wife, Judy, said, "We should get a larger negative return, like seventy-five hundred dollars, just like Fairbanks-Carlisle did."

Ray tried to explain to her that they were not established or proven as were the others, and had just gotten their foot in the door. First they had to crawl, then walk, before they could really run with the ball.

But she convinced Mac that he should write a letter to Lou. Mac did, and early one morning Ray received a hot phone call from Lou, collect! "Who the fuck is Mac McMahan? I tried to do you a personal favor, Swede. Take it or leave it!"

"Mac's my partner, Lou, and he doesn't understand. I'll try to get him to accept your offer, Lou, and I really appreciate it."

"Okay, you nut. Wire me at once on the decision."

When Judy and Mac arrived at the office, Ray explained in great detail everything Lou had said, and also his final attitude. But Judy insisted that Mac write another letter to Diamond, which he did. But no answer was ever to arrive. Lou Diamond had dropped dead of a massive heart attack the night before, and no record was filed regarding their agreement.

The bubble had burst. No deal. They finally had to sell the reels to Jerry Fairbanks at a loss. So near, yet so far. And so much for *Here's How* and how not.

The failure of *Here's How* had Ray scrambling around Hollywood for odd jobs. He was weary of all the traveling, and had decided to stick around home for a while. Also, he did not want to go back to Fairbanks. But he had a friend, Eddie Shuessler, who was casting director for Hughes Productions in Hollywood. When Ray told him about the *Here's How* reels after they were returned from New York, Eddie asked to show them to his boss, Howard Hughes.

The following day, Ray received a call asking him to meet with Hughes, who inquired about an air hostess training for Braniff. "Who's the tall, gorgeous brunette in the blue uniform taking the aptitude test?" he asked. "The one that is really endowed?"

"That's Rosalie Schach of Dallas," Ray told Howard.

"Can you get her on the phone, Swede, and ask her if she wants to come to Hollywood for a screen test?"

"Give me the phone."

When Ray told Rosalie about the screen test, she discussed it with her parents who knew Ray, and they gave permission only if she stayed with him and his wife. It was agreed. Hughes flew her to Hollywood on one of his planes, and Ray and Jerry met her at the airport.

Hughes hired a prominent director, I believe Howard Hawkes, and Tom Conway played opposite Rosalie in the test. Hughes didn't like the dress she was wearing, so he designed another. This time directed the test himself. He asked Rosalie to sign a contract, for she was perfect for the lead role in an up and coming blockbuster movie he was planning. But Rosalie had someone in Dallas to whom she had gotten engaged and turned Howard Hughes down flat. She had decided to return home and get married. The next girl Hughes chose for the part was Jane Russell. The movie, *The Outlaw*, was released in 1943.

Authors note: The only connection multimillionaire Howard Hughes had with Walt Disney was that his studio RKO Radio Pictures distributed 129

Rosalie Schach in Dallas, Texas.

the Disney films in the late forties and for much of the fifties, and that they both knew Ray "Swede" Fernstrom.

Swede was also the connection Hughes had with Rosalie Schach, Hughes' first choice for the part of Rio in the Outlaw movie. Ray was also the link between Hughes and Ray's old pal Russell Birdwell from the earlier newsreel days. It will be remembered that Russ Birdwell was the only man to film Lindbergh's takeoff on the historic flight and who now was a renowned publicist and Hughes' choice to promote the movie. Swede Fernstrom could very forcefully promote people he admired, and giants like Walt and Howard listened to him.

It is here that we will bring up Howard Hughes' fetish for large breasts. The moment he ogled Rosalie Schach's thirty-eight-inch endowment on the screen from Ray's Here's How Braniff Airlines short, he was hooked. After her ensuing screen test where Howard personally designed her revealing blouse and took over the direction filming her boobs from every possible angle, he wanted to sign her to a contract immediately. After Rosalie turned him down, Hughes interviewed over seven hundred applicants for the part before selecting a Rosalie Schach look-alike, also with a thirty-eight-inch bust, Jane Russell. Thereafter Miss Russell's breast's remained a fixation of his for the rest of his career in movies, especially during the shooting of The Outlaw, where he again photographed boobs from every conceivable angle. Could this be another reason why Rosalie had turned Hughes down? Later, according to Jane Russell, she said that *she was "as green as grass" and didn't realize what Howard was doing when he made her bend over so much.*

We recently discovered a pinup photograph that Swede had of Rosalie Schach's original Hughes screen test. It was taken in a Quonset hut in Africa during World War II. Swede obviously had a copy he had saved and hung on the wall for all the guys to enjoy. To the left of Rosalie's picture are two other popular pinups, Rita Hayworth, the fabulous Gilda, and ironically the other, Rosalie Schach's successor, Jane Russell.

This photo was taken by Swede in Africa during WW2. The soldier is admiring a publicity photo of Rosalie Schach, Jane Russell and Rita Hayworth that came from the Hughes Studio.

Hartley Harrison called Swede to meet with a Canadian film producer, Leon Shelly, who was about to film a series in Canada to be called *Beautiful British Columbia*, and Hartley had told Leon that Ray was his man. It would take about a year, so Ray decided to move the entire family to Vancouver.

Leon Shelley gave Ray the outline of what he had planned for *Beautiful British Columbia*, the subjects, locations etcetera. But he had been advised by Hartley Harrison to give Ray a free rein and let his imagination take over on all compositions. "Let the Swede create with his camera and you'll be amazed."

Swede had the latest in color film advancements, some of the most beautiful virgin scenery in the world and no restrictions on his ideas for capturing this magnificent beauty on film. He was Rembrandt again to create at will. Hartley had given Ray his latest lenses and filters to try out and the Master of Motion Paintings went to work.

The resulting photography Swede captured with the serene lakes reflecting giant snow capped mountains set a standard of excellence in the industry that is still emulated to this day in photographic composition.

Ray had just finished the films for Shelly, when he decided it was time to head home to California, as clouds of war were thickening and surely Canada, allied so closely with Britain, would be among the first to join.

It was in late 1939 that Swede had a torrid affair and Jerry became fully aware of his indiscretions. Up to this point, she had heard innuendos and had her suspicions, but the following brought it fully to light.

One night while Swede was having a few drinks at a popular little hangout in Manhattan Beach near El Segundo, Ray met a little hot Mexican spitfire named Lupe Velez. Thus began a tryst that would last for several months. Lupe had met her match in Ray "Swede" Fernstrom, and it took World War II to separate them.

Author's note: Lupe Velez was notorious as a man-eater; her sexual drive was beyond comprehension. She had recently been divorced from Tarzan Johnny Weismuller. She had an insatiable lust for handsome men. She was a childlike creature and one of the party-going breed that lived only for the moment. It was nothing for her to lift up her dress over her head, with nary a stitch of undergarments beneath, for everyone to see, and exclaim, "You like?"

Lupe would not pay her debts, and always had that give-a-shit attitude that proclaimed, "the world owes me a living," which seemed to infect so many stars of that time. Later, she became pregnant by another or her conquests and because of religious beliefs, refused to have an abortion. Again, one of the stars of that era opted for suicide. She killed herself on 14 December 1944, in her Rodeo Drive home, Beverly Hills, California. Swede was stunned by the news. The Cloud had once again struck very close to home.

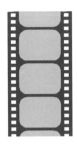

CHAPTER SIX

Swede Goes to War

Ray and his boss, Del Frazier, walked along the main street of Warner Brothers Studio. It was late 1939, and they were working on a series of color shorts about sports called *The Sports Parade*. A thought came to Del. "Hey, Swede, why don't you join our outfit? We have parties at Jack Warner's, Darryl Zanuck's, and all over town."

"Parties?" His meat. He asked how to go about joining. What was this outfit?

"We're affiliated with the research branch of the Academy and Signal Reserves."

Sounded interesting. Del sent Ray to meet a Major Levinson, the head of the Warner Brothers' sound department. He was pleasant and receptive, but unhappy to relate that all he had left for a cameraman was the rank of first lieutenant. He gave Ray the papers and soon Swede had a physical and a commission in the Signal Reserves' Signal Photo from Washington.

Then came a letter with several envelopes and an invitation to a party for General Melbourne, Chief US Army Signal Commander. Dress uniforms, Swede thought. I have no uniform. He rushed to Major Levinson for help.

"Swede, why don't you get one where Zanuck and I got ours?"

"Sure, Major. Where the hell is that?"

"Go to Western Costume Company, ask for Moe. He'll make you a beauty; take out your bowed legs, etcetera. He'll make you look like a West Pointer."

Three hundred dollars later, Ray strolled out of Western Costume looking exactly like Hitler in an American uniform. He wore jodhpurs, pinks, snappy tunic, US Signal Corps crossed flags, a Sam Brown belt, overcoat, gloves, jaunty cap, and silver bars on the shoulders. He didn't even know how to salute, but he was gorgeous.

The party was a success, with cocktails, dinner, and speeches, then Zanuck had the whole group pose for a picture. Most of the men had come in tuxedos, but Zanuck lined the uniforms up in the front row. Ray saw the picture later. Yep, there he was, big as life, looking more like Hitler than the Fuehrer ever did. He hung up the uniform and went back to work.

Swede in full regalia.

One Sunday morning while they were shooting from a camera car atop a hill in Hollywood, trying to finish and meet a film deadline on 1942 Fords, they ran knee-deep into antiaircraft guns. "You guys makin' movies, too?" Swede shouted.

"Turn on your radio," was the reply. It was 7 December 1941, Pearl Harbor Day.

Swede received his telegram. The gist of the message was, Report to Camp Haan for active duty and a physical, etcetera.

Ray dressed in full uniform and drove his 1939 Buick convertible up to the guard at the entrance gate into Camp Haan, Riverside, California, and got a snappy salute, his first, which he immediately copied. He presented his orders and was pointed up the hill to the giant flagpole with Old Glory waving in the breeze. "That's headquarters. Check in with the Adjutant, sir."

Ray parked the car and strode off, up the gravel path toward the Adjutant's office. A major came striding by and saluted him before he could get his saluting arm into the right swing. "But Major," he stammered bewildered, "I'm only a Lieutenant, sir."

The Major smiled. "But you walk like a Colonel," he replied, stomping off down the hill.

"Oh, another Hollywood officer, eh?" was his greeting from the fat adjutant. "Sign in." He was in the army.

Ray turned to the officer. "Sir, where can a guy get a drink around here?"

134

"Yes, it's about the right time. Come on, we'll go up to the officers' club." They drove off together up to the highest point on the hill, and Swede was introduced to the club, the bar, and Colonel Collins, the camp commander.

Each officer had his own bottle with his name on it, and the bartending corporal knew every one of them. Ray had a drink from the Adjutant's bottle, then one from the Colonel's. "Fernstrom; that's Swedish, isn't it?" the Colonel asked.

"Yes, sir, I was born in Massachusetts, but my folks took me to Sweden when I was three, and didn't get back until I was thirteen." The Colonel then proceeded to spiel off as fine a line of Swedish as Ray had ever heard from any Swede. Colonel Collins had held a government position in Sweden years before. And that's when he decided that while Swede was stationed at Camp Haan, he would be the official base photographer.

Swede in the cock-pit of a P-38 Lockheed "Lightning" at Camp Haan in the early days of World War Two. Ray was named base photographer. This base today is March Air Force Base.

One of Ray's first challenges after reporting in to Camp Haan was filming aerial bomb raids. The photography was lousy, horrible, as one might remember from early World War II newsreels of bombing runs. The films were shaky and not easy to view. How could this be improved? Swede had always flown in smaller planes with mostly hand-held cameras.

135

World War II created a whole new dilemma for the combat cameraman. Huge planes with multi-engines and very large aircraft created giant vibrations. If only the camera could match the shaking of the plane. One night, it came to him. Years before, he had watched his son Russell play with a toy spring-loaded handgun, which had a number of projectiles with rubber suction cups on the tips. Splat! One would stick to the door. Splat! Another to the ceiling. Russ had even walked up to him with a dart stuck to his forehead. "That's it!"

The next morning, Ray went over to the signal corps work unit and asked the brains there to fashion a rubber suction cup on the front of his hand-held camera. That was little problem, and the finished product looked professional. But would it work?

Ray scheduled a flight on the noisiest, most vibratory plane in the camp. He would film a mock bombing run simulating real combat conditions. They took off in the noisy shaker while Ray dampened the inside of the suction cup affixed to the front of the camera, and stuck it to the Plexiglas bubble from which he would shoot. Foowap! It held so well he could actually let go of the camera.

They arrived back at camp and Ray rushed the film to the lab for development, then anxiously awaited the screening. It was a picture-perfect bomb run; no vibrations.

Ray in the tail of a B-25 with his camera.

He was satisfied, for now the brass as well as the public could see the action as clearly as the pilot dropping the bombs, the bombardier who held his finger on the trigger. The "fum-pod" was born, and it changed aerial photography forever.

Swede with his beautiful B-25 bomber. Note camera stuck to the side of the plane by Ray's invention, the "fum-pod."

Orders finally came to ship out to Fort Monmouth and Astoria on Long Island, New York, his old home area. It was just a short hop over the river to the borough of Manhattan. Here was the Signal Corps Photographic Center, and almost from the beginning of his assignment to SCPC, he began shooting film for the air corps, as they had not yet developed their motion picture units.

He made two feature-length productions with locations throughout the country, from coast to coast and border to border. One was, *We Fight for China*, with an all-Chinese cast of pilots in training, who almost killed the American crew every time they flew with them. But that's another story. The other picture was *First Patrol*, about Latin Americans being trained by Uncle Sam, as had the Chinese, to fly and fight. The Chinese were fighter pilots, while the Latins were bombers.

Not long after Ray completed the two pictures, he received orders of a rather secret nature. He was sent, along with the rest of the unit, to the tip of Cape Cod, in Massachusetts, his home territory, and sealed into Provincetown by the military police. The whole town was closed off during the filming.

They were to make a complete production film for something radically new and requested by General Somerall, which were seagoing trucks called *Dukws*, and which immediately became known as Ducks, and were made within forty-five days of the demand from our industry. Soon they were coming off the assembly lines like sausages.

New orders arrived. Things were moving quickly. Oh, God! Swede thought. This is it. I am going to war! He sat down and wrote two hasty letters, one to his wife, the other to his parents.

As he walked up the gangplank of the troop ship, he shot a glance through a crack in the canvas-covered walkway. There was the *Mariposa*, one of the former Matson line Hawaiian luxury liners, now painted gray and equipped as a military ship.

They were chased by U-boats, then Rio was the first stop. War or no war, Swede figured on having a hell of a good time on shore leave. None was granted. The vessel had picked up an unwanted passenger, measles. Shit, Ray thought, why me? But he didn't come down with them, but passed the time playing gin rummy and won some needed bucks. The service pay was rotten.

The *Mariposa* was refueled and resupplied, then slipped out of Rio Bay early one dawning, and didn't stop until one night when she laid quiet in the water to fool old Von Bratwurst and his U-boats. Then she swung far to the south until her decks froze from the Antarctic temperatures, reminding Ray of Sweden.

Lieutenant Fernstrom was bored, so he organized an illegal crap game while the ship headed north around South Africa, passed Madagascar, and finally dropped anchor at Aden. Their destination was Suez. Ray swallowed a lump in his throat as they passed the *Queen Mary*, anchored in an Ethiopian harbor. The sight of the *Queen*, dressed in drab gray was almost too much, as she unloaded her army of British soldiers. Swede remembered happier days and colors of red, white and black and how he had influenced Sweden's liners to be painted white.

The quarantine was again lifted outside Cairo, Egypt, in Heliopolis. "I hope to hell these kids get over their fucking measles once and for all," Swede grumbled. It was no sooner lifted than Ray had two visitors, Captain Sam Greenwald and Major Felton. Swede had worked with the Captain for years at Paramount News. Felton was an aide to the American Theater Commander, General Brererton.

"What the hell are you doing in the signal corps?" bellowed Sam, who wore air corps insignias.

"Damned if I know," Ray admitted. "It's boring as hell."

"Listen, Swede, I need newsreel men like you. Someone who can do the job alone, tell the stories on film, do the daily news stories," conned Sam. Ray was listening. It sounded exciting. "You belong in the air corps, you crazy Swede, doing what you do best, flying and shooting the interesting stuff. Not this indoctrination crap."

"Well, Sam, I don't know." He remembered being suckered into a few tough jobs by Sam in the past.

"Don't you want flight pay? Maybe send home some wings for your sons?" The bait was taken. Obviously, Captain Greenwald had done his homework. "Don't worry; Major Felton will arrange everything with the General back at headquarters."

Two days later, Ray received the news. He and his small camera unit were being sent to join the Twelfth Bomber Group to cover all the daily aspects of activities on the ground and in the air. Swede strolled into Captain Sam's office to say good-bye and thank you, then listened carefully as Sam explained. "The Chiefs of Staff get these reports flown to them as soon as we receive them, and they are in a hell of a hurry!" As usual, the name of the game is speed, and I am well versed at that, thought Swede. Sam went on. "You'll have plenty of 35 mm cameras and black and white film. We'll keep you supplied." Swede nodded approval. Sam gestured toward a canvas covered pile of stuff in a corner and instructed Ray to "please take all that shit and bury it somewhere in the sand."

Ray's heart skipped a beat when he looked under the tarp and discovered two 16 mm Victor movie cameras and a tremendous load of Kodachrome 16 mm color film. Color! His mind raced. He turned to Greenwald and spelled out his new idea. He could make a color documentary of the bomber group, a sort of history of what they were doing. He'd have Technicolor blow it up to 35 mm to be shown in the theaters back home.

"Go ahead, Swede; I like it," Sam beamed.

Ray hurried back to his quarters, packed his clothes and heavy camera equipment, and headed straight into his next adventure.

Swede writes:

There was a storm, a blasting desert sand storm, as we lumbered toward an invisible landing strip. I'll never forget that helpless feeling as I looked to the rear of the aircraft. The tail section on the monster was swaying back and forth from the gale force of the winds, I swear, as much as fifteen to twenty feet, first to the left then to the right. I was sitting over the wing section, and was, needless to say, scared shitless. I'd done a hell of a lot of flying in my time, a lot of it under strenuous and sometimes scary conditions, but never in anything like that.

I had a totally helpless feeling and had put all my faith in our pilot and the Man Above. Suddenly, an unbelievably violent gust of wind blew us some fifty feet to the right of the strip, and at about a forty-five degree angle, just as the pilot tried to touch down. We all thought this was it.

The pilot revved the engines to full throttle, and to a screeching whine I had never heard before. I thought the giant engines would tear off the wings. Skillfully, he banked around for another try, and with God's help, between wind blasts we touched the sand.

I had made it one more time. I can't say why, but I have a tremendous faith that my luck would never run out, and it had held true once again.

Outside the huge plane, the blowing sand was so thick we scrambled for shelter. I looked back at the dim outline of our plane and remember thinking that what we had just accomplished was impossible. I shouldn't be here. I believed things in life happened for a reason. There must be things I still have to do.

Ray felt physically and mentally bruised from the harrowing plane trip. Now his ego was about to be badly beaten as well, in the form of his new commanding officer, Colonel Backus.

Lieutenant Fernstrom and his small, elite group reported at once to the Colonel, and immediately their ears began to burn. "So, we have another bunch of Hollywood prima donnas in our midst," he began. "We had a guy from your ninth combat camera unit here before." Ray's collar began to tighten. "That pansy camera jerk caused us nothing but trouble. Stupid crybaby. I kicked the bastard out." Backus roared on. "We're fighting a war here, real bombs and bullets. There is no time to pose while you guys sit on your asses shooting pictures for a hobby!"

Ray tried to explain, but was silenced.

"Did you hear me? It's no deal. You are dismissed!"

Swede was caught off balance. He had expected a little welcoming drink to be poured; instead he got a royal kick in the behind. Well, there's more than one way to skin this desert rat, he thought. As much as he hated it, it was kiss-ass time. Better butter up the old bastard. That is, if he got a chance to talk to him.

"Lieutenant Fernstrom, sir, you are wanted in the C.O.'s office." As Ray was ushered into the Colonel's office, he was riveted with an icy stare. "Why in hell are you and your group still here? I dismissed the whole worthless bunch of you." Swede remembered Colonel Carmichael, the crusty Texas Ranger and figured an air corps colonel could be handled the same way.

Three days had passed since their first meeting, and Ray had his pitch polished and ready. The glib-tongued Swede applied the balm of his charm on the old warrior. "Sir," he began, "you can fight all the wars, fly all the bombers, drop all the bombs in hell, fire all the bullets you can get a hold of, but we are the only ones who can record it all. No one will remember you were ever here." The Colonel listened as he leaned back in his chair, eyes closed. Warming to his success, Ray continued. "We'll even make a Technicolor historical film of your every effort for the brass to see back in Washington." That did it. The crusty old Colonel grabbed a bottle of Johnny Walker Red, poured two hefty blasts, and they drank, shook hands, and soon became fast friends.

Once the Colonel had seen some of Ray's footage, he changed his mind completely. He watched his war in full color. When he flew a mission with Swede, he became an animated finger, pointing this way and that, while yelling at Ray to get every shot of ack-ack puffs in black, poised against the blue skies and whipped cream of billowy white clouds floating amid, and Ray shot it all.

"My God, Swede, the flack is so thick we could walk on it!" shouted the Colonel.

"Colonel, you sure have come a long way," Swede said smiling. "I'm glad you're enjoying my hobby." Ray wondered what he would call this fabulous color film that was developing. He was spending every waking moment on it, as he had assigned the rest of the men the other duties, daily reports and routines. That was what he needed to do a first-class, never-before-attempted color masterpiece.

Sam Greenwald, true to his word, sent all the film to Technicolor. He had even sold his old pal Hap Arnold, Chief of Staff of the air force, on the film. Things were looking up. Arnold was a friend of all the newsreel cameramen on the West Coast, and for a very good reason. He had been champion of Bombers Galore when he had his old Martin Bombers at March Field (formerly Camp Haan) in Riverside, California. In the past, he had sought out publicity through all five major newsreels for his bomber ideas, and all the cameramen had dreamed up features about bombers in formation.

They had soared over the highest mountain, Mount Whitney, down to the depths of Death Valley. There had been all sorts of excitement, and the public ate it up. Sam Greenwald had handled everything. If two reports came in on the same subject, he would meld the best of them together and give full credit to both reels, much to everyone's satisfaction, especially Hap Arnold's, Major US Army Air Corps.   141

Author's note: "Hap" Arnold would later become the only air force five-star general of World War II and was to yield to the medics' advice keeping Swede out of the invasion of Normandie.

Ray's group had two liaison officers from the British Eighth Army with them. They tented together, and supplied the intelligence needed for the next bombing runs. The Englishmen had been gone for a few days to survey the effect of the B-25s massive attacks on Rommel and his elite Afrika Corps. When they returned from the front, they were in jolly good spirits, laughing and carrying on, each holding a bottle of Scotch. "Blimey, Swede, you should have been there. The Billy Mitchell bombers came over in waves and saturated old Jerry. It was a veritable earthquake!"

"That's it! That's what we'll call it, *The Earthquakers.*" A story and a movie were born. Ray immediately started spreading the name, giving chalk to all his gang, who wrote *The Earthquakers* on every bomb in the group.

"The Earthquakers"

The Colonel's tent became the Tremor Room. Operations was called the Seismograph Room, and they renamed the crash trucks Earthquakers Nightmare. The artists on each flight crew painted the name on the engine cowlings of every bomber in large bold script. The name stuck.

As the war raged on, the reality of losing planes and fellow warriors came home to roost. The influence the older men had on the younger pilots, bombardiers, navigators, and crew members was tremendous. Especially the old Swede, with his wondrous tales of unbelievable adventure, his booming, gravelly-strong voice and fuck 'em attitude toward the Krauts was inspiring. But especially his humor.

On Ray's mother's (Lydia's) side, he was descended from the Von Ungers, who had a title of Count he could have claimed in Germany. This came in handy when Ray entertained his combat compadres at the desert officers' club. If playing a German, Ray would strut and parade with his whip and sometimes false Hitler mustache like a true Prussian aristocrat just graduating from Heidelburg.

Once after a German raid on their position, a couple of German aircraft were shot down by ground fire, and the pilots had parachuted to safety. There was nowhere for them to escape in the desert, no POW camps, so the German fliers were invited to the officers' club tent, and both enemies proceeded to get merrily drunk while swapping war stories.

Swede decided to look up his false mustache and commandeered two MPs to sneak into the Germans' tent and borrow a German officer's uniform. Unannounced, they marched into the officers' club. There in the entrance stood Ray, the Count Von Unger, in all his glory with an MP on each arm, Hollywood mustache in place and his hair combed over his forehead. There was complete silence as the German officers went ghostly white. One slapped his forehead and exclaimed, "All is lost, for they have captured Hitler, too!" The place erupted into convulsive laughter, and this scene was talked about for years to come during reunions on both sides of the Atlantic.

Photo of Swede with his boss Sam Greenwald somewhere in Africa 1943.   143

Swede could always be counted on to liven up the dull moments. During gatherings around the mess tent, he would act out his triumphant return home as a wounded veteran. One highlight was his first visit to the Stork Club in New York where he would occupy two chairs, one for his gimpy leg, while all his female admirers swarmed around to hear his tall tales and rattle his medals.

This last scene was prophesied correctly, even to the medals. On the last bombing raid on that continent, Swede was the only crew member to get hit.

The B-25 Billy Mitchells were great aircraft. The pilots loved them. They were also rugged and could take a lot and still remain in the air. The first B-25 Cs and Ds arrived at a most critical time. Field Marshall Rommel's (the Desert Fox) Afrika Corps had just blitzed their way to within seventy short miles of Alexandria, Egypt. They had stopped at El Alamein to reform their victorious armies for the final push through Alexandria, they thought. Then on to Cairo, and the greatest prize of all, the Suez Canal. But the war was reversed at that point.

The Mitchells gave the Allies the air superiority they had been lacking. Together with other bombers which had been operating against overwhelming odds, the Mitchells blasted and softened Rommel's crack troops and Mussolini's tired-of-it-all legions, until the British Eighth Army forced them to withdraw from their strong El Alamein positions.

The British Army, eager for revenge, then drove them back. From then on, the enemy was plastered and blasted from every stand they attempted, and were pushed over two thousand miles across the North African front into Tunisia.

The first group of B-25s to be sent to the North African front consisted of four squadrons, which were the Earthquakers and who earned the title for record breaking attacks made on the enemy. They had replaced the American bomb racks with British ones and carried British bombs which were mounted eight in the belly and eight on the wing racks. They flew in waves of eighteen, and the Jerries called them the Golden Eighteen, as the Mitchells were painted tan and looked golden against the blue sky.

In the space of a few months, the four Earthquaker squadrons dropped fifty-five thousand bombs on Rommel's fleeing forces. Later during the offensive, other B-25 groups joined the battle, and they also dropped hundreds of tons of unmerciful bombs.

It is no wonder that the axis made what will probably go down in history as the world's fastest and longest retreat. Rommel will undoubtedly be known as one of the most able and brilliant desert commanders the world has ever known. He was at a loss as to why his supposedly superb antiaircraft defenses were so futile against the B-25s. Actually they were efficient enough, but it was the ruggedness of the aircraft and the skilled crews that flew them so evasively that had them baffled.

On one occasion, Rommel focused extremely accurate and concentrated 88 ack-ack fire on a flight of eighteen B-25s, and all were hit, some extensively with 160 jagged gashes, a few of which were over a foot in diameter. But in spite of the heavy pounding and sustained damage, all eighteen returned to base.

The ground crews worked through the night, and made necessary repairs, some temporary, thus enabling the same airplanes to shuttle more bombs on the exact same positions the next day.

What a beating that airplane can take, thought Swede. And how many times had he heard it since? The Mitchells operated out of axis-made airfields, just a short distance from Rommel's fleeing corps. As soon as the strips were captured and de-mined, the squadrons would move in. On these fields en route, they would see the twisted wreckage of masses of enemy aircraft and vehicles of all descriptions, the result of the bombings the boys had done a few days earlier.

Actual photograph taken by Swede during a bombing run of "The Golden Eighteen" B-25s, while chasing Rommel out of Africa.

It was on the last bombing raid that Swede caught a chunk of shrapnel in his leg from an eighty-eight blast. It was 17 April 1943. The Captain was grinding out pictures of bombs that had just been dropped over the Cape Bon area.

"Hey, Hugh, take it easy on my new pinks," Swede hollered to Sergeant Hugh Wade, a crack cameraman. Ray thought Hugh had kicked him. Actually, the fragment had found its mark in his left leg above the 145 knee. No one else on the Mitchell was injured, and the plane flew home safely.

Back at the base the story took on a different character. For weeks, Ray had been trying to get shots of a wounded airman being lifted from a plane right after a mission. This was his chance and he didn't want to lose it. A cameraman obliged and took the pictures.

Ray's wound was not serious, but he had completed his assignment and was ordered back to the United States for rehabilitation. Sometime during his desert tenure, he became known as Sandstorm. The nickname stuck with him and in all correspondence and reunions, he was always referred to as Sandstorm.

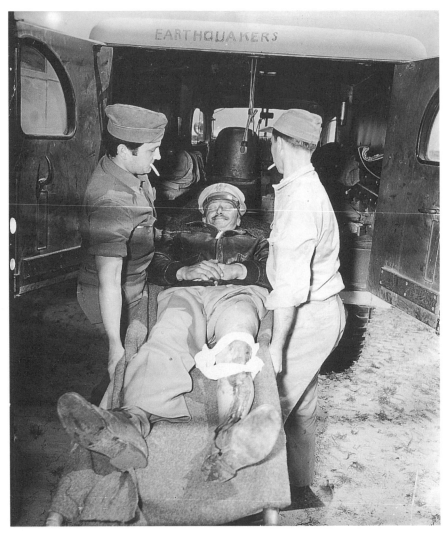

Swede, the wounded warrior.

At a later date, a similar documentary to the Earthquakers on B-17s in Europe was filmed, and Ray was second camera unit. That popular version was known as *The Memphis Belle*.

While recovering from his wound, Ray was made Officer in Charge (OIC) of combat camera training at the air force's first motion picture camera unit in California. Then he was shipped out for his second combat tour and ended up with sixty-five other officers at Jefferson Barracks. There, his leg wound ruptured, and he was back in the hospital again. He wrote Hap Arnold and asked to get out of the hospital but it did not help. His group of cameramen were shipped to Europe to film and record the invasion and victory in Europe, and his only consolation and satisfaction was their overwhelming success, for he had given them combat camera training for photographic excellence.

The war was over for Swede. He did a few publicity photos with other Hollywood men like Clark Gable outside the Selznick studios and was mustered out. For the rest of the world, the end of the war was very near also.

His medals clinked in his knapsack as he headed for the Fernstrom Estate in Sharon, via the Stork Club, to fulfill a promise then on to see his family, his mother and father, and to gather up his wife and children, Barbara, Russell, Eric and Selma, and take them back to California.

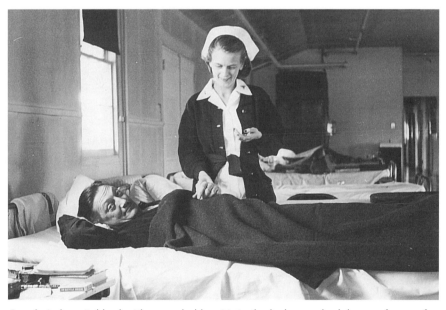

Swede in hospital bed with wounded leg. Note the lecherous look he was famous for.

Swede second from right and Clark Gable third from left just before mustering out of service. Picture was taken outside of the old Selznick and later Hal Roach Studios in Culver City, California.

Swede's regards to Rommel.

149

WAR DEPARTMENT

HEADQUARTERS OF THE ARMY AIR FORCES

WASHINGTON

2 8 MAR 1944

Capt. Raymond C. I. Fernstrom
Ward E-5, Station Hospital
Jefferson Barracks, Missouri

Dear Ray:

I received your letter of March 11th and immediately
had your status at Jefferson Barracks checked. The medicos
assured us that every effort was being, and would be made, to
get you in shape in time to leave with your shipment. However,
in the event you aren't able to depart on time, they informed
us that only a short delay was anticipated.

If you are unable to depart with your shipment, Jefferson Barracks has been directed to keep us advised and when you
are shipshape efforts will be made to get air transportation arranged for you, if at that time the airlines aren't too crowded.

I believe you will agree with me that it just isn't
good business to disregard the advice of the medicos, so my
advice to you is to make the best of your stay there and give
the doctors your full cooperation in order that you can get
away as soon as possible.

Wishing you a speedy recovery, I am

Yours truly,

H. H. Arnold,
General, U. S. Army,
Commanding General, Army Air Forces.

Hap's official reply to Swede. The original now hangs in the March Air Force Base
Museum.

18 JUN 1948

Mr. Raymond G. I. Fernstrom
1714 Strand
Hermosa Beach
California

Dear Mr. Fernstrom:

Your letter of 2 June 1948 concerning the first horizontal movie camera is acknowledged with thanks and appreciation.

The new camera would appear to possess considerable merit for certain types of Air Force use. I, therefore, request that you furnish details of its characteristics to the Photographic Laboratory, Engineering Division, Headquarters, Air Materiel Command, Wright-Patterson Air Force Base, Dayton, Ohio. In addition, if your camera is sufficiently developed, it is suggested that you contact the Photographic Laboratory to arrange for a demonstration of its manner of operation. A copy of your letter of 2 June 1948, also a copy of this correspondence is being forwarded to the Photographic Laboratory.

Your documentary color film "Earthquakers" was screened for me and I enjoyed it very much. The release of this film to the public has not been accomplished due to the high cost of reproduction of prints in color; however, it has received wide distribution within the Air Force.

Sincerely yours,

HOYT S. VANDENBERG
Chief of Staff, United States Air Force

Letter to Swede from General Hoyt S. Vandenberg. Obviously Ray had developed a new camera that the Air Force was interested in. Another big name that knew Swede Fernstrom.

151

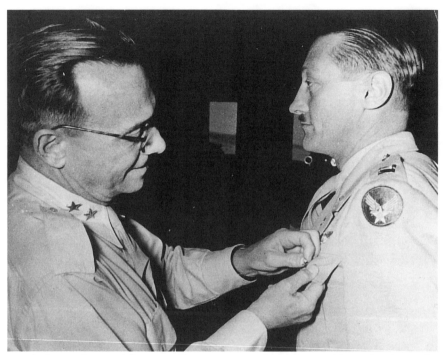

Swede being decorated by General Brererton. He looked more like Hitler than "The Fuhrer."

CHAPTER SEVEN
After the War

Ray returned to Hollywood with his family and went into a very hard period of readjustment like so many other returning warriors. The long separation during the war years had left Ray and Jerry far apart. Little love was left between them. His infidelity and reputation as the "horizontal captain" had reached Jerry's ears and had driven an irreconcilable wedge between them. Ray, never to take no for an answer when it came to sexual activity, had to make one final conquest. Christina Clara was born four years after Selma Rae, as had been the time also between all the other children, four years apart. This should give the reader some hint as to how often the Phantom Swede visited his family. If there was ever a man not cut out to be a family man, it was Ray Fernstrom. *Author's note: Jerry would always refer to Christina (Tina) as her daughter of sorrow.*

Jerry borrowed five hundred dollars from her mother and filed for divorce, having grown to hate the Fernstrom name. She always said the divorce was worth every penny of it. Jerry had become very religious, and it is believed that her new beliefs had a lot to do with the end of their marriage also. She and Ray saw little of each other from that point on. She would soon take up with a gigolo-type fellow, ironically named Raymond—Ray Manville, a guitar-playing, happy-go-lucky Texan. They were soon married and just as soon divorced, for he was an absolutely worthless individual. But Jerry keeps his name to this day.

Parties were the Hollywood name of the game and, of course, Swede was in his glory hosting many of them. Most of these bashes were rather like the Hughes takeoff movie, *The Carpetbaggers*, when Carol Baker swung from the chandelier while slurping a martini. But in real life, everyone would be dead drunk and she wouldn't have any panties on while challenging any would-be Tarzans to catch her with no holds barred. It was at one of these *teas* that Swede wandered into the study of one of his very influential friend's estate. Just another wild evening of fun and frolic that only Hollywood can produce. There before the fireplace, semi-passed-out lay this gorgeous, shapely brunette. Never one to let an obvious opportunity for an easy conquest escape his grasp, our Swede proceeded to make mad passionate love to the more than willing voluptuous beauty. Our Swedish Tarzan had met his Jane.

It was a few months later that Jane announced to Ray that Boy was on the way and your authors were informed that we now had a brand-new stepmother. Hooray for Hollywood!

Jane would later take Ray to the cleaners like no woman had done before. She turned out to be a very smart cookie during their inevitable divorce. Ray said she was really something. We were to see her only two times. Once when they arrived at the family house in Manhattan Beach in a front wheel drive, pearl-gray Graham-Paige beauty, a very expensive car (They were probably there to bring Jerry some minimal child support), and the second time was during their visit to our home in Riverside after Russ' marriage to Beverly, when Ray drove out with Jane and their son Mark. We never saw nor heard from Mark, Russ' half brother, again.

Ray picked up a lot of commercial work for General Motors, Ford, and Chrysler, and also newsreel piecework with various reels and the new kid looming on the horizon, television.

Photo by Floyd McCarty

Reunion

When the Oldsmobile commercial was shot here recently, it was like old friends getting together. Standing: Ray Fernstrom, ASC., Rosemary Clooney and Les Martinson, director. Seated Johnny Mercer and Bing Crosby.

Clipping from American Cinematographer. This is the only copy I have of this reunion Swede had with a few familiar people.

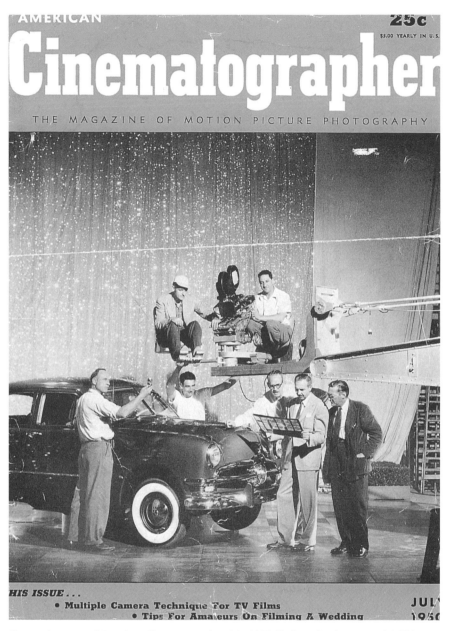

AMERICAN

Cinematographer

THE MAGAZINE OF MOTION PICTURE PHOTOGRAPHY

25c

$3.00 YEARLY IN U.S.

HIS ISSUE . . .
* Multiple Camera Technique For TV Films
* Tips For Amateurs On Filming A Wedding

JUL
1950

Ray on the cover of American Cinematographer, July 1950, filming a Ford commercial. This was not the only time Swede would grace the cover of this magazine.

The Hughes H-Four Flying Boat

Author's note: We have only Swede's word from conversations and his references in memoirs and picture credits about the following event, but after some checking with people within the Hughes organization and getting a nod of yes, there seems to be no dispute. He states in his notes that Howard Hughes hired him and that he was filming it for NBC Television Newsreel. It could be that he was doing it for both. A long time ago, or was it at the Spruce Goose display in Long Beach, we saw Ray with camera on his shoulder walking down the gangplank with Howard Hughes' arm around Swede's shoulder. We have never seen this newsreel again.

Swede had first met Howard Hughes over the *Here's How* Braniff Airline stewardess event and Rosalie Schach, the original choice for the female lead in the motion picture *The Outlaw*. Later, Howard commissioned Ray to do a color special called *A Boy Named Joey*, in Houston. Hughes showed the movie all over Texas to help raise funds for the new Shriners' Crippled Children's Hospital.

Later, he had Swede do another film of the hospital after its completion and during full operation. So, the two were in touch over the years, and Howard knew full well about Ray's talents.

In 1947, Swede was hired to film Hughes taxiing his huge Hercules flying boat around Long Beach Harbor as a test of its giant engines and ability to maneuver.

Swede had discussed this with Howard Hughes as to where he should position himself and the camera to get the best shots. He had been given a film camera, but no sound equipment, which created a new idea for Ray that he would later pursue with Howard. *Author's note: The gist was a new lightweight sound camera that would bring sound interviews to television, which was limited to cable lengths and close-ups. This would be called Teletalks. Several of the movie newsreels were covering them too, but all soundless.*

Howard was in contact with Ray when the giant Hercules taxied for position. "Do you have any stock left in the mag, Swede?" he asked.

"Sure do!"

"Well, keep it rolling; I'm going to take 'er up." Hughes pushed the throttles to full speed and aimed straight for Swede's camera. The plane broke the waves, and the awesome monster slowly gained altitude as Ray ground away. The seaplane gained an altitude of about twenty feet off the harbor water.

Swede was disappointed that he didn't have sound, for he would have liked to interview Hughes after the flight. Ray later told Russell that Hughes knew instantly that the Hercules flying boat would never fly. He told Swede, "It took every ounce of my strength and flying skill to keep her level for the descent of just twenty feet to water." Of course, he never flew it again. Hughes also told Swede, "I can't stand the name *Spruce Goose!*" regarding the great seaplane.

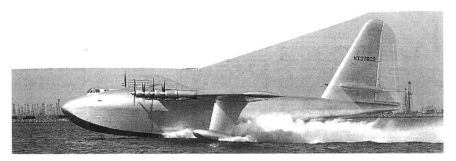

The "Spruce Goose" piloted by Howard Hughes speeds by Swede's camera just as she touched down. The first and only flight.

Two Masters of Color

One day somewhere over the Grand Canyon a plane hovered on a peculiar mission. The plan was that of following the movements of a large American bald eagle as it soared over the gorges, some a mile deep. The aircraft imitated the turns and swoops of the great bird, seeing what the eagle observed from its great height. The cameraman and the eventual viewer became that eagle. The passing moments and scenes would be seen and lived over and over again, and accompanied by music from the pen of a genius, for behind the lens of the camera, Ray was filming another masterpiece of color in motion picture painting for Walt Disney. It was to be relived by millions of earth bound people in theaters and schools the world over, with the music of Ferde Grofe's *Grand Canyon Suite*. It was this film that brought Ray to the height of his personal acme in photographic exhilaration.

Swede lectured around the country to the screening of the film and related his experiences and interesting sidelights about Mr. Disney. The motion picture *Grand Canyon* was so beautifully thought out and perfectly filmed that it won the Academy Award for aerial photographic excellence.

In the following years, Walt Disney hired Swede to do *Circarama*, a spectacle screened at the 1968 Brussels World's Fair in a special, unique theater built next to the US pavilion. The film was shot in the circarama method and ran continuously for the world to see and learn about our beautiful country and people spreading good will. The project of making the film took over a year, and was shot from Pilot Frank Tallman's specially equipped B-25, with eleven cameras adapted to a boom, shooting in a 360-degree panorama. A specially equipped station wagon did the ground sequences. The itinerary covered the entire country. After completion of the World's Fair, a special exhibit was set up at Disneyland, and   157

Ray Fernstrom photographed "Circarama" for Walt Disney Productions. It was an awesome film to view and showed to millions at Disneyland. Swede can be seen to the left checking the camera.

Frank Tallman's converted B-25 bomber. Notice the circular camera boom housing the eleven cameras on the belly of the plane.

literally millions of people the world over were inspired for years to come.

Later, Ray wrote to Roy Disney, Walt's brother, to film another script he and Walt had been working on called *Magic Carpet USA*. According to Swede, it was Walt Disney's dream to make an aerial pictorial symphony of the entire United States put to music. But Swede said, "We were working on it, when Walt passed on when my back was turned." He told Roy that Walt's last dream had been in his heart and mind ever since.

But Roy turned down the request, citing lack of funds from the Ford Foundation, who had paid for most of *Grand Canyon*. It was a dream that would never be fulfilled.

Ray Fernstrom A.S.C.
P.O. Box 1722
Newport Beach, California
92663

Executive Group   Easter Sunday, 1973
Walt Disney Productions Inc.,
Alameda Street
Burbank, California

Dear Friends,

Iam not the least bit superstitious, nor psychic, but it is as if Walt were standing behind me telling to write you this!

You, Bob Gibeaut now have Walt's aerial script I mailed. Evidently it was something he dreamed of completing. Roy said no, due to our having shot up all the Ford Foundation money, so Walt's "MAGIC CARPET, U.S.A." was never finished. Weonly had those Cinemascope scenes that appeared in the " GRAND CANYON" Special, that won the 1958 Academy Award for such produc- yions.

As you see by studying his cript....he had added scenes from all the U.S.A. for not only Circarama but "Canyon" and "MAGIC CARPET"...which was never developed into full script form, but I'm certain he would have done it if we had not run out of Foundation money.

Surely somewherethere must be Foundation money for a big screen Tribute to the Memory of Walt? How better spent than another Disney aerial symph- oney such as " GRAND CANYON"....even an hour long! " Walt Disney's Dream; An aerial, pictorial symphony".

I'd like to shoot it and I'll tell you why; Ever since 1925 I have flown with a camera over every pictorial spot Walt had in mind, during my career at one time or another. With present day steady ,vibrationless equipment undercranking from a good jet helicopter makes the dream a reality, from every technical angle. (No one has done more Helicopter shooting than I have in every conceivable chopper.) My artistic eye is just as good as ever, and since I quit booze three years ago, I'm better than ever, even though retired. I've been shooting pictorial impressions ever since, drivin around the land in my old Cad.

The thought of doing Walt's last dream has been in my heart and mind ever since he passed on when my back was turned.

May I have your thoughtful imaginative consideration of Walt's and now, my dream?

          Sincerely

Ray's letter to Roy Disney. Unfortunately, Roy turned down the proposition.   159

Shortly after Walt Disney and Swede met, approximately in the early 1930s, Ray had a meeting with Walt, and afterward asked him if he could take a couple of pictures of the life-size dolls, Mickey and Minnie Mouse.

"Sure, Swede," retorted Walt. "Take some shots with your kids. They're about the same height." Ray took the dolls outside and posed Bobbie, Russ' sister, and Russ, with the old Burbank studio as a background. Bobbie held hands with Minnie, while Russ hung on to Mickey. The dolls are now famous, and this book, it is believed, contains the only photo in existence of the two of them at that time. The only other photo seen by the authors was taken two years later and shows Walt Disney holding Mickey (a half-body shot) and standing next to his wife. There appears to be none of Minnie or of the two together. The cartoon characters were called the Charlotte Clarke dolls, as they were presented to Walt by Charlotte Clarke. The photo is dated December 1933. Russ was two years old.

Russ and Bobbie with the Charlotte Clarke dolls.

Television

The late fifties and sixties proved to be perfect for Swede. Television, with the short half-hour shows in black and white and a prewritten script, were old habits for him; the newsreels all over again, only easier, and the Director of Photography title to go with it.

He went from commercials to the half-hour weekly series, *Bourbon Street Beat* and *Surfside Six*, both with Van Williams, who went on to become the modern day version of the Lone Ranger and his friend Tonto, as the Green Hornet and his faithful companion Kato, who was also to gain fame as the Karate guru Bruce Lee. (The Cloud would soon claim Bruce Lee and later his son.)

The television days of black and white were a cake walk for Swede, for none could touch him with experience. He had lost his love, color, but went on experimenting with different contrasts and angles of black and white, creating new shades and exciting new techniques for the enjoyment of the fledgling television audience. He was in great demand and was kept busier than he had ever been in his career.

Swede and star Dorothy Provine on the set of "The Roaring Twenties." Ray always said that Dorothy wouldn't let anyone but him photograph her because he made her look like a teenager—thanks to Hartley Harrision's diffusion lenses.

Dorothy Provine and 007 Roger Moore in a scene of "The Roaring Twenties."

Some of his credits include *Mr. Roberts, Arrest and Trial, McHale's Navy, Channing, The Roaring Twenties, Maverick, Surfside Six,* and *Cheyenne,* to name a few.

The only break Ray got from colorless television was his reputation as the very best in aerial photography. There was a series of air force films and, of course, Swede was called on for the aerial work. He passed their rugged physicals like a kid of twenty. His three most memorable films were *On the Threshold of Space, A Gathering of Eagles,* and with another great aerial photographer, Bill Clothier, *Lafayette Escadrille.* The latter was filmed in black and white.

Two of Swede's lifelong pals and great daredevil pilots were Paul Mantz and Frank Tallman. Ray was an ace photographer and always

Ray filming another hit television series "Cheyenne" in the heyday of the black and white era. Ray can be seen standing by his trusty camera directly in front of the tent.

demanded the finest pilots. In the old days, it had to be Bert Acosta who flew the first aerial shots for William Wellman's *Wings*. Frank and Paul were his modern counterparts. Paul wrote about Ray's war efforts in his book, *Hollywood Pilot*, and referred to Swede's documentary *The Earthquakers*. Paul was killed in a weird aircraft accident while filming the movie *Flight of the Phoenix*. The ominous Cloud had struck once again very close to Swede.

Ray was in a state of shock over Paul's death and relied heavily on Frank Tallman thereafter. He spent a lot of time flying with Frank out of his air museum at Tallmantz Aviation at Orange County Airport, now John Wayne Airport. Frank's modified B-25 bomber, used in so many pictures, might still be there.

Tallman supplied the planes for the World War I adventure *Lafayette Escadrille* about the American volunteers who flew with the French Air Corps before America's entry into the conflict. The film was based on Wellman's experience as a member of the original flying group. It starred his nineteen-year-old son Bill, Jr., who portrayed his father. Later, Bill, Jr. was in Swede's last film, *A Swingin' Summer*.

Tallman supplied the ancient aircraft, Spads, Fokkers, Sopwith Camels, and Neiuports necessary for the ground and air sequences of the 1915-1917 vintage. Many of the aircraft were located in museums, and putting them in flying condition was no simple task.

Ray was fresh from his high altitude jet filming of Twentieth's *On the Threshold of Space* and RKO's *Back from Eternity*, and had to resurrect old flying film techniques to shoot the low and slow aerials needed to record the World War I story.

"It seemed strange," said Swede, "to put aside the plastic crash helmet, so necessary in today's flying, for the leather helmet and goggles of old, but I love it!"

Tallman was at a complete loss, trying to find an airplane that would provide a forward shooting position, yet fly at the fantastically slow speeds, in order to film the 1910 Bleriot. Suddenly, Bill Clothier remembered using a Curtiss Pusher in a Pete Smith short about twenty years before.

It was a typical zany Pete Smith short subject, *How to Do It* (Reminiscent of Swede's defunct *Here's How*?) story on shooting coyotes from an airplane. "You know," Bill recalled, "that plane flew so slow that we had trouble keeping up with the coyotes!" Tallman located a Curtiss Pusher labeled the *Blue Duck* and with a Ryan Navion, provided the two camera ships necessary.

"I never saw such a crazy cameraman," remarked Frank Tallman. "I'd be up there stunting my head off, and as I'd come out of a snap-roll, I could see the Curtiss Pusher out of the corner of my eye right behind me. And there, hanging half out of the cockpit, would be Swede, with his eye

Swede, complete with antique outfit and camera in the Curtiss pusher "Blue Duck." Pilot is unidentified.

glued to the viewfinder, following every move I made. Honestly, he scared me!" The movie was a masterpiece.

Lafayette Escadrille also starred Tab Hunter and David Janssen, two heartthrobs of the time. The movie was shot in black and white to denote the time period, and Swede enjoyed filming in the antique birds he knew so well.

An unexplained mystery occurred a few years later. Frank Tallman, ace stunt pilot, while flying on a clear day over territory that none knew better, flew his plane straight into an Orange County mountain. The only believable explanation for the accident was that Frank must have suffered a massive heart attack. And with this crash, an amazing era came to an end. Another Hollywood great and personal friend felled by The Cloud.

Television finally developed color acceptable to the viewing public and TV sets were at a premium. It caught on like wildfire. Swede was assigned to one of the best of the color series, *Death Valley Days*, with a longtime friend, Ronald Reagan. It was to be the last television series for both, as Ron went on to a successful career in politics, and an aging but spry Swede on to make motion pictures.

State of California
GOVERNOR'S OFFICE
SACRAMENTO 95814

June 19, 1974

Mr. Ray Fernstrom
Post Office Box 1722
Newport Beach, California 92663

Dear Ray:

Thanks very much for your note and for sending
me the clipping. My, what memories that story
brought back. I guess everything takes on a
little rosy hue with time. If we don't watch
out, we'll be calling those the good old days
and forgetting what tragedies there were and
the fine young men who never came back.

Again, thanks, and all the best to you.

Sincerely,

RONALD REAGAN
Governor

*A letter from then Governor Ronald Reagan. The clipping he refers to describes a reunion
between old war buddies.*

Heartthrob Tab Hunter takes a break on the set of "Lafayette Escadrille."

The Mountain High

Ray was still married to the lady named Jane when they paid us a call when Grandmother and Grandfather Fernstrom flew out from Sharon to visit us. I don't think Ray could comprehend that he had a fully grown son who was now a man and not little Russell. He was never a family man, and now had another son, Mark, on his hands. Another thing that must have affected him at the time was that Beverly was pregnant with his first grandchild.

It was in 1960-61 that the heat, smog, and progression in our area from rural country environment to a congestive city were more than Bev and I could endure, so up into the mountains we went, where we built a business in real estate selling mountain cabins (second homes), a house, and a new life. On one exceptionally beautiful day, the Phantom drove up in his new Imperial convertible with a brand new third wife, Evelyn.

Swede and Russ proceeded to bar hop and wound up at Big Bear Lake, where Ray told Russ, "I can't believe you're my son. You're more like a brother." Swede took to the mountains, fresh air, and natural beauty, and a whole new adventure opened up. Beverly and I had a new father.

"Swede," Ray, "Dad" invited me to Warner Brothers Studios to watch him film an episode of "Maverick" with James Garner and Jack Kelly. I asked if I could bring along a buddy, Harry Dudletts. "Sure," bellowed Swede, "bring the S. O. B. with you!" This is the only photograph of my father and I together.

He visited us often, and one day informed us that he would be making a movie at Lake Arrowhead. Could he remain with us for a while?

"Sure, why not?" During his stay, we had a great time listening to all the tales he had to tell. Russ was fascinated and the idea for the book you are reading was born!

A Swingin' Summer, the movie, was to be shot in the old Arrowhead Village, now demolished and completely rebuilt, with a lot of names in the music industry. The budding new star who was to be promoted was a lovely redhead named Quinn O'Hara. But Swede told me to keep an eye on the young unknown beauty, whom he thought under his direction as cinematographer, would become a real star. She became known as Raquel Welch. This was her first movie, and for some reason she doesn't seem to want to remember that.

Ray directing young star Raquel Welch.

Swede scouted the area for over a week, doing his homework regarding the scenic Lake Arrowhead, and was ready to begin the picture. At this time, he moved from our home to the Arrowhead Lodge, which was to be the headquarters during filming.

The first shooting was in the colorful ice cream shop in the old downtown village, with the blue lake as a background. It was the first time that quartz-iodine lights would be used in daytime on a Technicolor film. The old pioneer was still experimenting.

The old "Swede" on the set of his last picture. Shown with Ray are Rusty Meek, Assistant Director, and Charles Rosen, Gaffer. William Wellman, Sr. would later remark to Swede that

it was the most beautiful color he had ever seen.

Photo: "A Swinging Summer," starring Raquel Welch and James Stacy.

We were invited to view the water skiing and beach sequences and were thrilled at his mastery. However, he was oblivious to our presence as he was totally engrossed in his work, as he took color readings and barked orders to cameramen and actors. Then Raquel Welch arrived for her takes. Swede took one look at all the makeup plastered on her face and instructed her abruptly in his subtle meat-ax approach to, "Go wash all that crap off your face! I'll do the makeup for you with my lenses. You want to become a star, don't you?" Raquel left in tears while the whole troupe took a break.

When they resumed, a poised Raquel appeared as had been instructed, and Ray said, "Now that's better, sweetheart. Wait'll you see yourself on   171 film now." Her natural beauty did shine through at the screening. Raquel went on to her next film, which also required the natural look, *One Million B.C.*, where she skyrocketed to instant stardom.

Her love interest in *A Swingin' Summer* was James Stacy. He was later to be maimed in a motorcycle accident while riding with his girlfriend, losing an arm and a leg. The musical interests in the flick were the Righteous Brothers, Gary Lewis and the Playboys, the Rip Chords, and Donnie Brooks, which made it chock full of good music and dance.

One dance scene that Raquel did after she let her hair down in the movie was unforgettable and most likely responsible for her future stardom. Ray said, "I've had more damned fun on this picture, and it'll show kids what a swinging fun summer can be like at beautiful Lake Arrowhead."

This was Ray's last photographic assignment. He left Hollywood forever, except maybe for an infrequent visit or two to old friends.

It wasn't long after this picture that Beverly and I began to tire of living full time in the mountains. In the middle of a six-foot snowstorm, while both of us were shoveling snow off our roof, the snowplow had just taken the rear quarter panel off our station wagon and the septic tank had just backed up, that I looked over at my beloved wife and exclaimed, "We've got to be out of our frigging minds! We live in Southern California!" A week later, we locked up the house and moved to Newport Beach.

Ray was having marital problems with his third attempt at holy matrimony and was soon to move also. A whole new life opened up for us, as we fell in love with the climate and the area. I continued my real estate career with the biggest names in the new home industry during the largest boom in history, the explosive growth of Orange County. And Ray found a new home among his old motion picture buddies who were all retiring in Newport Beach.

Memory Lane and the Colonel's Ring

"Russ," remarked Swede, "let's go visit all the old haunts in Hollywood and see Hartley Harrison, Frank and Vita Kowalski, and have lunch at the Cock and Bull."

"Go have fun with your dad," said Beverly, who had overheard Swede's request. It was a beautiful morning, so with light hearts off we went. First stop, Harrison and Harrison Optics and Hartley, Swede's best friend.

Hartley greeted us warmly and gave us a tour of his plant, which reflected years of experimentation, for Hartley never threw away anything. Later in his office, Hartley showed us a three-dimensional postcard he was analyzing, and listened to our opinions and observations.

If ever there was a gentle, thoroughly scientific individual, it was Hartley Harrison. One could realize instantly why he and Swede had hit it off so well over the years. Two genius giants from different ends of the spectrum, matching wits and ideas and enjoying obvious admiration for each other and the lifelong bond between them. We were to see Hartley one more time when he visited Ray at our home, and another grand reunion was enjoyed over a bottle of Chevis Regal while the strains of Old Joe Doakes were banged out on the organ by Harrison.

At the Kowalskis, behind Reginald Denny's model airplane shop, we climbed the familiar stairs and knocked at the door of the old brown two-story house. Vita answered with a genuine smile. During our visit, we had coffee and covered the past thirty years like they were yesterday. Then after hugs and kisses, it was off on the grand tour down memory lane. We drove to a spot where my uncle used to live, which is now part of the Hollywood freeway, then past our old place on Fountain Avenue, over to Paramount Studios and the little place where Jerry and Ray had lived so many years ago.

Just before noon, we stopped off at the American Society of Cinematographers headquarters. The jovial old black bartender was tickled to see the Swede, and they rapped for half an hour while I toured the Museum of Photographic History. There on the wall was a picture of Swede with the Kings of Denmark and Sweden and his old Wilart camera.

We stopped at Disney's Burbank studio, then made a quick stop at Barney's Beanery so the Swede could exchange smiles and handshakes with his old pal Barney. Swede was to comment on the way to lunch, "Russ, we're in the very heart of old Hollywood. Not Paris, Rome, Culver City, Beverly Hills, Burbank, or North Hollywood, but the one and only Hollywood. I love her."

We arrived at the stars' old haunt, the famous Cock and Bull Bar and Restaurant. The bartender beamed when he saw Swede. "Where in the hell have you been keeping yourself, Ray?" he bellowed, as he poured two cold beers for us. They reminisced about their old drinking buddies, like Jack Wrather and the likes. (Jack now owns the Disneyland Hotel, the *Queen Mary*, and Hughes' *Spruce Goose*.) Finally, I noticed Swede eyeing the large gold and jade ring I wore. I explained that when Beverly and I had visited Grandma Lagerloef back in Weehawken, New Jersey, she had asked if there was anything in the house we would like to have. I declined, but she gave Beverly a pair of gold and jade earrings, then handed me Grandpa's old German beer steins. Then she told me she had an old Lagerloef family ring that Grandfather Hans had wanted me to have. It had been in the family for generations, and I was to care for it and pass it on in the tradition. She identified it as the ring of the Lowenskolds, or the General's ring.

Ray asked to look at it more closely, so I slipped it off my finger and gave it to him, remembering how much he and Hans had hated each other. "Dad, try it on and wear it for a couple of weeks if you like. Just take care of it, and remember that it belongs to me."

Ray turned on a lecherous face and commented, "I'll bet the old bastard's turning over in his grave with this ring on my finger." It fit him perfectly. We had one more cold one, then left the bar.

As we pulled up to a stoplight, Swede casually flipped his cigarette butt out the window, and it flew directly into the window of the car next to us.

"The Colonel" Hans Lagerloef would turn over in his grave, according to Swede.

The light stayed red as the car door opened and a huge six-foot-five, two-hundred-and-fifty-pound black giant ambled up to Swede's window.

"Did you throw that cigarette at me on purpose?"

"I beg your pardon," Swede answered casually.

"Did you throw that cigarette at me intentionally?" the giant repeated.

"I'm sorry, my good man, but I don't smoke!" Swede informed him as he rolled up the window.

The light turned green and I floorboarded the accelerator as I peered in the rearview mirror at the bewildered gentleman still standing there. The perfect ending to a most memorable day.

It was a couple or weeks after the Hollywood sojourn that I saw my illustrious father again. He casually drove up early one morning and came in for coffee and one of his quick visits. Swede could stand the home life about fifteen minutes before he had to be off to some bar or on the road again. I noticed the Colonel's ring was no longer on his finger.

"Did you decide to return the ring to me, Dad?" I asked casually.

"I don't have it."

"What?" I yelled. "What in hell did you do with it?"

"Russ, I had so much fun in Hollywood that I went back the next day and hung one on. I ran short of money and hocked it with the bartender for twenty bucks."

"For Christ sake, Mother will kill me!" I was furious as we raced, screeching into the parking lot of the Cock and Bull. The bartender was off-duty, so I had Ray call him at home. Half an hour later and twenty bucks lighter, I had the precious ring in my hand. That was the last time Swede ever saw it.

Swede Fernstrom was also Swede Fernstrom the ham actor. He had received a permanent disability from the government for his leg wound in the war. Many times he would go to the Veterans' Hospital at Sawtelle and Long Beach for ailments that were attributed to the service-connected injury. Many tests were run on his old carcass, especially his liver for sclerosis, only to find out his body had held up well after all those years of boozing. He always came away with a clean bill of health. But while there, he would lose weight and stop smoking, and the nurses would cater to him. As far as he was concerned, it was a health spa.

Many times, Beverly and I were commandeered to take him to the hospital, and later it was always Long Beach after he moved near us. He liked to cry wolf. He was a master at it. One day, after dropping Swede off at the "V.A. Hilton" (as he liked to call it) in Long Beach, Bev and I planned a little mini-vacation at our favorite hangout in Ensenada, Mexico. Just as we were about to walk out the door of our home, the phone rang.

"Is this Russ Fernstrom?" the dire voice asked.

"Yes, it is. What can I do for you?"

"This is the administration office at the Long Beach Veterans' Hospital. Your father is in intensive care and asking for you." I immediately suggested they notify his wife, Evelyn, in Van Nuys, and told him that we would be there as fast as possible.

"Please hurry. He would like to see you before . . . "

So much for Mexico, as I floored the accelerator toward Long Beach, Bev beside me. We rushed in, asking for Mr. Fernstrom in the intensive care section. "Oh, Mr. Fernstrom was transferred to Room 306 this morning." So up to 306 we dashed. No Dad. What the hell is going on?

"Nurse, do you have any idea where my father, Mr. Fernstrom, is? We understand he is dying."

"Dying! Why, he's going to be discharged tomorrow. He's in perfect health. I think he went to lunch in his wheelchair."

We searched the hospital for half an hour and finally found him back in Room 306, sorting through his mail. "Dad! What in hell is this all about? We were told you were on your deathbed, and I almost got a ticket getting here so fast. You look pretty damned healthy to me!"

"Oh, I just wanted to see you for some company, and I didn't think you would come. So I just made sure."

This was to happen a couple of times more, with variations. One time, while taking him for his recuperation visit, as we neared the hospital Ray took a long drag from his cigarette, tossed it out the window, and bent over in a horrible, whooping cough.

"Christ, Dad. What's the matter? What can I do to help?"

"Oh, nothing," he replied, sitting up. "Just getting in a little practice for the doctors." When we drove into the entrance of the hospital, he asked me to pull into the emergency entrance.

"Dad, we can't do that. This isn't an emergency."

"Well, then park as close to the admission desk as possible, and get me a wheelchair."

"Wheelchair! You didn't have any problem getting to the car at home!"

Ray could be a very pushy individual. Probably from his newsreel days; get the picture at any cost. And he always dubbed me "Sweet Jesus." So there I was, pushing the great ham in his wheelchair past all the other people patiently waiting to be called. We went up to the admissions desk. "I've got to get into bed immediately," Ray said, coughing. And red-faced as hell, I pushed him into the adjoining emergency room, where they admitted him without question. But the emergency crap would come back to haunt me, for after many, many wild goose chases to the V.A. Hilton, I was to receive a call one night in June.

"Come to the hospital immediately. Your father is in critical condition." I informed the caller that his wife, Evelyn, lived in Van Nuys, and to call her. I didn't believe the old fart. He had cried wolf once too often.

Raymond G. I. "Swede" Fernstrom succumbed at 6:00 A.M., D-Day, 6 June 1978, at the Long Beach Veterans' Hospital of total liver failure.

Epilogue

by Beverly Fernstrom

It was a chilly, rainy morning in June when Evelyn called. She delivered four words, "Your father is dead." Russ went numb, while my mind spun through the past. I recalled my first meeting with my father-in-law in 1956.

We lived in Riverside, California and had planned an exciting visit with Lydia and Emil. I was pregnant with our first son, Raymond's first grandchild, and loathe to meet this Hollywood flash. As an ex-model, I felt fat, frumpy, and very pregnant.

We had a long driveway, and when Ray pulled in, I had time to examine his car. It was a dusty, dirty Alfa-Romeo, stuffed to the hilt with camera equipment.

Swede with his Alfa-Romeo just before he came to visit us in Riverside, California. Outside Warner Brothers Studios, 1955.

177

Ray extracted his second wife, Jane, from the mess, then introduced us to their nine-year-old son, Mark, who promptly removed himself from our company, headed for the bathroom and spent the rest of the day flushing the toilet. Raymond and Jane paid no attention.

While Russ and Jane were getting acquainted in the living room, Ray followed me into the kitchen to "help out" his newly-found daughter-in-law. Showing no scruples nor practicing any, he made a pass at me. I slapped his hand away in surprise and anger, fixed him with a cold stare, and hissed, "Don't you ever touch me again!" He never did. I had gained his respect, perhaps. As I look back, I was the only woman he did respect as the years passed. We rejoined Russ and Jane in the living room, where nothing was mentioned.

I sent up a silent prayer, since I was convinced that Russ would have decked his father on the spot had he known.

The kid kept flushing. When they left, the sinks and bathtub were full to overflowing from backed-up sewerage, as we had already had plumbing problems, and the front yard looked like a lake.

I shook myself from my memories and looked at my watch. It was five o'clock on the evening of Swede's death. "Russ," I said softly, laying my hand on my husband's arm, "we don't even know the funeral plans."

The next day, we decided to call Evelyn. There was no answer. When we finally reached her, she explained that Ray would be cremated and his remains placed in the catacombs of the Veterans' Sawtelle Hospital in California, since this was all she could afford. Cremation? That was news to us. Ray had never mentioned it.

Troubled, I went to bed early the second night after Ray's death, but Russ sat up until the wee hours of the morning, thinking.

I awoke and startled Russ, yelling, "No! No! Not Sawtelle!" We stayed up the rest of the morning, discussing the burial arrangements and realizing that Ray's wife, Evelyn, had full control, as it should be.

The next morning, we hurried to Newport Beach, California to attend our boat that we had docked there. I am sure the errand was needed to keep our minds otherwise occupied. As we drove down Newport Boulevard, we were greeted by a huge, brand new billboard painted in Swedish colors of blue and yellow—PACIFIC VIEW MEMORIAL PARK, located in beautiful Corona Del Mar, which is a part of Newport Beach.

"Well, how do you like that for a coincidence?" I asked Russ. Neither of us had ever known such a place existed. Russ pulled a U-turn, and we raced home to call Evelyn. Would she permit us to arrange for a final resting place that we knew Ray would have approved of? Russ asked gently. We would pay all the costs. She graciously acquiesced.

We had discussed life and death with Ray several times in the past. His philosophy was that he didn't care, for he had made his pact with Almighty during life. He said, "Donate my carcass to the UCLA Medical Research Center for study or just throw it overboard way out at sea, Viking style. Any body that could put up with what I did and the booze

I've consumed should aid research. Oh, by the way Russ," he continued, "I don't have to worry about a thing anyway. You, 'Sweet Jesus', will take care of me in the very best style. I've always known that!"

And you know, we did!

The arrangements were made quite easily, and we felt a little lighter of heart. Now came the tough part. Evelyn had signed all the releases required, but it would be up to Russ and I to transfer that strange box of ashes. Some sort of legality between counties and funeral arrangers.

Evelyn called again and informed us that it would take ten days for the cremation. Ten long days and nights of thinking. Many memories could march through the corridors of the mind during that time.

It was in 1967 that I became very, very ill with lobar pneumonia. I had two sons, was crazy with fever, and barely able to draw a breath. I had asked my mother and mother-in-law for help. None was given. But the "Great I Am," yet another nickname I had attached to my father-in-law, stepped in. How really great he was! He attended to my every need. I was sweaty and stank of illness, but he stayed by my side. He was kind and thoughtful and nursed me back to health.

When I recovered, Ray finally enticed me to spend a day with him in Newport Beach, and paid a baby-sitter for our sons. I should have known better, for spots don't change on a maverick the likes of Ray. He brought me home about four o'clock in the afternoon, and did have the guts to face his son Russ, who was furious at our drunkenness. I flopped in bed, drank quarts of water during the night, and awakened with the hangover of the century. The "Great I Am" was on Russ' shit list for weeks. I was second on the same list!

Apparently, Ray had spent his time of suspension in deep thought, for he arrived later at the door with a gentle smile on his face, holding a bouquet of flowers. Now how do you deal with that?

As the days of our lonely wake ticked by, my mind constantly slipped into the past that we were about to put to rest. One evening I smiled, startling my brooding husband. "You know, Russ," I reminded him, "your daddy was pretty good with nicknames, too." He had dubbed our oldest son, Roy, whose IQ was above the graph, "the Little Professor," and after sizing up Kris' talents as an artist, coined him "Rembrandt." It was good to see Russ smile again.

What a pity Ray never knew or cared about his other grandchildren, who have all excelled in excellence, one of whom is now beginning a promising career in photography.

It was not unusual for Ray, still the swinger, to bring a new-found frightened cutie to our home after a day of bar hopping. We'd send the poor girl home in a cab and dump Ray in the guest room. Always the next morning, he'd be up first, making coffee. No regrets; no apologies. Take your choice. You either liked the guy or didn't. We had times when we didn't like him very much.

179

On the evening of the ninth day, Russ found me in the kitchen carefully ironing out yards of yellow ribbon I had saved from a flower arrangement Ray had given me. "What are you doing?"

"I'll give you three guesses, and the first two don't count." Tomorrow would be a long day for us, but I was up early and into my garden. The blue Plumbago winked at me, and I winked back. I made a beautiful spray, tied it with a huge bow of ribbon, and said in my heart, "This is not a funeral spray, Ray; it's just a special thing in your colors to comfort you while we return you home to your Newport Beach." I swallowed a lump, brushed away a tear, stuck a decent expression on my face, and tried to enjoy a cup of coffee with Russ before we left for the crematorium in Westwood.

The trip was soundless as we were tucked away in our own memories. Anything now would only add pressure to the guilt we both felt. We hadn't been with Swede at the end. But we'd had every good reason not to be. He'd dragged us through so many deathbed performances in the past. The feeling lies heavy on the heart. Evelyn had been with him and told us he just looked beyond her, smiled, and was gone. As we passed through Long Beach, Russ and I automatically glanced at the Veterans' Hospital on the horizon, where Swede had died ten long days before.

A crematorium is not a pleasant place. It smells of death and makes the flesh crawl. I sighed as I grabbed Russ' hand, and we entered the place to collect what we had come for. There were reams of papers to be filled out and signed. Russ' hand was unsteady. Finally, the strange, cold, heavy box was placed in my husband's hands. His face went ashen. I managed to walk beside him as we left the dreaded place out into the sunshine, but my legs turned to marshmallows before we got to the car.

Then we began probably the longest funeral procession ever. All the way on Swede's freeway, from Westwood to Newport Beach, it was just the three of us again. Swede had never been concerned with other family, now or ever.

To add softness to our hard task, we placed the blue and yellow spray of flowers on top of that heavy box wrapped in plain brown paper on the journey home. Then Russ and I agreed to one last kind of strange goodbye. We drove down to Newport Bay with "the box" on the back seat, bought three cans of Ray's favorite beer, drank them, and gave Ray a final *Skål*.

Then we headed up the hill of Pacific View Memorial Park, the flowers still as fresh as our memories.

The Raymond G. I. Fernstrom, A.S.C., 1900-1978 with the Mason symbol and DAD plaque would be installed later. It was arranged, and we returned home.

A short time later, as we were cruising Newport Harbor in our boat, we saw the flowers and wreaths floating in front of John Wayne's home. The little triangular flag with the wild goose on it, representing Duke's converted mine sweeper of the same name, was flying at half mast.

Yes, the Duke was gone too, and a feeling that a great Hollywood era had just passed overwhelmed me. It was in 1968 when the Duke had yelled to Swede, "Come on aboard and bring your camera. Let's chase that beautiful Portuguese sailing ship and get some good memories of that classic. It's her last voyage!"

Ray grabbed the needed equipment from the trunk and hopped aboard. One of the results or that fun-filled day Duke and Swede enjoyed hangs proudly in our home in a gilded, round frame.

The ring of the telephone brought me up to the present. Ray's plaque had been installed, and we were welcome to inspect it.

The Duke had been buried at the same cemetery a short time before and security was heavy when we pulled into the parking lot. No unwelcome visitors were allowed. We had to register to enter past the heavily guarded gate, beneath the flagpole where there were mountains of floral wreaths from Wayne's funeral. He had been buried in the wee hours of the prior morning in complete secrecy, and his burial spot, because of the Charles Chaplin grave desecration, is kept from the public.

We drove through the lovely, peaceful place nestled high in the cliffs overlooking the blue Pacific, up to the highest point to a building appropriately called "Memories." Security eyes watched us.

The plaque was in place, brightened by the warm California sunshine, and we remarked to each other about the magnificent panoramic view with gentle green rolling hills, past the quaint little town of Corona Del Mar, and sweeping down to the sparkling blue and silver waters of the ocean Ray so dearly loved. Big, white billowy clouds arranged to meet us that day as a final farewell was made and a prayer said.

Raymond G. I. Fernstrom, Cameraman, rests in our memories surrounded by the one thing he loved the most—color, of course.

Epilogue for the Family

Raymond and Acky, his sister, remained close through correspondence until his last days, even though she lived on the East Coast in order to be near Gunhild's and her own children. Acky was also close to Emil and Lydia, staying with them until the end, then opting to live out her life in the little Fernstrom town of Sharon, Massachusetts.

Carl lived near Los Angeles with his wife and rather large family. The brothers, Ray and Carl, were not close and of entirely different natures. Carl died recently of acute pneumonia, of which he was not aware until it was too late.

Emil passed away first, but Lydia was not alone or heartbroken for long. On her ninetieth birthday, before her death, she danced in a beautiful blue dress that matched her eyes, sporting not one but two corsages—a costume she requested to wear at her burial. The request was fulfilled.

Less than a year after Emil's death, Lydia followed. She was enjoying noon coffee and pizza with a friend at a local pizza parlor, and it was over in an instant. When Emil came back to claim his beloved wife, he could not have been more gentle.

Evelyn, Ray's third wife and sole heir, was most instrumental in preserving Swede's memoirs and fulfilling the wishes of her husband for Russ to finish his work. She passed away in December 1993.

As of this writing Acky, Ray's sister, and Mabel (Jerry), my mother, are still alive and well.

"I've done more in one lifetime than most people could possibly do in three."

—Ray "Swede" Fernstrom